Illness or Deviance?

Jennifer Murphy

Illness or Deviance?

Drug Courts, Drug Treatment,
and the Ambiguity of Addiction

TEMPLE UNIVERSITY PRESS
Philadelphia • Rome • Tokyo

TEMPLE UNIVERSITY PRESS
Philadelphia, Pennsylvania 19122
www.temple.edu/tempress

Library of Congress Cataloging-in-Publication Data

Murphy, Jennifer, author.
Illness or deviance? : drug courts, drug treatment, and the ambiguity
of addiction / Jennifer Murphy.
        p. ; cm.
Includes bibliographical references and index.
ISBN 978-1-4399-1022-1 (cloth : alk. paper)
ISBN 978-1-4399-1023-8 (pbk. : alk. paper)
ISBN 978-1-4399-1024-5 (e-book)
I. Title.
[DNLM: 1. Substance-Related Disorders—therapy—United
States.   2. Drug and Narcotic Control—legislation & jurisprudence—
United States.   3. Health Policy—United States.   4. Medicalization—
United States.   5. Social Stigma—United States.   6. Substance-Related
Disorders—psychology—United States. WM 270]
RC564 .M8728 2015
362.29—dc23

                                                          2014044767

Printed in the United States of America

9 8 7 6 5 4 3 2 1

Contents

Acknowledgments

This book would not have been possible without the cooperation of those involved in Capital City's Drug Court and the staff and clients of Southside and Westview drug treatment programs. Before I started my research, I was very concerned that those in the treatment programs would find my observations and interviews intrusive, but I could not have been more warmly accepted by those working in and receiving treatment from these programs. I thank all of them for their brutal honesty in the interviews and for sharing such personal things with me. I wish I could recognize each of them here by name, but that would break the confidentiality of those I am trying to protect. I am also very grateful to those who helped me transcribe the interviews, including Kaitlyn Crescenzo, Lynda Laughlin, Pangri Mehta, and Morgan Robinson.

California State University, Sacramento (CSUS) has been a wonderful place to begin my academic career. Thank you to my sociology colleagues for their helpful guidance along the way and to Todd Migliaccio and Kathryn Hadley for giving me feedback on my book prospectus. I am also extremely grateful for the institutional support I received through the Provost's Probationary Faculty Development Grant and the College of Social Science and Interdisciplinary Studies' Summer Research Grant. The Interlibrary Loan Department at CSUS was extremely helpful and efficient, allowing me to broaden my sources to a much wider range. The Sacramento Public Library and Sacramento's Coffee Garden and Old Soul coffeehouses provided writing space (and caffeine!) that gave me the needed break from my office. Much of this book was written in those public spaces.

Because this book started as my dissertation, I want to thank the many people who helped me along the journey through graduate school. Julia Ericksen,

Kim Goyette, Susan Markens, and Shanyang Zhao, were especially helpful in clarifying the initial research project, both by reading earlier drafts and talking with me about my ideas. Thank you to my fellow graduate students who helped during the proposal writing process; the comments of Josh Freely, Rosemary Feeley, Lynda Laughlin, Wendy Sedlak, and Richard Smith were especially helpful. Thank you also to Bob Sterling for his encouragement during graduate school and his help in getting my data collection approved. I am indebted to my dissertation committee members Gretchen Condran, Kevin Delaney, and Bob Kidder for helping me become a better researcher and scholar. George Dowdall offered some extremely helpful comments as I began the transition from dissertation to book.

To my husband, Paul, who has stayed almost as close to this project for the past few years as I have, your endless support and fabulous editing skills made this book happen. Zoe and Alec gave me the necessary breaks from writing and always helped to remind me what is most important in life. Finally, to Mom and Dad, thank you for your encouragement and patience throughout graduate school and life. None of this would have been possible without your love and support at every turn.

Illness or Deviance?

1

Drug Addiction

Illness or Deviance?

On a cold February morning, a group of ten men and women gather inside the Westview Outpatient Substance Abuse Treatment facility. They sit in a circle in a large room along with the therapist who moderates the group, a white woman in her early twenties. All of the group members are black, ranging in age from about twenty to fifty, with the exception of one white male who looks like he is about twenty years old. The group members take turns "checking in" to the group therapy session, reporting their first name, the drug(s) for which they are in treatment, and the number of "clean days" they have. About fifteen minutes into the group meeting, the door opens and another therapist escorts an additional group member into the room, a black man who appears to be in his early thirties. The therapist hands the group therapist a small piece of paper and leaves the room. After reading what is written on the paper, the group therapist looks at the late group member with exaggerated shock and disappointment. He sits down in one of the open seats, laughing nervously and pulling his knit hat over his face. The other group members start muttering to each other and several say, "Oh, Steve!"

> THERAPIST [*looking at Steve*]: Well, I guess we definitely have something to talk about now! Steve, would you like to share?
> STEVE [*laughs, pulls his hat over his face again, and says quietly*]: I used last week.
> MARTY (black male, about forty): What did you use?
> STEVE: Wet [PCP] . . . I was just under a lot of stress and, I don't know . . . I just did. It's not a big deal, though. I don't have to use again. I mean

everyone uses something to relax, right? Like some people smoke and some people gotta have coffee. It's just my thing.

[*Many people in the group appear agitated.*]

MARTY: Whoa, whoa! Wait a minute here. Are you sayin' that you gonna use again then?

STEVE: No. I was just . . . I mean, my car . . . I got problems with my car and my girl's been getting to me. And my car was in the shop, and then it got hit by two other cars there. I don't know; I just felt all frustrated. I used it to relax me.

[*Group members appear to get increasingly agitated.*]

ESTER (black female, early forties): What?! Oh, you're just in denial. You don't think there's anything wrong with that?

HARRISON (black male, probably early forties): You know what they say denial stands for? Don't Even Know I Am Lying! 'Cause that's the truth. I mean, if you don't even think you're an addict.

STEVE: I'm just sayin'. I mean, I was just feeling, like my car and my girl getting on my nerves. And I didn't see what the big harm would be.

BERNADETTE (black female, probably mid- to late forties): Steve, don't you see that you're an addict?

STEVE: I don't know.

BERNADETTE: Do you even know what an addict is?

STEVE: Yeah. It's like when someone goes out on the street and has to use and tries to buy drugs.

SARAH (black female, probably mid- to late forties): He don't even know what an addict is!

BERNADETTE: Is that what you think? Like just someone you see out coppin' on the street?

STEVE: Well, no . . . I mean . . .

BERNADETTE: 'Cause, guess what? You're an addict! And it don't matter what drug. PCP is just as powerful as crack! Let me find the definition of "addict" that NA [Narcotics Anonymous] gives [*pulls out a pamphlet from her purse and begins reading*]. "An addict is a man or woman whose life is controlled by drugs. We are people in the grip of a continuing and progressive illness whose ends are always the same: jails, institutions, and death." [*Turns to Steve*] Steve, are you even working the program? Do you know this stuff?

[*Steve shrugs.*]

MARTY: When you're an addict, you're an addict for life!

STEVE: See, I don't see it that way.

HARRISON: Man, why are you here then?

MARTY: Yeah, what are you doing here?

ESTER: Is it because of court?

STEVE: Well . . .

ESTER: Let me guess. You got picked up and it was either jail or come here. So you chose to come here. Well, until you come to terms with who you are, you just gonna go back out and use.

MARTY: See, man. 'Cause once you're an addict, you're always an addict. An addict isn't just that person down there on the street tryin' to buy something. I could be clean for like ten years, never use in ten years. But you know what? I'm still an addict! That's what you don't understand.

[*Several group members agree and nod their heads.*]

TIM (white male, about twenty years old): See, I don't agree with that, about always being an addict. I mean, if you haven't used in ten years, then I don't think you're still an addict.

THERAPIST: It doesn't even have to be drugs. You can be addicted to other things, too, right? Like John . . . He tells me how he feels when he sells drugs. Like that feeling he gets is the same feeling as other people get from *using*. So I tell him, selling drugs for you is an addiction!

BERNADETTE: Steve, you better go to a meeting. There's one here right after group.

THERAPIST: Yeah, we'll make it part of your treatment schedule. Now you *have* to go!

STEVE: Oh . . . [*doesn't sound enthusiastic*]

HARRISON: Yeah, man . . . you gotta start going to meetings and workin' the program.

ESTER: You first got to realize what you are!

What is drug addiction? Is it a disease that can be treated or is it a crime that should be punished? Is it a temporary condition or an incurable illness? What causes it—bad genes or a bad upbringing, a lack of responsibility or a lack of spirituality? While most Americans agree with the notion that drug addiction is a disease, these questions still have no clear answers. Decades of research and an ongoing war against drugs have not brought us any closer to a definitive method of defining and dealing with drug addiction. Just as the previous scene illustrates how those in drug treatment have varied perspectives about addiction, we have myriad ways of handling it. Some drug users will go to treatment while others will go to jail. Some drug users will be labeled lifelong addicts while others will never receive or accept such a designation.

The opening scene highlights the confusion and contradictions about labeling addiction that I observed during my fieldwork in two institutions designated as authorities in managing drug users: a drug court and an outpatient drug treatment facility. The scene comes from my observations of group therapy meetings at the drug treatment facility. Many of the interactions between those in treatment had to do with negotiating what the "addict" label means. As the scene shows, most subscribed to the notion that addiction is a lifelong disease with no cure, the view promoted by twelve-step groups like Alcoholics Anonymous and Narcotics Anonymous. This definition was even extended to behaviors that did not include drug use, like selling drugs. Others, however, were skeptical about this definition. Ultimately, individuals in both institutions had to accept the definition of "addict" that was assigned to them in order to progress through the programs. Steve, the individual in the scene who was reluctant about labeling himself an addict, was ultimately discharged from the drug treatment program. Because he was referred into treatment by the criminal justice system, his failure to complete treatment also likely resulted in his being sent to prison. While his continued drug use certainly contributed to that outcome, his resistance to accept the "addict" label also played a role in the clinic deciding that he was not progressing appropriately in treatment. If he had accepted that he was an addict and articulated his relapse as a sign that his addiction problem was out of his control, he likely would have been sent to a more intensive treatment program, such as inpatient, rather than to prison.

While I initially expected to find a lot of variation in the construction of addiction across these settings because of their different underlying orientations (the criminal justice system versus treatment), there was instead a great deal of consistency. Everybody in both settings tended to enforce the disease label of addiction, yet their management tactics overlapped treatment with punishment. This overlap of therapeutic and punitive approaches to managing addiction, a practice I term "therapeutic punishment," occurred in both drug treatment and drug court. In the drug court, the staff viewed the client as a criminal with an addiction problem. In treatment, counselors often had the same view of those in the program, especially if they had been referred to treatment by the criminal justice system. Even if they were not explicitly viewed as criminals, addicts were thought of as untrustworthy and immoral. This view justified the use of punishment in both treatment and the court, although it was framed as therapy, a way of "helping" clients come to terms with their addiction problem and their lack of socially appropriate values. Those going through these programs, however, viewed the sanctions as purely punitive.

It is not a surprise that the "managers" of drug addicts viewed the drug users they encountered as immoral, irresponsible, and often criminal. I offer two main reasons for this, both of which relate to the ongoing stigma that surrounds drug use and abuse.

First, our cultural discourse about drugs and addiction overlaps therapeutic and punitive perspectives. For the past twenty-five years, we have been inundated by federally funded drug "prevention" announcements on television and school programs like D.A.R.E. (Drug Abuse Resistance Education). The messages are clear: drugs turn ordinarily good people into immoral, bad addicts. The only way not to become a low-life addict is to *choose* not to use drugs in the first place. Drug users, often portrayed as scary (and poor racial minorities), should be avoided at all costs and essentially removed from society. One individual in drug treatment that I interviewed discussed the impact these messages had on his own family. The day before our interview, his daughter had come home from elementary school and when he asked her what she had done in school that day, she mentioned attending a program where they learned about "bad people who use drugs." The father felt horrible and reluctant to reveal his drug problem to his daughter because of this message. These "educational" messages also conflate any drug use with abuse; all drug users become bad drug addicts. This leads Americans to the conclusion that the only possible solutions to our drug problems are treatment (for those who deserve it) or incarceration (for most everyone else), or some overlap of the two. That drug treatment facilities in urban areas are often in poor neighborhoods populated by racial minorities furthers this moral perception of drug users and addiction.

Second, the criminal justice system has essentially colonized drug treatment. The criminal justice system has become the largest referral source for those in treatment (more so than doctors, self-referrals, or any other source). The majority of adults in treatment for using stimulants (including methamphetamine) or marijuana are there because of the criminal justice system (SAMHSA 2010a). Initiatives like drug courts have institutionalized the relationship between the criminal justice system and drug treatment by putting a judge at the forefront of both the client's criminal offense and his or her drug problem. This relationship has been effective because of our cultural discourse about drug users (sick people who need to be punished) and Americans' sense that while drug addiction might be a disease, at the same time, drug users need to be punished. As a result, any alternative approach to drug policy becomes silenced; any "new" initiative is about diverting offenders into treatment rather than reforming our drug laws. Our drug policy solidifies the notion that any drug use is abuse that requires treatment. As my research shows, even those who do not meet traditional diagnostic criteria for drug abuse or addiction are labeled addicts in need of drug treatment.

I began this project with a very open-ended question: What frameworks for defining and managing addiction operate in two settings that, on the surface, appear to represent competing authorities of addiction management (medical and criminal)? In these settings, is addiction framed and managed primarily as an illness, a criminal problem, or a moral issue? To represent those competing authorities, I chose an outpatient drug treatment facility and an adult drug court as my research sites. Both were located in the same large city, which I have given the pseudonym "Capital City." While I was aware that overlapping frameworks could exist in one setting (and they did), I chose sites that at least institutionally reflected different authorities. That is, in the court, a judge was the ultimate authority in handling the drug-addicted clients; in the treatment facility, a psychiatrist or therapist was the ultimate authority in determining treatment success or failure. Because of this institutional focus, the findings illuminate the institutional arrangements of labeling and managing drug users, in a sense, the "production" of addiction. Therefore, it is more a study about organizations than about individuals.

To answer such a broad research question, I utilized a "grounded theory" approach (Glaser and Strauss 1967). I had no preconceived hypotheses; the study began as largely exploratory. I wanted to hear how people in these settings talked about addiction, how they revealed their views of addiction in their daily actions and written materials, and how they thought it best to manage people diagnosed as addicts. I attempted to learn the "natural language" of the organizations (Manning 1970: 256). Because I focused on how these institutions communicated definitions of addiction to their clients, my research fits into the paradigm of "institutional ethnography" (Smith 2002, 2006a, 2006b). Institutional ethnography is not incompatible with a grounded theory approach; it just directs the focus to social processes that influence individual behavior. Observations and open-ended interviews were the primary tools I used to gather data. In addition, to connect these discrete settings to larger institutional processes and meanings, I examined national data about drug treatment and drug courts along with documents from national organizations related to drug treatment and drug courts. Themes emerged from the data and helped guide my subsequent data collection, which occurred between June 2005 and May 2007. See the appendix for a more detailed discussion of my methodological approach.

While the research in this book focuses on one particular city's drug court program and an affiliated treatment facility, the findings have a broader application to the institutional arrangements of drug treatment and the criminal justice system. While drug courts vary by locale, they have many components in common (NADCP 1997). Thus, examining one program in great detail can help readers better understand drug court programs as a whole, even if all of the findings do not apply to every drug court program. Capital City's court also had served as a "model court" for those who were planning drug courts in their own communities, indicating that its practices were promoted by the preeminent national organization of drug courts. For similar reasons, the outpatient treatment facility that I studied in Capital City offers crucial insight into treatment programs across the United States. Outpatient drug treatment is now the most common treatment modality in the United States and these programs are governed by a similar set of state and federal guidelines, ensuring a high degree of similarity. While the interactions in Capital City's drug court and treatment facility undoubtedly reflect some degree of local peculiarities, this study transcends the local by exploring issues related to drug courts and treatment programs throughout the United States.

Other scholars have discussed the deviance-versus-disease contradiction of drug addiction, but most focus on the macro level, tracing policy developments over time or placing them in a historical context (for example, Conrad and Schneider [1980] 1999; Reinarman 2005; Tiger 2013). One of the strengths of this book is its "microsociological" focus on how this contradiction gets worked out in the day-to-day activities of institutions that label and manage drug addicts. It is a qualitative study of the front line of addiction work. Research on drug courts and drug treatment has been overwhelmingly dominated by quantitative evaluation studies. Even the relatively few qualitative studies of drug treatment and drug courts (for example, Nolan 2001; Paik 2011; Shavelson 2001; Tiger 2013; Whiteacre 2008) do not typically investigate the coordination between treatment and the criminal justice system. This is a serious gap in the research on drug addiction, considering that the criminal justice system and drug treatment are so intertwined. This book serves as an important contribution to filling that gap and to better understanding the treatment and punishment overlap.

This book also adds a new perspective to the existing literature by contextualizing the findings within theories of medical sociology as well as criminology. I specifically draw on the ideas of two broad sociological areas that have been used to study deviance: medicalization and the labeling perspective. The medicalization of deviance thesis argues that many of our definitions of deviant categories have shifted from moral conceptions to medical ones, especially in recent years (Conrad and Schneider [1980] 1999). It is a macro sociological perspective in that it attempts to trace social processes over time to identify larger cultural patterns of how we define and manage deviance. While the case of drug addiction somewhat fits into this medicalization thesis, I also show how medicalization falls short at explaining the lingering moral frameworks that still exist to describe drug users. Our current view, in terms of both cultural discourse and established drug policy, is that drug addicts are both diseased *and* deviant. That is, they are on the one hand sick individuals in need of treatment, but on the other hand still immoral outsiders who require punishment and resocialization. Additionally, this overlap of both medical and moral frameworks for describing drug users is reinforced by policy and discourse so it appears to be a stagnant designation; as a result, we are not necessarily moving toward further medicalization despite the millions of dollars spent annually to test and develop various pharmaceuticals to treat addiction.

I also frame my research findings from a labeling perspective (Becker 1963; Scheff 1999; Szasz 1974). A labeling perspective of deviance emphasizes the microsociological processes involved in the application and enforcement of deviant labels. Because my research focuses on the interactions between those in the court and the treatment programs to understand how addiction is defined and managed, a labeling perspective is appropriate. The rest of this chapter briefly reviews these attempts to understand deviance and integrates them to explore the use of therapeutic punishment in the drug court and drug treatment facility.

Medicalization and Deviance

> A disease is no absolute physical entity but a complex intellectual construct, an amalgam of biological state and social definition. (Rosenberg 1962: 5)

The previous quotation is from Charles Rosenberg's book *The Cholera Years*, which documented the various explanations people gave for the causes of cholera during three nineteenth-century epidemics. During the 1832 and 1849 epidemics, the disease was framed in very moralistic terms; those who contracted it were seen as sinners who indulged in vices because of their weak moral character. By the 1866 epidemic, however, the general consensus on how diseases were contracted and how they manifested within the body had changed markedly. By the time of the third epidemic, most people believed disease to be an entity that could be distinguished from both the individual sufferer and other diseases. Disease was no longer a judgment from God, but often environmental in origin, and could be isolated and treated (Rosenberg 1962). While changes in scientific understanding certainly contributed to this shift in how people thought about disease, they were not the only factors. Rosenberg focused on these cholera epidemics to illustrate how concepts of disease reflect larger social and cultural values. Indeed, disease categories are never stagnant; they are constantly being negotiated within the medical establishment, within other institutions in society, and between the medical establishment and other institutions. This process, along with the historical forces that shape it, is called the "social construction" of disease (Aronowitz 1991).

Medicalization is one specific mechanism that may operate in the social construction of disease. Medicalization refers to the process by which conditions not previously considered to be illnesses become redefined as such. Medicalization can occur at a conceptual level, where medical language is used to describe a behavior or condition, or at an institutional level, where treatment of the behavior or condition becomes more firmly placed within the realm of the medical community (Conrad 2007). Medicalization could include the redefining of a moral problem into a medical one. An example of this would be the emergence of attention deficit disorder (ADD) in the 1970s and 1980s to replace the notion of "bad" or unruly children (Conrad and Schneider [1980] 1999). Medicalization could also involve the movement of issues previously seen as "natural" or nonclinical into the realm of medicine. An example of this would be the increasing medicalization of women's bodies and processes, the view that menstruation, childbirth, menopause, and premenstrual syndrome are pathological conditions and/or require medical intervention (Markens 1996; Martin 1999; Riessman 1983; Wertz and Wertz 1989).

Medicalization would not be as widespread without the success of the medical profession in increasing its power and prestige, thereby enforcing its expertise over all areas that can be perceived as medical in nature (Freidson 1989; Starr 1982). Medicine's expert control over technologically advanced procedures and treatments, as well as its increasing use of genetic research to trace the possible causes of certain diseases and behaviors, has fueled further interventions by medical professionals into treating more contested areas (Conrad 2000; Ragoné and Willis 2000).

Medicalization, however, is not always a top-down process, where the medical profession imposes a new medical label on a behavior or event without the consent of the general population. Ballard and Elston (2005) argued that the earlier descriptions of medicalization overemphasized the medical profession's desire to expand its own dominance and underplayed the benefits of medicine that people perceived. Indeed, there are many instances in which patients themselves demand that a medical label be attached to their condition. For example, Vietnam veterans actively persuaded psychologists to diagnosis them with posttraumatic stress disorder (PTSD) and those suffering from chronic fatigue syndrome (CFS) sought the medical label to legitimize their illness (Aronowitz 1992; Mechanic 1995; Scott 1990).[1] Alcoholics Anonymous (AA), founded in 1935, promoted the idea that alcoholism was a progressive disease even before the medical establishment had universally agreed that it was a medical problem (Schneider 1978). Many of the subsequent notions about addiction as a progressive disease have come from this early definition proposed by AA. Similarly, the disease view supported by AA has resulted in the development of other twelve-step programs, including Narcotics Anonymous, Cocaine Anonymous, and most recently, Marijuana Anonymous. These examples show that the medical profession is sometimes only marginally involved in the process of medicalization. That is, Americans value a disease explanation and will often seek out a medical label themselves if none exists.

Medicalization has both positive and negative consequences. Certainly, some conditions become less stigmatized when they are framed as medical problems. The individual is no longer at fault for having a disease, as they were perceived to be during the early nineteenth-century cholera outbreaks. Viewing a problem in a medical way relieves the individual of blame, although not entirely. Some will still view the person as responsible for contracting the disease, such as in the case of lung cancer or HIV/AIDS. However, even if they view the person as responsible, most will acknowledge that the individual still deserves treatment for the condition. Medicalization also draws attention to issues that we may have neglected in the past, like PTSD. However, medicalization has the drawback of further individualizing and depoliticizing social problems. That is, medicalization contributes to the increasing neglect of the social, economic, or political context that may be related to certain problems (Conrad and Schneider [1980] 1999; Fox 1989; Lee and Mysyk 2004; Zola 1972). Instead of looking within the social structure or culture, medicalization ensures that we attempt to isolate the cause of the problem within the individual.

The Medicalization of Addiction

Although not all medicalized conditions have advanced in this progression, there has been a tendency to move from sin to crime to illness in categorizing and treating a variety of behaviors (Fox 1977). Like many other behaviors once considered deviant, drug abuse has been medicalizing, especially during the latter half of the twentieth century.[2] The increasing use of pharmacological treatments (such as methadone and buprenorphine for opiate addiction) is one example of medicalization; the expansion of health insurance coverage for addiction treatment is another. Powerful institutions like the National Institute on Drug Abuse (NIDA) and the National Institute on Alcohol Abuse and Alcoholism (NIAAA) also strongly advocate a disease view of addiction, as evidenced by the types of projects they seek and fund. Undeniably, scientific and clinical "experts" have become more involved in framing our understanding and management of addiction during the last seventy years, since the first addiction research studies at the "narcotic farms" in the 1930s and 1940s.

Perhaps the strongest evidence for the medicalization of drug addiction is the public consensus that drug addiction is in fact a disease. Labeling drug addiction as a disease is hardly a new phenomenon; twelve-step groups like AA have called addiction a disease for more than fifty years. They promote the belief that the disease has no cure, but that it can be put into remission through total abstinence. While there is some opposition to framing addiction as a disease (for example, Peele 1989; Szasz 1975; Walters 1999), this view does not appear to be widespread. That is, other research, as well as popular culture, largely shows that Americans are quite open to the idea of labeling addiction as a disease. For instance, at the beginning of the twenty-first century, 52 percent of Americans believed that drug use should be treated as a disease compared to 35 percent who favored treating it as a crime (from a Pew Research Center poll cited in Lock, Timberlake, and Rasinski 2002). More recently, a 2006 *USA Today* and HBO poll randomly selected Americans who had an immediate family member with an alcohol or drug addiction. Seventy-six percent of the respondents indicated that "addiction is a disease," the vast majority of whom described addiction as both a physical and psychological disease (*USA Today* 2006).

Further examination of some of the polling data, however, reveals a contradiction in how the disease label is used. For example, in that same *USA Today* and HBO poll, a majority of respondents indicated that "lacking willpower" is a major factor of addiction (*USA Today* 2006). A recent statewide survey in Ohio also revealed conflicting views about addiction; while 59 percent reported that addiction to drugs or alcohol is a disease, many more (83 percent) indicated that mental illness is a disease ("Ohio Survey" 2010). This survey also found much higher levels of stigma against people with addiction compared to people with mental illness; 43 percent of respondents indicated that addiction is a "weakness," while only 13 percent said the same about mental illness. These research studies reveal that people's views of addiction are multifaceted and can overlap both medical and moral frameworks, even when subscribing to the notion that addiction is a "disease."[3] This ambiguity about the addiction label could also relate to its widespread application across a variety of phenomena, including gambling, sex, shopping, and eating (Reinarman 2005).

Some are also hostile to expanding the addiction label to behaviors beyond drug use. Walters and Gilbert (2000) interviewed both addiction "experts" and prison inmates about their notions of addiction. The experts were more likely to spontaneously express dissatisfaction with the concept of addiction and the application of the term to behaviors that do not involve drugs, while none of the inmates offered these critiques. The authors theorized that the inmates may not have been concerned with the generalization of addiction to other behaviors because their view of addiction was more about a state of mind than discrete behaviors. Another possible interpretation is that the inmates viewed the broadening of addiction to other behaviors positively because they interpreted it as a sign that the addict label was becoming less stigmatizing. Certainly, the broadening of the addict concept widens the net of not only behaviors to be labeled addictive but also to the types of people labeled addicts (that is, more middle- and upper-class individuals)[4] and by extension might decrease the stigma associated with all types of addiction.

Similarly, research on Americans' attitudes about how best to handle drug offenders, and drug addiction in general, also shows that our beliefs with regard to addiction are complex and sometimes contradictory (Cullen, Fisher, and Applegate 2000). For instance, California voters passed landmark legislation in 2000 (Proposition 36), which diverts nonviolent drug offenders who were arrested for simple drug possession directly into treatment, with less court supervision than other criminal justice initiatives like drug courts. Such legislation indicates that the public supports increasing access to drug treatment for nonviolent drug offenders in lieu of incarceration. Still, California voters decidedly rejected a ballot proposition in 2008 (Proposition 5), which would have further expanded treatment for drug offenses. The public seems to support treatment for drug offenses to an extent, but they become uncomfortable with treatment that is not tied to some level of punishment. Similarly, Americans will subscribe to vague notions about the need for criminal offenses to be harshly punished, yet when they are forced to choose between specific ways to handle drug offenders, they are shown to favor increased spending for drug treatment versus typical criminal justice approaches, such as money for prison construction (Cohen, Rust, and Steen 2006; Lock, Timberlake and Rasinski 2002). It appears that we want it both ways: we want the disease to be treated, but also the offender to be punished.

Polling and survey data, however, can only tell us so much about American views of drug addiction. These views do not operate in a vacuum; they are both the reflection and the perpetuation of larger discourses in society about drug use and addiction. One can agree that addiction is a disease, but these data do not give us enough context about *why* the person thinks of it as a disease or how individuals justify using different frameworks (medical and moral) for explaining addiction.

While various theories of the causes of drug addiction continue to exist, the current director of NIDA, Dr. Nora Volkow, a research psychiatrist, has been quite successful in promoting the view that addiction is a disease to the medical community, political leaders, and the wider society. NIDA's mission is "to lead the Nation in bringing the power of science to bear on drug abuse and addiction" (NIDA 2006). This mission is annually supported with more than $1 billion in federal funds, most of which is awarded to researchers studying the causes of addiction as well as new treatments for the disease (often pharmacological). NIDA's mission is reinforced with addiction researchers' claims that addiction is a chronic illness (McLellan et al. 2000), a "brain disease" (NIDA 2006). The reports disseminating this research argue that addiction is like other physical diseases that we are familiar with, such as asthma, heart disease, or diabetes, though their tone suggests that researchers still perceive the need to convince treatment professionals and the public to accept this scientific perspective. Even though others argue that drug addiction is more of an acute condition rather than a chronic one (for example, Heyman 2001), NIDA's brain disease model has become the dominant theory of addiction in the United States today.

Volkow's research used imaging technology to illustrate how drugs affected certain areas of the brain, causing damage and leading to the user's inability to control further drug use. She indicated that the same effects were produced by a variety of different substances (heroin, cocaine, marijuana), and might even extend to a broader concept of "addiction" that does not just involve drugs or alcohol. For instance, she and her colleagues found similar results in brain images of obese, "pathological" eaters (Volkow 2007). She explained in a 2006 interview that this broad notion of addiction could lead to the eventual production of medications that would not be addiction-specific: "If you're developing a medication, you don't necessarily need to address it [as] a medication for cocaine addiction, but rather a medication for addiction in general. And then you can start to recognize that, indeed, the market could be very large" (National Public Radio, "Talk of the Nation," 2006). Volkow also mentioned, however, that pharmaceutical companies were not actively researching and developing such medications. She cited the stigmatization of drug addiction as one possible reason, saying that people might be reluctant to take such drugs and therefore would not produce a profit for the pharmaceutical company. Since methadone is such a commonly prescribed drug for opiate addiction, it is not entirely clear to what Volkow was referring. The stigma might instead lie in the medical community since they are most often not the ones treating addiction. Linking the treatment for drug addiction to treatment for obesity would definitely expand the market for pharmacological treatments, and could place addiction treatment in the physician's realm. But as the history of addiction treatment reveals, physicians are typically uncomfortable having such direct involvement with drug addicts.

While drug abuse has become more medicalized, that process has not been complete. Several contradictions are apparent in the framing of addiction as a disease. First, research shows that medical professionals (those who, following the medicalization thesis, would be eager advocates of medicalization) are often unknowledgeable about addiction science and resistant to a medical model of addiction. Addiction specialist Charles O'Brien, M.D., Ph.D., said, "When you say that [addiction is a brain disease] to [an audience], people get very angry. It's something we have to continue selling" (Vastag 2003). Physicians still stigmatize patients who abuse drugs and often encourage nonmedical treatments for drug/alcohol problems. For instance, Freed (2010) found that the physicians he interviewed (all of whom were considered "experts" in addiction medicine or psychiatry) frequently advocated twelve-step meetings as treatment for their patients. One physician he interviewed, a former president of the American Association of Addiction Psychiatry, said, "I can tell you that if I were stuck with only one treatment it would be twelve-step" (151). Another physician equated twelve-step meetings to cognitive-behavioral therapy sessions. That there are two conflicting disciplines designated as the authorities of addiction, "addiction medicine" and "addiction psychiatry," reveals how medical professionals can have quite different views of addiction (Freed 2010). In addition, the fact that physicians embrace twelve-step methods is evidence of twelve-step ideology's hegemonic position in addiction treatment, but also reveals that physicians are often reluctant to treat addiction with medications (Rychtarik et al. 2000). Inherent to this debate is the idea that pharmaceuticals might replace one drug addiction with another. The idea that addiction is a moral choice creeps into these debates about whether or not pharmaceuticals should be used to treat drug problems. That is, if addiction is perceived to be a matter of self-control, then those who still abuse drugs are perceived to have a character weakness or a moral or spiritual problem. From this perspective, using medications to alleviate craving or withdrawal would be seen as cheating or not really being "clean." This fear of substituting different drugs that could be abused could also be related to the history of addiction treatment, when physicians in the early twentieth century prescribed various narcotics (like heroin) to treat alcohol problems (Musto 2002). Physicians also were seen as responsible for the large numbers of opiate addicts at the turn of the twentieth century, who became addicted after being prescribed opiates by their physician.

Other research has shown that physicians are not comfortable diagnosing drug problems and lack knowledge about addiction. The 1999 *CASA National Survey of Primary Care Physicians and Patients on Substance Abuse* found that 41 percent of pediatricians failed to diagnose drug abuse when presented with a classic description of an adolescent patient with symptoms of drug abuse. The same survey found that the majority of patients with addiction problems said their primary-care physician did nothing about their substance abuse; in fact, fewer than 20 percent of primary-care physicians considered themselves "very prepared" to identify alcoholism or illegal drug use. This is not surprising, considering that a majority of general-practice physicians and nurses believed no available medical or health-care interventions would be effective in treating addiction (McLellan et al. 2000).

When a problem has been medicalized, the response is typically to treat it with more "medical" methods. However, pharmaceutical treatments for addiction have not been developed at the same rate as other diseases and the federal regulations around their use is far stricter than for almost any other medication. While methadone has been accepted as a legitimate treatment in drug treatment facilities since the early 1970s, regulations still mandate that a patient visit a clinic several times a week, most often daily, to receive the medication (where the patient is then monitored to make sure he or she consumes it on-site). While buprenorphine was developed as an alternative to methadone in that physicians could prescribe it just like any other medication, it has not achieved the same popularity, most likely because of the low rates of insurance coverage and barriers that physicians encounter when attempting to get authorized to prescribe the medication (Walley et al. 2008). An additional complication in the framing of addiction as a medical problem is the ongoing issue of insurance plans not fully covering medical treatment for addiction. It was not until 2008 that the Paul Wellstone and Pete Domenici Mental Health Parity and Addiction Equity Act was passed, requiring most health plans to provide benefits for addiction and mental health treatment that are equivalent to those for other medical services (Smith, Lee, and Davidson 2010).

Drug problems also are still sanctioned and managed by the criminal justice system, creating further problems for the medicalization thesis. The overlap of institutions that are used to deal with drug addicts has resulted in a medical/legal/moral hybrid definition of addiction (Conrad 1992). This hybrid conceptualization both reflects the existing stigma around drug addiction and perpetuates it. Some of the stigma around drug use is due to its association with an illegal act; since drug users break the law, they are perceived to be bad people. We are constantly being socialized by a moral view of drug addiction through tax-funded public service announcements aimed at discouraging drug use (often through graphic images) and drug prevention education programs. These mechanisms continuously produce "moral panics" about drugs and drug use (Ben-Yehuda 2009; Cohen 1972; Reinarman and Levine 1997), where the public's fear of drugs and drug users becomes disproportional to their actual prevalence.

Research illustrates how pervasive this moral perspective is, even in the context of increased medicalization. For instance, a recent study found that Americans were more likely to view a drug addict as "blameworthy" and "dangerous" than someone with a mental illness or physical disability (Corrigan, Kuwabara, and O'Shaughnessy 2009). Similarly, Abide, Richards, and Ramsay (2001), in a survey of undergraduate students, found that those who considered alcohol and drug use to be "morally wrong" were less likely to use those substances than those who felt that using was not a matter of right or wrong. As one of the students articulated, "I always thought . . . drugs, marijuana, . . . they were wrong simply because you were told they were wrong. You were brought up with that" (380).

Race and class also become intertwined in this moral framework of addiction, since many Americans see drug addiction as primarily a problem of poor minorities in urban areas. This could be due to media representations like the poor black "crack mothers" of the 1980s (Boyd 2004; Humphries 1999) and the disproportionate number of African Americans and Latinos currently in prison for drug offenses (King 2008; Reinarman and Levine 2004). While most drug users are not poor people of color, the media and our criminal justice system suggest otherwise. This misrepresentation also has seeped into our subconscious: a growing body of literature finds that, when asked to envision a drug addict or violent criminal, most white people imagine the offender to be black (Beckett et al. 2005; Tonry 2011). Because of the overrepresentation of addicts as poor and of color, it is difficult to disentangle why Americans view drug addicts as more "dangerous" than those with a mental illness: is it racism, classism, or moralism? In reality, it is likely some combination of all three.

If we want to understand what it means for something to be considered a medical problem or a "disease," then we need to have a more nuanced understanding of how such terminology gets used and exactly what treatment looks like. Even though something is considered a disease, it might still elicit a moral response, even in the treatment realm. In this book, I illustrate that the medicalization of drug addiction is an ongoing and incomplete process that involves the continuous negotiation and renegotiation of the disease label with other competing conceptual frameworks. Rather than the therapeutic replacing the punitive, I show that we actually have an overlap of the two in philosophy and institutional practice. In many ways, this allows the criminal justice system and the treatment establishment to coexist and even cooperate since both essentially view the person in treatment the same way: as someone who is diseased but also needs to be reformed by learning responsibility and better values.

Labeling Perspective

Theories of deviant behavior often focus on why an individual engages in illegal (or what some in society might consider immoral) activities. The labeling perspective, in contrast, moves the discussion away from asking why an individual engages in deviant behavior to instead asking how the deviant label is applied and reinforced. Sociologists who developed this perspective, largely in the 1960s, turned the research focus away from individual behavior and highlighted policies, institutions, and the *consequences* of applying deviant labels such as identity transformation and stigma (Becker 1963; Goffman 1963; Scheff 1966; Schur 1965; Szasz 1974).[5]

Early research using the labeling perspective focused primarily on crime and mental illness and discussed the power that certain individuals and institutions had in applying deviant labels in these areas. Thomas Szasz, in his book *The Myth of Mental Illness*, argued that mental disorders were externally imposed by the "moral and political enterprise" of psychiatry (1974: xii). He contended that psychiatric diagnoses were stigmatizing labels applied to people with annoying or offensive behaviors with the goal of social control. He strongly advocated against the medicalization of mental illness and addiction, arguing that neither were actual diseases. Thomas Scheff (1966) also emphasized the social control aspect of labeling mental illness and the negative effects that being labeled mentally ill can have. Scheff (1999) argued that we are socialized to view mental illness in a negative way, which reaffirms the negative stereotypes we have of the mentally ill. Duckworth et al. (2003) explored this idea through a content analysis of newspaper references to schizophrenia. They found that the news media inappropriately used the word "schizophrenic" to describe things such as weather and sports teams. Scheff's point about socialization also can be applied to drug addiction. Even though we have a medicalized view of addiction (as a disease that can be diagnosed and treated), the negative images of drug users and addicts that are reinforced in our media and other social discourse make it impossible for us to fully accept the idea that addiction is a disease rather than a moral failing.

Labels are often imposed by powerful forces in society in an effort to extinguish undesirable behaviors (Becker 1963). That is, the "rules" of appropriate conduct are not always universally agreed to; they are imposed on the less powerful in society. Various organizations and institutions enforce these rules, leading some to accept a certain role (such as being mentally ill) even if they do not want to (Scheff 1999). Research using a labeling perspective often highlights how groups of lower status (via social class, race, and gender) disproportionately receive deviant labels (for example, Becker 1963; Chambliss 1973; Duster 1970; Scheff 1999) for behaviors that may be considered "normal" for those of higher status. This is especially true for those labeled "addicts." The addict population in 1900 was most commonly found in higher social classes, but by 1920, addicts were considered to be primarily from lower classes (Duster 1970). Not coincidentally, when the demographics shifted, the criminal penalties increased.

In addition, the process of labeling can be ambiguous and imprecise. For instance, Scheff (1999) argued that the *Diagnostic and Statistical Manual of Mental Disorders* (*DSM*) is problematic in that most people's symptoms do not cohere in the way that the *DSM* organizes them. The *DSM* has been edited and reorganized several times (the *DSM-V* was published in May 2013), reflecting changes to how certain disorders are labeled and diagnosed. Homosexuality, for instance, was removed from the *DSM* in 1974 largely because of the social movement of gay activists who fought to demedicalize the label (Conrad and Schneider [1980] 1999). Today, many treatment programs use the *DSM* to diagnose addiction, although other instruments are also commonly used (such as the Addiction Severity Index) that do not necessarily reflect the *DSM*'s classification.

Labeling can ultimately lead to an identity transformation because of the stigma and "outsider" status that comes with it (Becker 1963; Duster 1970). Scheff (1999: 45) saw stigma as "the single most important aspect of the societal reaction to deviance." In addition, the formal structures of punishment and treatment never fully remove this stigma, even when the individual returns to the wider society (Scheff 1999). Rains (2007) studied unmarried pregnant girls in maternity homes and found that these girls applied the public image of an illegitimately pregnant girl to themselves, often expecting harsh reactions from society even before they occurred. Organizations are powerful socialization forces; by giving groups a certain label, like addict, individuals end up associating with others who have been given the same label (Manning 1970). For instance, twelve-step groups are immensely popular among those who have been labeled addicts (either by the criminal justice system, by family members, or by self-definition). These organizations then reinforce the meaning of the label through their language and activities. Drug courts also have become an important socializing agent for instructing individuals on how to assume the "addict" role. Indeed, self-knowledge and identity cannot be separated from structure and institutions (Somers 1994).

Labeling someone as deviant can have real consequences for that individual; labels are often very stigmatizing. A 2004 study by the Substance Abuse and Mental Health Services Administration (SAMHSA) found that stigma around drug abuse was one of the main reasons why individuals did not seek treatment. Similarly, a study of nearly three hundred methamphetamine users found that those who perceived stigma around their drug use were less likely to enter treatment (Semple, Grant, and Patterson 2005). Being labeled deviant also could lead to engaging in more serious deviant behavior because the labeled individual ends up believing that he or she will always be a deviant (Becker 1963). That is, they internalize the social response they receive and act accordingly (Goffman 1963). The stigma of being labeled deviant also could lead to withdrawal because of societal discrimination (Link et al. 1989). In addition, stigma has been linked to other negative long-lasting effects like low self-esteem, lower quality of life, shrinking of social networks, illicit drug use, income loss, and unemployment (Li and Moore 2001; Link 1987; Link et al. 1989; Markowitz 1998; Rosenfield 1997). Research also shows that even those close to individuals labeled mentally ill or addicts, like family members, can hold stigmatizing attitudes that impact how the labeled individuals view themselves (Markowitz, Angell, and Greenberg 2011).

It is very difficult to shed a deviant label. Even a label that is temporary in its assignment (such as a "convict" who is in prison) often can become the dominant framework for looking at a person for the rest of his or her life. Those released from prison face this problem every time they apply for a job and have to indicate that they have a criminal record; prospective employers then perceive them as "criminal" above any other identifying characteristic (Pager 2003). Other "invisible punishments" that stay with an ex-criminal include loss of voting rights in some states and the inability to apply for federal housing benefits (Travis 2002). Similarly, the hegemonic view about the characteristics of drug addiction makes the drug addict a lifelong label. Even those who have not used drugs or alcohol in decades might still refer to themselves as "addicts," perhaps clarifying the label by adding the adjective "recovering." The use of a noun suggests that the label is not changing, but is instead a permanent status.

Some who initially embrace the addict label might attempt to delabel themselves at some point. Howard (2006) interviewed twenty-nine individuals, some of them self-identified as "addicts," who went through a process of delabeling themselves. While they found the recovery identity to be useful for understanding their past behavior, they also found it to be limiting in that the label became all-consuming and an end in itself. One of the women Howard inter-viewed was critical of Alcoholics Anonymous members who blamed every problem in their life on their "alcoholic thinking" (318). These delabelers found that the addict label prevented them from moving forward. Many, however, cannot simply exit their deviant role even if they want to; most deviant labels become that person's "master status" through which all other identifying char-acteristics are filtered (Becker 1963; Duster 1970).

Critics severely attacked the labeling perspective, especially in the 1980s (Best 2004). These critics argued that the negative outcomes associated with a deviant label were due to the illness itself, not the stigma of labeling (for example, Gove 1982). Other critics argued that the stigma of labeling did not predict further deviance, that the social control emphasis was overstated, and that being labeled deviant could actually have positive outcomes (Best 2004; Grattet 2011; Kalkhoff, Djurich, and Burke 2007; Thoits 2011). For instance, Thoits (2011) argued that most people seek mental health services voluntarily and that the effects of stigma are often moderate in intensity. Others also argued that the effect of stigma is negligible and can actually be beneficial because it brings the problem to society's attention and leads those who need them to access necessary services (see Link et al. 1989 and Rosenfield 1997 for a discussion of research that makes these critiques). Furst et al. (1999), in their interview study of a poor, drug-infested urban area, found those who did not end up using crack cocaine often cited the "crackhead" stigma as one reason for not using. However, supporters of the labeling perspective argued that many of these studies were flawed in their mea-surement of stigma (Link et al. 1989) and did not appreciate the complexity of the labeling perspective (Paternoster and Iovanni 1989). Because of the severe level of criticism the labeling perspective received, much of the contemporary researchers who employ its foundational ideas do not even identify labeling as their analytic perspective. In fact, Grattet (2011) argued that scholarship using a labeling perspective has actually grown in the past thirty years, especially regarding the consequences of labeling (stigma) and the management of devi-ance by social control agencies. However, much of this research never cites classical labeling perspective theorists or even uses the terminology. For instance, Pager's (2003) widely cited study of the potential barriers that those labeled as convicted felons face on the job market in many ways used a labeling perspective yet never identified it as such.

This book examines drug addiction within a labeling framework, but also recognizes the complexity involved in constructing addiction. Addiction is not just a label used by the powerful in society to exert social control over the less powerful (although it often is), but it is also used by addicts themselves in an attempt to better understand their own predicaments and to foster community among those who may be struggling to change their lives. The label might be used to reduce stigma, but it also might stigmatize the individual more because of the assumption that an addict is immoral or weak-willed. Similarly, it can be used for both altruistic and selfish reasons by the medical community. Many addiction researchers have the genuine goal of easing drug problems, both on the individual and societal level, while others are merely seeking profits from the development of a new pharmaceutical drug to treat the disease.

My contribution to labeling theory more generally involves the illustration of how institutions both shape the way labels are created and applied and how they are also shaped by discourses in the greater society. Other ethnographies, especially those done in urban settings, have effectively shown how institutions shape culture (that is, Dohan 2003; Wilson 1996). Similarly, my research shows how institutions like drug treatment programs and drug courts are able to construct what addiction is through their selection and labeling of individuals as drug addicts. These institutions, at the same time, are shaped by the discourses of addiction that are widespread in our culture. Those working in the drug court and drug treatment programs base their conception of addiction on who they are encountering most in their program: poor, black individuals with low levels of education. Their perception of addicts as immoral, irresponsible, and child-like cannot be separated from their stereotypical views of the population they are dealing with. As the history of drug policy shows, we cannot separate addiction from the drug addict (Courtwright 2001; Musto 1999). All of the characteristics that the counselors and court staff see as undesirable—unemployed, living in poverty, having family problems—become symptoms of addiction. Addiction becomes the source of other social problems rather than the result of those problems. All of the individual's life circumstances become framed as "signs" of addiction and are used to make sense of their behavior (Duster 1970). This situation of the institution as a proverbial "middle man" in enforcing what the label of addict means is legitimized because the institutions borrow messages about addiction from the larger society. These are messages that the individuals in these institutions have been exposed to throughout their lives; they are then reinforced by the drug court and drug treatment programs. This interinstitutional analysis contributes to a more nuanced use of the labeling perspective (Grattet 2011).

Therapeutic Punishment

In this book, I explore how addiction is conceptualized and managed in two institutions that are designated as authorities for handling people with drug problems: a drug court and a drug treatment facility. Through observations in each setting and interviews with staff and clients, I reveal the ambiguity and contradiction involved in the labeling of addiction and the methods used to "treat" it. The implication is that if you label something a disease, then you manage it therapeutically. On the flip side, if you label it a crime, then you manage it punitively. This study shows that both frameworks overlap in both settings.

The use of such a broad and ambiguous definition justifies the mixture of therapeutic and punitive methods used as "treatment." These methods, which I call "therapeutic punishment," are discrete punishments packaged as extensions of therapy; their goal is to extinguish the allegedly poor values and irresponsible behavior inherent in drug addicts. In both the court setting and the treatment programs, clients are exposed to punishments that are intended to be therapeutic. For instance, a client might be sanctioned and sent to a recovery house (also known as a "halfway house") for not following a program requirement. Clients consistently viewed this sanction as one of the worst punishments; the highly structured living environment reminded them of prison. The staff, however, viewed a recovery house as a place where a client would be forced to learn responsibility and accountability. The use of therapeutic punishment implied that drug abuse is caused by inadequate socialization more so than by physiological defects. Worse, the view that drug addicts need to be both clinically treated *and* punished perpetuates the stigma associated with drug use. Thus, even though polling data and other research studies show that many people agree with the notion that drug addiction is a disease that requires treatment, because of the way our society still handles drug issues (largely as a moral problem), we cannot move past the social stigma associated with drug addiction. Instead, we have institutionalized an ambiguous definition of addiction that encourages both medical and moral explanations for addiction along with both clinical and punitive techniques for treatment. The result is a model where treatment becomes intertwined with punishment. This model has economic benefits to both the criminal justice system and drug treatment programs. It also reflects and perpetuates the disjuncture between our beliefs about addiction and how we elect to manage it.

Organization of the Book

Chapter 2 explores the historical tension inherent in our approach to managing drug users: the simultaneous increase in both the medicalization *and* the criminalization of drug problems. Drug policy has consistently overlapped two dimensions of managing drugs—treatment and law enforcement. Only by understanding the evolution of that policy do we fully understand the current relationship between drug treatment and the criminal justice system and how this relationship relates to broader conceptualizations of drug problems. The overarching theme of the chapter is that both medicalized and punitive methods for dealing with drug users have continuously coexisted despite attempts to frame them as separate ways to handle drug problems. This overlap has intensified with recent developments such as drug courts.

In Chapters 3–5, I explore the larger issues of medicalization and labeling addiction in two locations: a drug court and a drug treatment facility. I attempt to take those larger frameworks for understanding addiction (medical, moral, criminal) and see how they work themselves out at the day-to-day level in both locations. Both the court and the treatment facility have overlapping therapeutic and punitive methods for labeling and managing drug problems. Institutionally, they are in agreement about how to handle the client's addiction. In Chapter 3,

I explore how Capital City's drug court promoted a medicalized notion of addiction while balancing its role as part of the criminal justice system. What appeared on the surface to be contradicting frameworks for understanding drug problems actually operated in a rather harmonious fashion, mostly because the court was able to become both the legal *and* the medical authority of the client's drug issues. Chapter 4 takes the reader into two outpatient drug treatment programs to further explore how addiction is labeled and managed in drug treatment. The facility utilized a cornucopia of treatment methods including group therapy, methadone maintenance, individual counseling, and twelve-step meetings. The result was a rather ambiguous notion of addiction and the client was left to navigate what treatments worked best for them. At the same time, they had to self-label as an addict to show that they were appropriately progressing through the treatment program. Those working in this facility also promoted the view that addiction is a disease, although symptoms of disease severity were broadly constructed to include what they viewed as signs of irresponsibility (such as unemployment), as well as signs of physical drug use. Chapter 5 describes the main method that both the drug court and the treatment facility used in their daily management of drug users: therapeutic punishment. This method reflects the simultaneous medicalization and criminalization of drugs that has occurred on a structural level. The main purpose of therapeutic punishment is to resocialize the clients into responsible citizens with good values. The staff at both the court and the treatment facility saw personal transformation as the ultimate goal and used this method of social control to achieve it.

In Chapter 6, the conclusion, I revisit the main questions that guide this study about the implications of a medicalized view of addiction. Despite the framing and managing of addiction as a "disease," there is no evidence that the stigma of drug addiction has declined in power. Instead, through criminal justice initiatives that include drug treatment, an individual is actually more stigmatized since they are labeled *both* a criminal and an addict. The medicalization of addiction can only operate within the boundaries set by existing laws and the criminal justice system, so the stigma of drug addiction will continue unless larger structural changes are made in our drug laws. I conclude with several policy implications that would shift our conversation away from how to stop illicit drug use to how we can effectively deal with the social reality that drug users will always exist in our society and how to best help those who need treatment.

2

Historic Tensions and the Development of Drug Treatment and Policy

On March 28, 2007, then senators Joseph Biden, Edward Kennedy, and Michael Enzi introduced Senate Bill 1011, the Recognizing Addiction as a Disease Act. The legislation aimed to change the name of the National Institute on Drug Abuse (NIDA) to the National Institute on Diseases of Addiction. In a press release, Biden asserted, "Addiction is a neurobiological disease, not a lifestyle choice, and it's about time we start treating it as such." He further explained that "by changing the way we talk about addiction, we change the way people think about addiction, both of which are critical steps in getting past the social stigma too often associated with the disease."[1] Even though the bill was never released from committee for a full Senate vote, the proposed name change illustrates the ongoing tension in our drug policy about how to characterize and treat drug addiction.[2] Even though Americans view addiction as a disease, there is still a strong stigma associated with addiction. However, would just changing NIDA's name make it a less stigmatizing condition? I would argue that it likely would not because of the criminalization of drug problems, the moral/punitive aspects of drug treatment, and the institutional overlap of drug treatment and the criminal justice system. This name change proposal failed to recognize how stigma exists largely because of the criminal designation of drugs and the moral frameworks we use to describe and treat drug users. In fact, NIDA has worked very closely with the criminal justice system in promoting how to use the medical model of addiction within the context of criminalization, rather than arguing for an alternative perspective (NIDA 2006). This cooperation between drug treatment and the criminal justice system is the result of decades of drug policy that has largely overlapped the medicalization and criminalization of drug use and addiction. This chapter explores the connection between the history of drug treatment and the evolution of U.S. drug policy during the last century. Today, there is a significant overlap between the funding of addiction treatment in the United States and the expansion of criminal sanctions for drug offenses. In other words, drug treatment has largely flourished because of the criminal penalties associated with drugs. This is particularly important because it directly affects the philosophy of drug treatment, especially as more individuals are entering treatment through the criminal justice system. During various times our policy might shift more toward medicalization than criminalization, but the pendulum never swings very far in the direction of medicalization. This is most apparent when we examine three areas: the development of formal drug treatment programs, how penalties for drug offenses have changed over time, and today's drug court system. As seen through these developments, the criminal justice system has explicitly resisted policy changes that would decrease their control over drug issues, even in the context of increasing use of medical terminology and methods for dealing with addiction. Exploring the evolution of drug treatment and drug policy in the United States provides the necessary context for understanding why overlapping frameworks of medicalization and criminalization exist in our drug treatment programs today.

The Evolution of Drug Treatment

Now addicts will no longer be merely sent to prison for what is really a weakness, but will be given the best medical treatment that science can afford in an atmosphere designed to rehabilitate them spiritually, mentally, and physically. (Dr. Lawrence Kolb, speaking at the 1935 opening of the first prison hospital in Lexington, Kentucky)

Instead of imprisoning an addict, Drug Courts insert hope and support into the very lives of people who the traditional justice system says are hopeless. (National Association of Drug Court Professionals Web site, 2013)

There has been a constant tension in drug policy between medicalization and criminalization. For instance, the previous two quotes reveal that the treatment of drug addiction has historically been closely tied to the criminal justice system. They also show how even medical perspectives of addiction can be tied to moral judgments (for instance, describing addiction as a "weakness"). Both the prison hospitals of the 1930s—or "narcotic farms," as they were more commonly called (Dr. Lawrence Kolb was the first director of the institution at Lexington)—and today's drug courts were designed around a similar purpose: to "rehabilitate" drug addicts by diverting them from the traditional prison setting into drug treatment. The history of drug treatment reveals the tenuous position it has had in our federal drug policy and the tethering of treatment to criminal justice as a means of institutional survival.

The federal government was largely uninvolved with drug treatment programs until the enforcement of drug laws in the 1920s (Campbell, Olsen, and Walden 2008). While concern for alcohol problems and the "disease" of inebriety can be traced back to colonial America, other drugs were not viewed as a similarly significant social issue until the late nineteenth/early twentieth century. The peak of narcotic addiction likely occurred in the mid-1890s, when it was estimated that there were about 4.59 addicts per thousand people (Courtwright 2001). The main cause of higher addiction rates was due to the medical profession administering opium and morphine to the point of addiction. While the number of addicts declined into the twentieth century, the demographics of the addict population shifted significantly during that time period. At the turn of the twentieth century, drug users were found among all social classes; the typical addict was actually a wealthy, middle-aged female. By 1920, however, the addict population was concentrated among the lower social class, and addicts were more likely to be young and male (Courtwright 2001). This demographic shift led to increased public concern for dealing with drug addicts (Acker 2002).

Alcohol consumption was also historically much higher in the nineteenth and twentieth centuries than it is today, leading to the creation of "inebriate homes" and abstinence societies like the Washingtonian Society; both efforts were designed to reform "drunkards" and opiate addicts in nonpunitive settings (Acker 2002; Lemanski 2001; Tracy 2005). Still, there was no dominant theoretical explanation for addiction at this time, so there was not much continuity across treatment approaches; many different explanations of addiction flourished (Acker 2002).

The evolution of drug treatment cannot be separated from the history and treatment of alcoholism. Linguistically, there is not much of a separation between drug addiction and alcoholism today; they are often lumped together into a general "substance abuse" framework. Similarly, many methods for dealing with drug addiction were born out of the treatment for alcoholism, including the twelve-step model derived from Alcoholics Anonymous (AA) (Lemanski 2001; White 1998). Even today, formal drug treatment programs (both privately and publicly funded) commonly employ the principles of AA in their treatment methods.

The Early Overlap of Medicalization and Criminalization: The Narcotic Farms

Drug addicts were arrested in record numbers in the 1920s because of aggressive enforcement of the 1914 Harrison Act, which essentially criminalized the use of opiates and cocaine (Campbell, Olsen, and Walden 2008). Formal drug treatment programs were virtually nonexistent at the time; the extent of treatment for opiate addiction was largely found in hospital wards that provided withdrawal and detoxification services (Acker 2002). These hospitals replaced the maintenance clinics that had existed before the Harrison Act essentially barred physicians from prescribing opiates to control addiction symptoms (Goldberg 1980).

Because of strict enforcement of the Harrison Act, by the late 1920s, one-third of all federal prisoners were imprisoned for drug charges (Campbell, Olsen, and Walden 2008). This dramatic increase in the drug-related prison population led Congress to pass a 1929 bill (the Porter Act) authorizing the creation of two prison hospitals, also known as "narcotic farms"; the first would open in 1935 in Lexington, Kentucky (the other opened three years later, in Fort Worth, Texas) (Musto 1999). These institutions were nicknamed "narcotic farms" because of their locations on open farmland and their requirements of vocational labor; most "patients" performed agricultural work as part of their treatment (Campbell, Olsen, and Walden 2008). They were hybrid prison hospitals that were designed to remove addicts from urban environments to deal with the growing social problem.

Referred to as a "New Deal for the drug addict," the purpose of these institutions was to "treat" drug-addicted offenders along with volunteer addicts from the general population (Campbell 2006). Volunteer patients made up about half of the institutional population; they were admitted if there was space available after the federal prisoners had been accommodated (Musto 2002). For decades, these institutions were among the only publicly available drug treatment facilities. Thus, the origin of formal drug treatment programs (even for those never arrested for a crime) cannot be separated from the criminal justice system. Medicalization and criminalization overlapped institutionally, as these narcotic farms were run jointly by the Bureau of Prisons and the Public Health Service. Their philosophy embraced this overlap; they viewed some combination of medical and legal authority as the way to solve the social problem of addiction (Campbell 2007).

Dr. Lawrence Kolb, the first director of Lexington, had developed a theory of addiction in the 1920s that he applied to the patients there. He viewed the source of addiction as a defective personality; his theory grouped addicts into six categories based on psychopathology (Acker 2002). This theory was the predominant view of addiction for many years and was promoted at Lexington. The treatment program was designed to last at least six months (volunteer patients were urged to stay for that long) and involved a combination of detoxification, psychotherapy, recreational activities, and vocational training (Inciardi and Martin 1993). The staff referred to the residents as "patients" rather than inmates (Campbell 2007).

Research at Lexington

Within the narcotic farm at Lexington, the Addiction Research Center (ARC) operated for the purpose of researching the causes and consequences of drug addiction (Campbell 2006). Through the ARC, many psychiatric residents were trained in these addiction treatment methods. The center was nationally recognized as a pioneer in addiction treatment. Researchers at Lexington even successfully convinced the World Health Organization to change the reference from addiction to "drug dependence" in the 1960s (Campbell 2007).

Researchers wanted to understand why some individuals became addicts and others did not, as well as why so many addicts relapsed after periods of abstinence (Campbell 2007). They also tested a number of pharmaceutical drugs on the prisoners in an effort to find a cure for addiction. The most prolific research occurred at the ARC during the 1950s because of the influx of prisoners due to new mandatory minimum sentencing for drug offenses (Campbell 2006). Volunteer patients at Lexington did not participate in research studies.

Some of the research methods were controversial. One study involved the deliberate addicting of inmates to morphine in order to study the full addiction cycle (Campbell, Olsen, and Walden 2008). Dr. Kolb rationalized the experiment by arguing that these research subjects would inevitably relapse at some point anyway. Other inmates participated in studies that involved the distribution of LSD and barbiturates. While participation in research was voluntary, those at the Public Health Service questioned the inherent coerciveness of the research, especially considering that inmates received time off their sentences for participating and, up until 1955, were even paid with drugs (Campbell, Olsen, and Walden 2008). Inmates from other federal prisons also were transferred to Lexington if they agreed to participate in research studies.

The ARC was eventually absorbed into NIDA in 1974. Research at Lexington ended in 1976; all federal prison research ended in 1976 after highly publicized scandals like the Stanford Prison Experiment and the Tuskegee Syphilis Study (Campbell 2007). Despite the controversial methods, many of the theoretical conclusions based on research findings that took place at Lexington are still widely accepted today. For instance, studies at the ARC through the 1940s and 1950s found that about 80 percent of their addict volunteers relapsed (Acker 2002). Addiction discourse today also emphasizes the likely occurrence of relapse (Gerstein and Lewin 1990). These research findings and other subsequent studies are often criticized, however, because they tend to be conducted with those arrested for drug offenses or those who have self-identified as addicts and are seeking treatment (Duster 1970). This was certainly the case at Lexington, where even those classified as "mildly addicted" had been excluded from research studies.

Changing Demographics
While the narcotic farms had initially enjoyed a relatively harmonious existence among inmates, volunteer patients, and staff, the shift in the prison population in the 1950s contributed to tension between these groups and an overall change in treatment philosophy. In the 1930s and early 1940s, most patients at Lexington were addicted to morphine or smoking opium. After World War II, however, the primary opiate of choice was heroin. The postwar inmate population also

was more likely to be younger and poorer than its earlier counterparts; a growing proportion was also African American. These newer patients were seen as unruly and undesirable and resulted in more conflict between the patients and the staff (Campbell 2007).

The overall numbers of prisoners also increased, especially because of the harsher criminal penalties for drug possession in the 1950s. This also helped change the racial makeup of Lexington. While in the late 1940s, two-thirds of the inmate population at Lexington was white, by 1955, two-thirds of the 1,100 drug offenders at Lexington were African Americans addicted to heroin. As the population increased and became more racially mixed, the initial humane focus also shifted to one that was more punitive and focused on social control (Acker 2002).

While the demographic shift contributed to a changing focus of the institution, the federal government also was growing more dissatisfied with the outcomes of those who went through Lexington's treatment program. The high relapse rate, which hovered around 90 percent throughout its years, suggested that the drug treatment focus was not successful. In 1974, Lexington was taken over by the Bureau of Prisons; today it is a designated Federal Medical Center, providing health care to seriously ill federal prisoners (Campbell, Olsen, and Walden 2008).

Alcoholics Anonymous and Twelve-Step Treatment

While the two narcotic farms operated through support from the federal government, the primary method of treating addiction post-Prohibition did not occur in institutional settings; the dominant "treatment" at the time was Alcoholics Anonymous (AA), founded in 1935 by two "reformed" alcoholics—Bill Wilson and Dr. Bob Smith. AA membership grew quickly; a 1941 report placed total membership at eight thousand, while estimates in the early 1950s put membership at one hundred thousand (White 1998). While the original principles of AA focused on alcohol problems, some seeking support for other drug problems found help through these meetings.

As membership in AA continued to grow throughout the second half of the twentieth century, its principles were also folded into the dominant model of addiction treatment that emerged in the 1940s and 1950s: the Minnesota Model. This model was first applied in two small treatment programs in Minnesota in the late 1940s, including Hazelden, a well-known treatment facility that continues to operate today (White 1998). The approach to treatment emphasized the components of AA, including the twelve steps, along with the disease concept of alcoholism that was developed by E. M. Jellinek through his work at the Yale Center on Alcohol Studies (Lemanski 2001). Jellinek's research on the causes and treatment of alcoholism became widely accepted through the 1950s and culminated in the 1960 publication of his book *The Disease Concept of Alcoholism*. In this book, he defined alcoholism as "any use of alcoholic beverages that causes any damage to the individual or society or both" (Jellinek 1960: 35). He proposed five "species" of alcoholism that were characterized by increased physical and psychological tolerance to alcohol, the presence of withdrawal symptoms with discontinued drinking, and the inability to abstain from alcohol. This became the dominant "disease model" of alcoholism, and was officially endorsed by the World Health Organization in 1951 and by the American Medical Association in 1956 (Faupel, Horowitz, and Weaver 2004). This acceptance of alcoholism as a disease led to an expansion of the alcohol treatment industry, with treatment operating in distinct institutions; treatment included detoxification procedures that further incorporated a medical view of treating alcohol addiction. At the same time, treatment also incorporated the philosophy of AA, which embraced this disease view of alcoholism.

AA, the disease concept of alcoholism, and the federal government intertwined to produce the drug treatment landscape that exists today. The relationship between the disease view of alcoholism and the principles of AA was codified by the creation of the National Committee for Education on Alcoholism in 1944, by Jellinek and AA's "first lady," Marty Mann (White 1998). The two founders of AA were listed as advisers in the early formation of the institution. This organization would eventually become the National Council on Alcoholism and Drug Dependence (NCADD), which still operates today. According to its Web site, the NCADD's purpose is to fight "America's number one health problem—alcoholism and drug addiction" (NCADD 2008). By the 1970s, this organization had close ties with the treatment industry, AA, and the federal government. Today, they produce educational materials and advocate for public policy around alcohol and drug issues (such as warning labels on alcoholic beverages). While one of their explicit goals is to fight the stigma around alcoholism and the perception that addiction is a "moral failure," much of their advocacy focuses on curbing underage drinking. Their focus on alcohol-related health problems and the costs of alcohol use appears to be their primary method of attempting to fight the stigma around alcoholism and drug addiction.

While AA and other drug-specific twelve-step groups promote a disease view of addiction, these groups are also resistant to promoting the further medicalization of addiction. For instance, alcoholism as a disease is widely accepted by AA members, but is not endorsed in AA's Big Book. Instead, the disease concept is used metaphorically (comparing addiction or alcoholism to an allergy) or related to the individual's lack of spirituality. The Big Book describes alcohol as "but a symptom of a spiritual disease stemming from resentment" (O'Halloran 2008: 211). Twelve-step groups also have been resistant to using pharmaceutical treatment for addiction, including methadone maintenance, which became widespread in the 1970s because of Nixon's "War on Drugs."

The War on Drugs and Methadone Maintenance

On June 17, 1971, President Richard Nixon declared drug abuse to be "public enemy number one in the United States" and that to fight this enemy, it was "necessary to wage a new, all-out offensive" (Massing 1998: 112). This moment is regarded as the official start of the contemporary War on Drugs. When Nixon took office, public concern about drugs was low, although that changed during the early years of his presidency. As Figure 2.1 shows, in 1970, only 3 percent of Americans named "drugs" as the most important problem facing the country, yet following the passage of the Controlled Substances Act of 1970, public concern about drug use exploded, with 20 percent naming it the most important problem two years later. As analysts have argued, public concern about drugs is often the aftermath of political rhetoric and legislation rather than the cause of it (Sharp 1994). That appears to be the case in the early 1970s, with very low public concern over drugs before 1970, the year that the federal government passed the Controlled Substances Act, which proved to be the cornerstone of drug policy for the rest of the twentieth century (Musto 2002). The increased public concern was likely due to the supposed link between heroin use and urban crime that became common rhetoric in the early 1970s (Goldberg 1980).

The beginning of the War on Drugs resulted in a continued push for criminal penalties associated with drug use, but it also resulted in large amounts of federal money going toward drug treatment (Tracy and Acker 2004). In his first budget after declaring a War on Drugs, Nixon requested $155 million in new funds, of which $105 million was designated for treating and rehabilitating drug

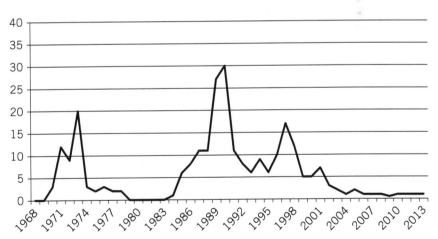

Figure 2.1 Percentage of Americans choosing the response "Drugs" as the most important problem facing the United States, 1968–2013. *Source*: Gallup Poll: Public Opinion, 1968–2013. *Note*: For years where the question was asked more than once, the highest percentage reported during the year is recorded.

abusers (Massing 1998). While the exact funding would differ from his request, this was the only time in history that more federal drug spending money went toward treatment and prevention than toward law enforcement.

This new policy on drugs, one that emphasized treatment, was related to Nixon's campaign promise of lowering crime. Several advisers in his administration had investigated the impact of methadone maintenance treatment on crime rates in large cities like Washington, DC (Massing 1998). They noticed dramatic declines in crime rates after the expansion of methadone maintenance programs. While methadone maintenance therapy had emerged because of the medical profession's growing dissent from the criminalization of addiction (Acker 2002), its appeal to lawmakers was one of pragmatism. Methadone was a commonly used drug for detoxification since the late 1940s, but it was not until the mid-1960s that practitioners began testing its effectiveness as a maintenance drug. Drs. Vincent P. Dole and Marie E. Nyswander of the Rockefeller Institute in New York City found that daily methadone doses could keep addicts from craving heroin or having withdrawal symptoms. In 1966, they published their work, which included the noteworthy finding that methadone maintenance had virtually eliminated all criminal activity among the addicts they studied (Goldberg 1980). Nixon needed to fulfill his campaign promise of lowering crime in urban areas in order to be reelected; methadone maintenance treatment looked like the answer (Sharp 1994).

In 1972, Nixon created a distinct agency that focused on treatment and prevention issues, the Special Action Office for Drug Abuse Prevention (SAODAP). The SAODAP was created to help coordinate the various agencies that were involved in drug treatment, such as the Veterans Administration, the Office of Economic Opportunity, and the National Institute on Mental Health. It had the power to oversee the drug treatment programs that were operating through these organizations and direct funding to those that seemed to be the most promising (Sharp 1994). It was through the SAODAP that funding for methadone maintenance treatment became a central focus of the Nixon administration. Despite research at the narcotic farms into the causes and consequences of addiction, formal training about addiction in medical schools was virtually nonexistent at this time. If a patient demonstrated a drug problem, his or her physician likely responded with general ignorance, or possibly even gross negligence (Lewis 1992). Until the expansion of methadone maintenance programs, opiate addicts had few opportunities for treatment outside of prisons (Inciardi and Martin 1993; Musto 2002). This treatment modality would unlikely be as prevalent today if it had not been for the increased funding that the Nixon administration put toward its implementation nationally in the early 1970s. Courtwright (2001) argued that the increased funding for methadone maintenance was also related to a demographic shift in heroin use, from the young blacks and Hispanics of the 1960s to the white suburbanites and Vietnam veterans of the 1970s. As methadone maintenance therapy became more widespread in the 1970s, federal regulations also made its distribution much stricter.

Physicians were no longer allowed to prescribe methadone for pain control; all methadone for maintenance therapy had to be dispensed in designated clinics under tight regulations (Lewis 1992).

The National Institute on Drug Abuse

In 1973, NIDA was created through the merging of the SAODAP and the Division of Narcotic Abuse and Drug Addiction (DNADA), which had its roots in the Addiction Research Center at the Lexington narcotic hospital (DuPont 2009). Prior to 1971, almost all federal drug prevention efforts were in the area of law enforcement; the focus shifted in the early 1970s to provide significant funding for addiction research and treatment as well. At the same time, while this strategy of "balancing" drug issues between criminalization and medicalization has operated under every subsequent presidential administration, the proportion of funding toward treatment and prevention has never been as high as it was in the early 1970s.

NIDA grew quickly to a staff of four hundred and an annual budget of $250 million (which would be more than $2 billion in today's dollars). While it was charged with overseeing treatment, prevention, research, and training operations, its early focus appeared to concentrate most heavily on research. Early studies examined the biology of addiction and the health effects of marijuana, with a big focus on the effectiveness of various drug-testing technologies (DuPont 2009).

Early research through NIDA also focused on the use of various medications for addiction, such as naltrexone and buprenorphine. This attempt to discover new medications for treating addiction continued through the 1980s and 1990s, when the primary goal was to develop a cocaine-blocking drug (DuPont 2009). As NIDA's promotion of addiction as a "brain disease" increased through the 1990s and 2000s, so did research into other possible pharmacological treatments. This also coincided with NIDA's movement into the National Institutes of Health (NIH) in 1992, with a far greater focus on pharmaceutical developments. NIDA's first director, Robert DuPont, lamented this increased focus on pharmacological treatments in a 2009 journal article; he views the bureaucratic placement of NIDA under the NIH umbrella as problematic because it shifted NIDA's focus away from prevention and the evaluation and development of other treatment methods. While DuPont celebrates the early years of NIDA because of its broad focus around drug issues, he sees the current institution as having "become increasingly divorced from the practical issues of treatment and prevention as it has allowed itself to be mesmerized by the study of the brain's reward system" (DuPont 2009: 11).

NIDA and the Brain Disease of Addiction

The current theory of addiction as a "brain disease" is directly related to the institutionalization of NIDA and its relationship with the NIH (Anderson,

Swan, and Lane 2010). While the medicalization of drug addiction through the twentieth century was related to a number of different theories including genetics and psychopathology, it clearly now resides within NIDA's brain disease theory, the result of brain imaging studies that show how addicted brains are fundamentally different from "normal" brains (Volkow, Fowler, and Wang 2003). This theory cites the source of addiction to be the damaged brain; the damaged areas are those that control impulses. In other words, addicts' brains become rewired after continued drug use, leading to the inability to control their subsequent drug use. David Courtwright (2010), a historian of drug policy, argued that this brain disease theory was popular among psychiatrists and physicians as far back as the 1920s; these early scientists just could not prove it. Critics argue that these brain changes do not necessarily equate to addiction; the brain's chemistry changes during many pleasurable activities and this could be considered a normal process (Aharon et al. 2001; Blakeslee 2002; Slate 2012).[3] Studies of non-addicted groups show that the brain can become rewired in response to a number of stimuli; a study of London cab drivers, for instance, revealed that their brains showed similar changes to "addicted" brains as they learned the quickest way to navigate the city (Jabr 2011). Others argue that the perspective overemphasizes pharmaceutical interventions as treatment; if the brain is the problem, then only getting the brain back to its "normal" chemistry would curb addiction (Satel 2001). Despite these criticisms, the brain disease theory is by far the dominant perspective among addiction researchers today.

From the mid-1980s forward, all of NIDA's directors have been neuroscientists (with one exception); this helped promote the brain disease theory in NIDA-funded studies and articulated a clear focus for finding the source of addiction. Despite this relatively hegemonic view of addiction currently held among researchers, evidence suggests that addiction educators and practitioners do not necessarily share the same theoretical perspective (Broadus et al. 2010). Because of this disconnect, the brain disease model is probably not well integrated into treatment programs. It certainly was not an integral component to either the drug court or the treatment facility that I observed.

On the surface, the brain disease view appears to be the most medicalized theory of addiction to date. It reduces addiction to damaged brain tissue and suggests that individuals have virtually no control over using drugs because their brains just do not allow them to. At the same time, ironically, this perspective fits very well with the criminalization of drugs. If addiction cannot be cured, then we need to reduce supply (Courtwright 2010). Historically, addiction research has always complimented punitive drug policy, leading to developments like the narcotic farms (Acker 2002). Today, the brain disease model legitimizes the use of court-mandated treatment and other types of coercion; the state must get involved to help addicts because they cannot stop on their own (Satel 2001). The medical view of addiction fits nicely into this paternalistic quality of drug policy (Burke 1992).

Drug Treatment in the Late Twentieth and Early Twenty-First Centuries

In 1970, Congress passed the Comprehensive Alcohol Abuse and Alcoholism Prevention, Treatment and Rehabilitation Act (also known as "the Hughes Act," named after former senator Harold Hughes, an active AA member who sponsored the bill) (Lemanski 2001). The bill established the National Institute on Alcohol Abuse and Alcoholism (NIAAA), which provided a large amount of federal money for treatment programs. Around this same time, major insurers such as Blue Cross and Aetna began to add coverage for addiction treatment to their plans. This coupling of federal dollars to support treatment programs, along with the expansion of insurance coverage, resulted in an explosion of addiction treatment facilities; one estimate supposed that the number of treatment facilities at least quadrupled between 1970 and 1990 (Lemanski 2001). Part of this explosion also was the result of middle-class demand for addiction treatment, which established many private treatment facilities (Acker 2002).

Twelve-step meetings and philosophy were at the foundation of these earlier treatment programs. Today, twelve-step methods remain the most powerful influence in drug treatment programs across the United States, even those funded by public dollars. While therapeutic communities (highly structured residential treatment programs with required stays of up to several years) were popular in the 1970s, they saw a decline in the 1980s and 1990s due to the length of the programs and their confrontational techniques (DeLeon 2000). The therapeutic community model exists today in a more limited form, often in prison settings, and may incorporate twelve-step philosophy.

Treatment programs today use a variety of techniques—cognitive behavioral therapy, psychoanalysis, methadone maintenance, twelve-step methods, and others. Still, even in programs that use multiple treatment modalities, it appears that the dominant treatment method comes from twelve-step philosophy. In a 2004 survey of publicly funded drug and alcohol treatment programs nationwide, about 60 percent of the programs' administrators reported that the twelve-step model "best characterized" their program, while another substantial proportion indicated that the twelve-step model was incorporated as one of several emphases. In addition, more than 64 percent of the programs required patients to attend twelve-step meetings during the course of treatment (Roman and Johnson 2004). Because of the hegemonic status that AA has for treating drug and alcohol problems, it is difficult to find a treatment program in the United States today that does *not* incorporate twelve-step philosophy, despite research that suggests it is not very effective (Lemanski 2001). While some also have questioned the constitutional legitimacy of public dollars going toward funding treatment programs that incorporate twelve-step methods (because of their quasi-religious focus), there has been no movement to dramatically change the structure of treatment programs. While the twelve-step model incorporates a disease view of addiction, it also promotes a moralistic view of addiction that stems from a spiritual void within the person. This overlap of medical and moral perspectives about addiction has historically been at the center of addiction treatment. As the next section of this chapter shows, these overlapping perspectives also have been at the heart of our drug policy for the last one hundred years.

The Waxing and Occasional Waning of Criminal Penalties for Drug Offenses

Despite the growing recognition that addiction is a disease, American legal responses to drug possession and use in the twentieth and early twenty-first centuries have been largely punitive. While the medicalization of addiction as a disease should have led to reduced stigma and more therapeutic responses to drug users, instead there has been an increase in the tension between treatment and punishment for drug offenders. To explore this connection, it is useful to outline major drug legislation from the twentieth century and the subsequent impact these laws have had on the criminal justice population. A common theme throughout the history of the criminalization of drugs is the use of "moral panics" around specific substances to increase Americans' fear of drugs and drug users (Goode and Ben-Yehuda 1994). These moral panics also capitalize on racial and social class tensions to legitimize the end result: increased penalties for drug offenses.

Early Legislation

The first federal legislation that criminalized drug possession was the Harrison Narcotic Act, passed in 1914. Concern over narcotics use increased considerably in the final thirty years of the nineteenth century. There had been growing concern over opiate use because of the perceived increase in the number of people using these drugs and also because the drug was increasingly tied to "undesirable" ethnic groups, particularly Chinese immigrants who had arrived in large numbers in the mid-nineteenth century (Courtwright 2001; Hickman 2000; Musto 1999). Before this federal legislation was created, several cities already had passed anti-opium ordinances, the first being San Francisco (Davenport-Hines 2002). Because the federal government has limited power regarding the criminalization of behavior, the Harrison Act was actually a tax imposed on the importers and distributors of opiates and cocaine (Sharp 1994; Spillane and McAllister 2003). The act required medical practitioners, as well as manufacturers and importers of these narcotics to register with the U.S. government, obtain a license, pay a small fee, and maintain paperwork on all transactions; those in unregistered possession of these drugs were violating the law (Davenport-Hines 2002, Spillane and McAllister 2003). The effect of the act was to criminalize narcotic possession and use, except for what was narrowly defined as "legitimate" medical purposes. Interestingly, the American Medical Association (AMA) supported the Harrison Act, despite how it limited physicians' power. The AMA was concerned with the perception that doctors were causing addiction by prescribing opiates; they saw the new law as a way to distance the profession from recreational users (Tracy and Acker 2004).

Several Supreme Court cases clarified the application of the Harrison Act. *Webb et al. v. United States* (1919) addressed the question of whether it was legal for physicians to prescribe opiates to addicts for "maintenance" purposes (that is, to prevent opiate addicts from experiencing withdrawal symptoms). While the physician, Dr. Webb, who had been prescribing narcotics to addicts, argued that he could do so under provisions of the Harrison Act, the court ruled that such uses were not legitimately medical and therefore were not permissible. However, this decision was essentially overturned in *Lindner v. United States* (1925), when the Court modified its previous stance on the prescription of opiates for maintenance purposes, and argued that in small amounts it could be legal. This decision was particularly notable because the Court wrote that those addicted to narcotics were "diseased and proper subjects for medical treatment" (cited in Faupel, Horowitz, and Weaver 2004). This position was advanced further in the 1962 case of *Robinson v. California*, which struck down a California statute that made it a misdemeanor to be "addicted to the use of narcotics" (Faupel, Horowitz, and Weaver 2004). The Supreme Court ruled that the status of being an addict could not be considered criminal since it would violate the Eighth Amendment's protection against cruel and unusual punishment (Bayer 1992). Thus, possession of an illicit substance was still illegal, but the status of being a "user" or "abuser" was not itself a crime.

Marijuana was criminalized in 1937 through the Marihuana Tax Act. During alcohol Prohibition, the legal consumption of marijuana had increased in visibility, with the development of "tea pads"—marijuana smoking establishments—in major cities across the United States (Brecher 1972). The federal government became increasingly concerned about marijuana consumption, so the Federal Bureau of Narcotics (FBN) began pushing for criminalization (Sharp 1994). The first head of this agency was Harry J. Anslinger, who served as U.S. commissioner of narcotics until 1962.[4] Anslinger served as a "moral entrepreneur" of sorts against the use of drugs, helping to create and pass antidrug legislation, while also facilitating the public's increasing intolerance of drugs (Becker 1963; Sharp 1994). He used racist and sensationalized propaganda to raise public concern over drugs, arguing that marijuana was a highly dangerous, violence-invoking drug associated with Mexican immigrants and African American jazz musicians (Musto 1999; Sharp 1994). Becker (1963) revealed a dramatic increase in the number of references to marijuana in popular magazines from 1937 to 1939, many of which explicitly cited the FBN as the source of facts and figures. One dramatic story was used repeatedly about a family murdered by their son while he was high on marijuana; even though the man had serious mental health problems, the marijuana smoking was touted as the chief reason for the murder.

The propaganda worked to raise public support for the criminalization of marijuana.

Increased Criminalization of the 1950s

Two other significant drug laws that were passed during Anslinger's tenure increased the legal sanctions associated with drug possession. The Boggs Act, passed in 1951, increased penalties for drug law violations and established uniform penalties for both narcotics and marijuana violations (Musto 2002; Sharp 1994). The Boggs Act also mandated a minimum sentence of two years for first-time possession of narcotics, essentially taking power away from judges to tailor punishments to an individual offender rather than a particular crime (Acker 2002; Goldberg 1980). The Narcotics Control Act of 1956 increased the penalties enacted by the Boggs Act (Massing 1998). The law also allowed for the sale of heroin to minors to be punishable by death. These stricter penalties were related to a growing concern about young Americans becoming addicted to heroin (Courtwright 2001). Both pieces of legislation also were effectively used as political weapons by members of Congress who had higher political aspirations and wanted to position themselves as being tough on crime (Sharp 1994). Since the wider society largely viewed drug users as immoral and unproductive, politicians were able to capitalize on the fear of drug-related crime to advance their own political careers. At the same time that penalties were increasing, the American Bar Association and the American Medical Association were becoming more vocal in their appeal for policies that recognized addiction as a medical problem rather than a criminal one (Tracy and Acker 2004). Despite these attempts, however, the criminalization of drug possession and selling expanded significantly in the 1950s.

While Nixon's War on Drugs in the 1970s focused heavily on expanding drug treatment, there were also increased penalties enacted at the same time. The Controlled Substances Act of 1970, for instance, reduced federal penalties for possession and distribution of marijuana, but also created mandatory minimum sentences of ten years and a maximum fine of $100,000 for first-time drug traffickers. Penalties for second-time offenders were even harsher. It also established new funding for drug law enforcement—$220 million over a three-year period. Another law passed in 1970, the Organized Crime Control Act, further strengthened the law enforcement side of drug policy. Title IX of that act, called the Racketeer Influenced and Corrupt Organizations (RICO) statute, granted law enforcement the power to seize property that was acquired through organized criminal activity (Sharp 1994). It also instituted severe penalties for drug law violators.

Nixon easily won reelection in 1972, and shortly afterward it became obvious that drugs were no longer one of the administration's central concerns. The federal budget for drug treatment and rehabilitation declined in 1973, while funding for drug law enforcement increased. This shift in policy priorities has led some to conclude that Nixon's focus on treatment was only an attempt to reduce crime in time for reelection and that he was actually philosophically opposed to large amounts of federal dollars going toward treatment and prevention (Sharp 1994). By 1974, the federal government had resumed its default position regarding drug addiction: calling it a "disease," but mostly treating it as a crime. Not surprisingly, after the political rhetoric and legislative action declined, there was also a significant decline in public concern over drugs (see Figure 2.1). In 1974, concern about drugs was back to the same low level (3 percent) that it had been in 1970, despite the increase in drug use through the 1970s (Gfroerer and Brodsky 1992).

While overall funding for drug control increased during the Ford and Carter administrations, the supply and demand sides of the budget were similar in proportion, and funding for treatment declined. By 1976, federal spending on drug law enforcement for the first time surpassed the amount spent on treatment and prevention (Massing 1998). For the most part, drugs were not mentioned as significant issues by politicians in the late 1970s; tactics of drug control continued more as part of the existing routine of various programs (Sharp 1994). Carter increased funding for drug prevention and education programs through the Alcohol and Drug Abuse Education Amendments in 1978. This legislation also authorized employee assistance programs, which are typically referrals or short-term counseling provided by employers to help employees with alcohol/drug or mental health problems. As Figure 2.1 shows, concern about drugs remained very low through the end of the 1970s. However, drugs reemerged as a significant political issue during the 1980s, and led to drastic increases in the number of arrests and prisoners for drug offenses.

Drug Policy in the 1980s and 1990s: Investing in Incarcerating

Drug policy issues again became a national priority after President Ronald Reagan took office. A series of laws that were enacted under his administration indicated a shift back to more punitive drug policies (Musto 1999). For instance, in 1984, Congress passed the Sentencing Reform Act, which reestablished mandatory minimum sentences for those convicted of drug offenses (Faupel, Horowitz, and Weaver 2004; Sharp 1994). Two years later, the Anti–Drug Abuse Act of 1986 further increased the penalties for drug-trafficking offenses and institutionalized the disparity in the penalties for crack cocaine versus powder cocaine (despite their being only different formulations of the same drug). Under this act, a person convicted of possessing 5 grams of crack cocaine was given the same penalty (five years) as someone convicted of possessing 500 grams of powder cocaine (Musto 1999). This difference in mandatory minimum sentences (known as the controversial "100-to-1" disparity) was the product of intense fear of the psychoactive effects of crack cocaine, which at the time were believed to be much stronger than powder cocaine and could provoke extremely violent behavior (Davenport-Hines 2002), despite research that showed otherwise (Cheung, Erickson, and Landau 1991; Waldorf, Reinarman, and Murphy 1991). Even though a 1996 article published in the *Journal of the American Medical Association* challenged the medical basis for this sentencing disparity, arguing that the physiological and psychoactive effects of the crack form were very similar to powder cocaine (Spillane 2000), the sentencing disparity continued until 2010, when it was reduced to a 13:1 disparity. The racial implications of such a policy were clear. Crack cocaine use in the 1980s was largely concentrated in poor, urban areas and more often used by racial minorities, while the typical powder cocaine user was wealthier and white (Musto 1999). As a result, the arrest and conviction rates of drug offenders through the 1980s and 1990s were disproportionately African American.

The 1986 legislation also increased funds for treatment and education for the first time in more than a decade, although the amount was insignificant compared to the funding for law enforcement tactics. In real dollars, the 1986 federal budget for drug treatment was barely one-fifth the amount it was in 1973 (Massing 1998). There would be no return to the budgets of the 1970s, with the larger proportion of funds going toward treatment and prevention. In fact, federal funding for drug control through the 1980s saw the share going toward law enforcement programs hovering between 70 and 83 percent.

Reagan took a very "supply-side" approach to fighting the war on drugs (Inciardi and Martin 1993). Although he spoke of "demand-side" tactics, they were largely symbolic and did not include significant funding or a detailed strategy about how they would be implemented (Acker 2002; Sharp 1994). A good example is Nancy Reagan's "Just Say No" campaign, where she highlighted the dangers of drug use, with no real plan of how to deal with drug users. While such drug "education" programs and media campaigns have been shown to have no real impact on drug use, the 1980s saw an increase in federal dollars going toward them (Caulkins and Reuter 2006). Still, these tactics were apparently successful at arousing public concern over drugs, since drugs again became an important national issue during the mid-1980s (see Figure 2.1). At the same time, the proportion of the drug control budget going toward treatment sank to an all-time low of 8 percent by the end of Reagan's term. Federal funding for prevention and treatment declined dramatically during the 1980s, while funding for drug law enforcement increased at the highest rate in history, rising to 80 percent of the budget (Burke 1992; Reuter 1992). These proportions reflect our larger philosophy about dealing with crime with reactive sanctioning rather than prevention (Garland 2001). Acker (2002) argued that this funding shift created a two-tier system for drug problems: poor addicts and people of color with drug problems would be incarcerated while the middle- and upper-class addict would go to private treatment facilities.

The Anti–Drug Abuse Act was passed again in 1988, with provisions added that increased penalties associated with drug abuse violations in other ways. For instance, the act reinstated the death penalty for major drug traffickers and expanded the government's right to seize the assets of individuals arrested for drug-related offenses. This legislation also institutionalized the Reagan administration's "zero-tolerance" policy of illegal drug possession, even in small amounts (Sharp 1994). It furthermore created a cabinet-level official whose job it would be to coordinate federal drug-control policy, informally named the "drug czar" (Sharp 1994).[5] The drug czar headed the new office of National Drug Control Policy and advised the president on organizational and budget matters involving drug enforcement agencies. The first "drug czar" was William Bennett; he was appointed by the newly elected George Bush and confirmed by the Senate in March 1989. Not surprisingly, Bennett's approach to fighting the drug war focused heavily on the law enforcement side; he was even quoted as saying that treatment was a form of "coddling" (Massing 1998: 195).

The 1988 act, along with the legislation of 1984 and 1986, profoundly affected the criminal justice system by crowding court dockets with drug offenses and dramatically increasing the prison population. Figure 2.2 shows the increase in arrests for drug abuse violations since 1980.[6] Figure 2.3 shows the increase in the number of people serving prison sentences for drug-related offenses (mostly due to possession and sales). These increases were also the result of more-aggressive arrest policies in the second half of the 1980s. Couple the increase in arrests with harsher penalties and longer sentences of incarceration enacted through the

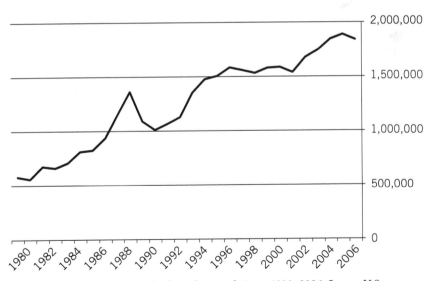

Figure 2.2 Number of arrests for drug abuse violations, 1980–2006. *Source*: U.S. Department of Justice, Office of Justice Programs, Bureau of Justice Statistics, http://www.bjs.gov/.

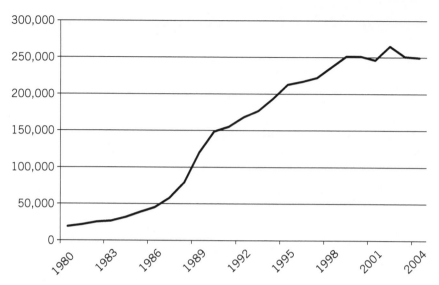

Figure 2.3 Number of persons in state correctional facilities for drug offenses, 1980–2004. *Source*: U.S. Department of Justice, Office of Justice Programs, Bureau of Justice Statistics, http://www.bjs.gov/.

1980s, and the result was a substantial increase in the overall prison population. These increases also were due to Congress requiring states to impose severe penalties for drug-related offenses on their own or face possible withholding of federal highway funds (Reuter 1992).

Presidents Reagan and Bush capitalized on the use of moral panics during the 1980s—especially those around the use of crack cocaine—to increase public's fear of drugs and acceptance of prioritizing law enforcement to deal with drug issues. One of the characteristics of moral panics is heightened concern over an issue. Exaggerated concern over drugs in the 1980s, despite the decrease in the overall use of drugs, was fueled by the media. Indeed, media reports promoted the idea that crack cocaine addiction was a serious epidemic; for instance, in 1986, the *New York Times* featured a cover story referring to crack as the "Issue of the Year" (Mauer 2004). Multiple studies of prime-time news reports found that illegal drug stories were dominant in the late 1980s (Jernigan and Dorfman 1996; Reuter 1992; Waldorf, Reinarman, and Murphy 1991). These stories used dramatic images and language: helicopters flying over the South American jungles (reminiscent of coverage during the Vietnam War), border agents discovering a drug tunnel under the U.S.-Mexico border, and anonymous black hands holding a dirty crack pipe are just a few examples (Jernigan and Dorfman 1996). Reports of feeble, underweight "crack babies" and their irresponsible (and, not coincidentally, poor and black) mothers also dominated headlines in the late 1980s, even though research would later reveal that such a "syndrome" never really existed (Humphries 1999). Also amid these reports were exaggerated claims about the prevalence of crack cocaine use, often with distorted graphs and statistics (Orcutt and Turner 1993). Indeed, media reports made it seem like crack use was a widespread problem despite a very small number of users compared to other drugs (Reinarman and Levine 2004).[7] Reagan himself promoted these exaggerated statistics by claiming in a nationally televised address that cocaine was "killing a whole generation of our children" (quoted in Waldorf, Reinarman, and Murphy 1991). This hyped rhetoric also emphasized the notion of choice in drug use (Hawdon 2001). For instance, Reagan said in the same televised address that the government would "continue to act aggressively, but nothing would be more effective than for *Americans simply to quit* using drugs" (cited in Hawdon 2001: 429, emphasis in original).

Moral panics also require a focus on "folk devils," stereotyped deviants responsible for the problem, in order to be successful. Stanley Cohen, the sociologist who first wrote about moral panics, highlighted the power that certain groups in society have to impose their views and interests on others (Ben-Yehuda 2009). For the crack cocaine moral panic, the folk devils were mostly poor urban black men and women. Media reports highlighted these folk devils concentrated in the inner city. The message to middle-class parents was clear: this menace was just one step away from their children unless the "problem" was eradicated. The medicalization of addiction was largely absent in the moral crusade regarding crack cocaine. Kohler-Hausmann (2010: 74) summarized it best when discussing the criminalization of drug addiction: "Pusher/addicts moved from being considered *diseased* to being cast *as the disease*" (emphasis in original). A notable example of this rhetoric was a televised address by President George H. W. Bush in September 1989, where he announced his drug strategy. During the speech, Bush famously held up a bag of crack cocaine that supposedly had been purchased in the park across from the White House, a dramatic image of how close the crack "epidemic" was to everyone.[8] In that speech, he specifically said, "We need more prisons, more jails, more courts, more prosecutors" (Sharp 1994: 60). Because of the crack hysteria, public concern over drugs swelled to a new high by 1989, with 27 percent of Americans indicating that "drugs" were the nation's most important problem. Bush's drug control strategy recommended increasing the number of drug arrests and expanding the nation's prison system. He proposed an increase in federal drug spending, including $1.6 billion for the federal prison system. While he also increased money for treatment, only 17–18 percent of the budget went toward treatment and prevention programs (Massing 1998). While this was certainly an improvement over the Reagan years, it was still quite low compared to the 1970s.

The War on Drugs continued through the 1990s, although the particular moral panic over crack cocaine subsided by around 1992 (Reinarman and Levine 1997). Clinton's 1994 drug control strategy proposed a 14.3 percent increase in funding for treatment and a proposed *decrease* in funding for drug interdiction efforts. His announcement of the strategy at a prison-based drug treatment program was particularly symbolic of what would prove to be the new approach to expanding treatment: via the criminal justice system. However, there was concern over new survey results that showed an increase in marijuana use among high school students, the first increase in fourteen years. Clinton's treatment initiative was cut as a result, and the subsequent budget had a smaller proportion of dollars going toward treatment and prevention—a comparable proportion as the final year of the Bush administration (Massing 1998). Clinton continued the trend toward increasing punishments for drug offenders. For instance, the 1994 Violent Crime Control and Law Enforcement Act tripled the maximum penalties for using children to distribute drugs near a school or playground. Clinton's well-known "Welfare Reform Act" (the Personal Responsibility and Work Reauthorization Act) restricted government benefits like housing benefits and cash assistance for those who were convicted of drug offenses. General Barry McCaffrey replaced Lee Brown as drug czar in 1996, and U.S. drug policy quickly moved back toward demand-side policies like attempts to destroy coca production in Columbia (known as "Plan Colombia").[9] There was a small increase in funding for treatment, but it was a rather trivial sum; most cities in the United States still had long waiting lists for drug treatment (Massing 1998). As a result, the arrest and incarceration rates for drug offenses continued to rise throughout the 1990s.

Regarding this escalation in the War on Drugs, historian David Courtwright (2010) pondered why the medical profession in the 1980s and 1990s did not fight this increasing criminalization of drug problems given the acceptance of the brain disease model. He concluded that it was largely because the brain disease model had not produced the "magic bullet" necessary to eradicate addiction. Anderson, Swan, and Lane (2010) made a similar argument in that the brain disease model is good for looking at the effects of addiction, but not at the causes. Courtwright (2010: 143) suggested that there would be "rapid medicalization of the field" with police and politicians giving full authority and control to physicians if there were a pharmaceutical drug to fully block the craving and euphoria of drugs. Based on the history of both drug policy and drug treatment, I disagree with his prediction. The medicalization of drug addiction has not reduced the stigma around drug use by very much. Moral messages about drugs and drug users flourish, even in the context of increased medicalization. Most significantly, the criminal justice system has successfully used medicalization to its advantage to retain control over drug issues. Punishment is perceived to be a legitimate way to treat addiction because of the "nature" of the disease.

Race and the War on Drugs

The impact that these policies have had on racial minorities, particularly African Americans, is impossible to overstate. Tonry (1994) argued that Reagan's and Bush's drug and crime control strategies of the 1980s and early 1990s were racially biased. The consequences of the policies support his argument. While arrest rates for drugs increased for all racial groups during the 1980s and 1990s, they increased much more dramatically for people of color. Between 1980 and 2003, the increase in drug arrests among whites was 70 percent, while for blacks it was 225 percent (King 2008). This disproportionate arrest rate is not due to increased drug use or trafficking among blacks, as surveys show that black respondents do not report statistically higher drug use or more drug-related crimes than whites (McBride et al. 2009; Tonry and Melewski 2008). Looking at national survey data of adolescents reveals that whites are actually *more* likely to use and sell drugs, yet African American youth are still more likely to be arrested for drug-related crimes (Kakade et al. 2012). This racial disparity in arrest during adolescence is then correlated with worse educational outcomes later.

Law enforcement strategies frequently target low-income communities with more public drug transactions rather than white suburban areas where drug dealing is less visible, leading to more arrests of people of color (Kennedy 2003). Even when whites deal drugs in open-air, urban places, police concentrate arrests in areas that have larger nonwhite populations (Beckett, Nyrop, and Pfingst 2006). Beckett et al. (2005) also show that law enforcement's disproportionate focus on crack—compared to other drugs sold more frequently—was the primary cause of the racial disparity in arrests for possession. The racial gap is then exacerbated by the higher likelihood of blacks or Hispanics receiving a prison sentence (Demuth and Steffensmeier 2004; Steen, Engen, and Gainey 2005).

Incarceration has profoundly negative impacts on people and communities, both economically and emotionally. Because of the disproportionate imprisonment of poor black men for drug offenses, these negative outcomes also are more likely to be concentrated among this group (Western 2006). Our drug policies have helped maintain white Americans' social, economic, and political dominance over blacks because of these negative outcomes, including higher unemployment and the elimination of voting rights (Davenport-Hines 2002; Tonry 2011). Wacquant (2001: 116) further argued that our prisons are "race making" institutions, largely because of these biased outcomes. Our prisons separate a largely nonwhite group from the mainstream population, creating the view that they are not deserving of full acceptance even when they are eventually released. Another result of these policies is the profound distrust within the African American community for law enforcement, especially concerning the War on Drugs. Bobo and Thompson (2006) found through surveys and focus groups that while 79 percent of whites believed drug laws were enforced fairly, only 34 percent of black respondents agreed. The War on Drugs also has increased whites' fears of people of color and the perception that they are criminals who need to be severely punished (Tonry 2011).

Further Moralization: Linking Drugs with the War on Terror

President George W. Bush issued his first National Drug Control Strategy in February 2002, which linked the drug war with the newly designated "War on Terror." In the introduction to the 2002 drug control strategy, he indicated that "Our fight against illegal drug use is a fight for our children's future, for struggling democracies, and against terrorism" (ONDCP 2002). He described drug profits as a way to fund terrorists. To introduce this link between drugs and terrorism, the White House funded television ads that promoted the connection. One such ad first ran during the 2002 Super Bowl and asked, "Where do terrorists get their money?" The ad then responded, "If you buy drugs, some of it might come from you." This new antidrug rhetoric reiterated the historical use of foreign threats to drive up the public's fear of drugs, similar to the use of anti-Mexican sentiment around the Marihuana Tax Act, or the threat of a communist take-over in the 1950s because of lax drug attitudes (McBride et al. 2009).

The largest overall budget item in Bush's drug policy was domestic law enforcement, which in Fiscal Year 2002, comprised more than 50 percent of total spending for federal drug control. Looking at the spending priorities from a "supply/demand" perspective shows that about 67 percent of the budget went toward "supply-side" tactics like law enforcement and interdiction, while only 33 percent went toward "demand-side" tactics like treatment and prevention (ONDCP 2002).[10]

How recent federal drug control strategies discuss drug problems reveals a conflation of medicalization and criminalization. For instance, in the 2006 National Drug Control Strategy, the only explicit treatment programs named in the report are drug courts, which are not what many would classify as treatment programs per se, but rather a criminal justice initiative that includes treatment with frequent court supervision. Obama's first drug control strategy (2010) continued this trend, putting drug courts in the "treatment" budget; this "treatment" budget item even included nontreatment-related aspects of drug courts like case management and "program coordination" as specific budget items. This appears to be an attempt to merge the "supply" and "demand" sides of funding, especially if drug courts are funded through the "treatment" portion of the budget. While Obama's initial drug control budget designated about one-third of funding toward treatment and prevention, the ambiguous designation of programs like drug courts (as both law enforcement and treatment programs) makes the proportion going toward actual treatment less clear.

Drug Policy Today and the Legacy of Criminalization

President Obama's first drug control strategy appeared to continue many of the policies of his predecessors, although the rhetoric in the published strategy called for moving drug addiction into the public health realm (ONDCP 2009).

While it is not yet clear if this new strategy will result in a fundamental shift in philosophy and practice, Obama did lift the ban on federal funding for needle exchange programs in 2009, and signed into law a reduction in the sentencing disparity between crack and powder cocaine, two contentious issues that his predecessors fought against.[11] Still, there have been more federal raids of medical marijuana dispensaries (legal in the states they are operating) under Obama than in previous administrations.

This overview of the history of drug policy in the past one hundred years reveals several common threads in how the United States has dealt with drug users. First, while the particular drug of focus would often change with the decade (marijuana in the 1930s, heroin in the 1970s, cocaine in the 1980s, methamphetamine today),[12] the policy strategies were strikingly similar: increase public's fear of the drug, often through sensationalized and racialized images, to garner support for more punitive policies. During each moral panic, drug problems were seen as a serious threat to the social fabric, yet U.S. drug use rates have never been exceptionally high compared to other countries (Caulkins and Reuter 2006). The strategies of increased enforcement also have done little to actually affect the supply of illicit drugs in the United States. Caulkins and Reuter (2006) found that as the incarceration rate for drug offenses skyrocketed during the late 1980s and 1990s, the price of cocaine and heroin dramatically decreased, the opposite outcome that would be expected. In addition, illegal drugs are not any more difficult to obtain today, considering the large amount of offenders in prison (Bushway and Reuter 2011). Second, while the medicalization of drug abuse and addiction also flourished during this time period and became integrated into policy, it never replaced the punitive nature of drug policy. As this chapter shows, the further medicalization of drug treatment within the increased criminalization of drug policy has led to the institutional overlap we have today. As discussed in the final section of this chapter, today's drug courts are the logical conclusion of our moralistic drug policy where we attempt to simultaneously treat and punish drug users.

Institutionalization Today: Drug Treatment and the Criminal Justice System

The history of drug policy in the United States reveals that the federal government has consistently favored moralistic and punitive approaches to controlling drug use. In addition, since the 1970s, the government's focus on treatment has been mostly tied to law enforcement rather than being an alternative approach to handling drug problems. This has led to a two-tiered approach to handling drug issues: the wealthy can access costly private drug treatment facilities, but the poor are faced with the criminal justice system as their primary way of accessing treatment (Campbell 2007; Mauer 2004).

Coerced Treatment

One strategy that overlaps medicalization and criminalization of drug use is the state's use of coerced treatment as an alternative to prison. The 1962 Supreme Court decision *Robinson v. United States*, in addition to overturning a state law that prosecuted those who consumed drugs, included a lesser-known provision that permitted a state to establish compulsory treatment for narcotic addiction, with penal sanctions for failure to comply with treatment (Inciardi and McBride 1991). California already had instituted its own Civil Addict Program in 1961, which involved the involuntary commitment of narcotic addicts for treatment. The 1966 Narcotic Addict Rehabilitation Act (NARA) permitted treatment to be used as an alternative to jail at the federal level. Most of these programs involved sending offenders to the narcotic farms described earlier, or versions of therapeutic communities with their harsh resocialization tactics (Faupel, Horowitz, and Weaver 2004).

Subsequent strategies have used coercion less overtly. The 1970 Controlled Substances Act authorized the diversion of primarily nonviolent, first-time drug offenders from the criminal justice system into addiction treatment programs (Inciardi and McBride 1991; Nolan 2001). This program became institutionalized in 1972, with the creation of the Treatment Alternatives to Street Crime (TASC) program. By this time, there was an increase in community-based treatment programs, and TASC diverted drug-involved offenders into those programs. The first TASC programs became operational in Wilmington, Delaware, and Philadelphia by the end of 1972 (Inciardi and McBride 1991).

TASC was based on three assumptions: that problems of drug abuse and addiction affect significant portions of the population, especially in metropolitan areas; that along with drug addiction comes a cycle of crime, arrest, incarceration, release, and often continued drug use; and that there are opportunities for the introduction of treatment alternatives to street crime because of the frequent contact between the addict and the criminal justice system (Inciardi and McBride 1991). The program also gave credit to two prevailing sociological theories of crime in the 1970s: labeling theory and social learning theory. Proponents of labeling theory argued that if a person who is arrested for a less serious, nonviolent crime (like drug possession) is given a strict sentence and labeled a criminal, he or she will then develop a criminal identity that leads to further, more serious criminal behavior. Social learning theorists argue that everything about criminal behavior is learned, so if you incarcerate an individual, that person will learn additional criminal techniques and have more opportunities for criminal behavior because of his or her association with other inmates. By initially focusing on pretrial diversion for first-time offenders, TASC was attempting to avoid both the use of the "criminal" label and the socialization of less serious offenders into career criminals (Inciardi and McBride 1991).

TASC expanded rapidly. By 1978, seventy-three projects in twenty-four states were being funded; the number of TASC programs increased to 178 by

1991 (Nolan 2001). TASC significantly increased the proportion of those in treatment who had criminal records (Inciardi and McBride 1991). While federal funding was completely withdrawn from TASC in 1982, it did have some funding restored in 1984 through block grants for programs aimed at drug-related crime. However, with no overseeing organization in place, TASC evolved in different ways in different settings. By the late 1980s, many of the TASC programs surveyed did not fit the original TASC model, and the kinds of services emphasized varied across programs (Inciardi and McBride 1991; Johnson and Waletzko 1992). TASC continues today as a broadly defined program that links offenders to drug treatment and provides case management services (Inciardi and Martin 1993).

Another way that treatment is incorporated into the criminal justice system is through prison-based treatment programs, which were first seen with the creation of narcotic farms in the 1930s. The 1986 Anti–Drug Abuse Act included millions of dollars for substance abuse treatment, of which a large proportion was directed at prison-based programs (Wexler 1994). Such programs expanded through the 1990s; a 1997 Substance Abuse and Mental Health Services Administration (SAMHSA) survey indicated that 40 percent of all correctional facilities nationwide had some sort of on-site substance abuse treatment, including detoxification and individual or group counseling (SAMHSA 2000). A more recent study found that the most prevalent services offered in prisons are group counseling (Taxman, Perdoni, and Harrison 2006). Many prison-based programs are modified therapeutic community programs; they aim to change the whole lifestyle of the inmate, including elimination of antisocial behavior and the development of prosocial attitudes in addition to abstinence from drugs (Inciardi and Martin 1993; Prendergast and Wexler 2004; Welsh and Zajac 2004). Despite their prevalence, the vast majority of drug offenders are not able to access drug treatment programs in prison; these programs have long waiting lists and recently have undergone major budget cuts (Johnson 2012; NIDA 2006; Taxman, Perdoni, and Harrison 2006; Wexler and Fletcher 2007).

While these initiatives (civil addict programs, TASC, prison-based drug treatment) were designed to deal with the increasing arrest rate and prison population of drug offenders, they all utilize some degree of coercion in their structure. Satel (2001) argued that the definition of addiction as a chronic brain disease actually makes it easier to advocate for coerced treatment because the implication is that the person cannot stop on his or her own. The disease view of addiction, then, actually promotes the paternalistic policy of coerced treatment, because the state is essentially saving sick people from themselves (Burke 1992).

Proponents of these programs who argue that the nature of drug addiction makes coercion necessary also cite research findings in support of the benefits of coerced treatment. NIDA claims that those who enter treatment because they are ordered by the court have as good if not better outcomes than those who are not (NIDA 2006). They also argue that for every dollar spent on drug treatment, there is a reduction of four to seven dollars in the cost of drug-related crimes.

Similarly, Burke and Gregoire (2007) found that those legally coerced into treatment had lower drug use and addiction severity at follow-up than those who entered treatment voluntarily. Other studies have found mostly positive outcomes from coerced treatment, including better retention in treatment and lower drug use and criminal activity after release (Polcin 2001). These positive outcomes could be related to length of time in treatment; those who are coerced into treatment through the criminal justice system typically stay in treatment longer (Hiller et al. 1998). Because of tight funding restrictions through private or public insurance programs, those who enter treatment voluntarily often do not have the benefit of remaining in drug treatment for as long a period of time. Some research also suggests that those who are coerced into treatment likely would not seek treatment on their own (Sterk, Elifson, and Theall 2000).

Other research, however, reveals that there is no clear benefit from coerced treatment. A national study revealed that the treatment dropout rate among persons legally coerced into treatment was no different than persons who attended treatment voluntarily (Perron 2007). McSweeney et al. (2007) followed 157 individuals in treatment across ten treatment centers in England and found that the coerced group had the same outcomes as far as future substance use and criminal activity as those who were not coerced. Another study of methadone maintenance patients in southern California showed similar treatment outcomes between those coerced and those not coerced (Brecht, Anglin, and Wang 1993). Norland, Sowell, and DiChiara (2003) also concluded that similar groups who do not receive any drug treatment have the same positive changes as those mandated to treatment.

A third body of research argues that outcomes are actually worse for those coerced into treatment (Farabee, Prendergast, and Anglin 1998; Seddon 2007). One study of methamphetamine users in a treatment facility found that the odds of relapse were actually 1.7 times higher for those reporting legal pressure to enter treatment than those reporting no such pressure (Brecht, Anglin, and Dylan 2005). Another study (Howard and McCaughrin 1996) found that programs with high rates of coerced clients (75 percent or more) had lower treatment plan compliance. In a review of eleven published studies, Farabee, Prendergast, and Anglin (1998) found that five showed positive relationships between coercion and treatment outcomes, four found no differences, and two found a negative relationship. The supposed positive effects found in coerced treatment research also are problematic because the studies often are based on small samples, lack generalizability, and rely on self-reports at follow-up, where those who are legally coerced would feel more pressure to report not using drugs because of perceived legal consequences than those not affiliated with the criminal justice system.

The inconsistent findings across research on coerced treatment suggest that the picture is more complicated than any one study might suggest. Coercion may be effective, but only for some groups, such as those with less serious drug problems (Powell et al. 2011; Salmon and Salmon 1983). Others argue that the positive effects seen for those coerced into treatment could be because many of those arrested for drug offenses do not actually have serious drug *use* problems (Norland, Sowell, and DiChiara 2003). This relates to my earlier point about the conflation of drug use with abuse, especially in criminal justice contexts. While those who are arrested do show higher drug use rates than the general population, there is likely extremely wide variation around how severe their drug use problem is, if they have one at all. Those with less serious drug problems would then likely show better outcomes compared to the voluntary treatment population. For instance, Sered and Norton-Hawk (2011) interviewed women who were court-mandated to attend AA/Narcotics Anonymous (NA) meetings and found that the majority attended as required but reported no personal benefit from attending.

In addition to the unclear benefits of coerced treatment, there are a number of ethical issues related to pressuring offenders into treatment. Seddon (2007) argued that forced treatment is a violation of basic human rights and that a person could actually get a longer sentence if he or she did not comply with treatment. He also argued that it creates further inequality in access to treatment; those arrested for a crime should not get access to treatment ahead of nonoffenders. Regardless of the ethical questions and equivocal research findings about the effectiveness of coerced treatment, it remains a fundamental principle of criminal justice initiatives that include drug treatment. It also underlies the philosophy and structure of today's drug court movement, called "enlightened coercion" by its advocates (Tiger 2013: 90).

Drug Courts

Perhaps the most significant criminal justice strategy that overlaps the medicalization and criminalization of drugs is the drug court movement. It also has been the most rapidly growing program for drug offenders in the past twenty-five years. The first drug court started in Miami, Florida, in 1989; today there are more than 2,700 nationwide. While drug courts vary by jurisdiction and include programs for both adult and juvenile drug offenders, the underlying principles that shaped their creation are supposed to be prevalent in all settings. These include the integration of drug treatment with criminal case processing, frequent meetings between drug court participants and the drug court judge (the chief monitor of their progress), and a system of graduated rewards and sanctions (Hora 2002). Most drug court programs restrict participation to nonviolent offenders with no more than one or two prior convictions. Programs vary in their designated length, but most are structured to last at least one year. Offenders typically are given a large incentive to participate: the possible expulsion of their offense from their record, a significant reward considering that many participants face felony charges. Alternatively, if they are evicted from the program because of noncompliance or rearrest, they most often are sentenced to a prison term depending on the offense and are not eligible for alternative programs or criminal court proceedings. This is because drug court participants typically plead guilty (nolo contendere) to their charges to enter the program. Proponents tout drug courts as the "most innovative, comprehensive, and successful alternatives to incarceration yet developed" (Hennessy 2001: 5), yet others argue that their philosophy and approach mirrors many previous criminal justice reforms from the Progressive Era and are not as innovative as they claim (Tiger 2013).

Drug courts have gained an extremely high level of support from many politicians, both Republicans and Democrats, and they are frequently mentioned in national drug court strategies (by both Republican and Democratic administrations). This broad acceptance is largely because drug courts overlap philosophies of both medicalization and criminalization. Those who are more sympathetic to the idea that drug offenders need treatment rather than incarceration appreciate the drug court model's emphasis on rehabilitation and access to treatment services. On the other side, those who are concerned about offenders getting off "too easy" are supportive of drug courts because of the strict requirements of the program and the drug court judge's tight supervision, including the "stick" he can threaten participants with: a prison sentence. The first drug court judge in Miami, Stanley Goldstein, articulated this perspective quite clearly when he lamented to a reporter at the start of Miami's drug court that the judicial system was so overloaded with drug possession cases that the vast majority of those arrested for possession of small amounts of cocaine were being released with "time served," even when they were convicted (Klein 1989). His comments suggest he felt that drug offenders were not being punished harshly enough and that drug courts could make sure offenders do not get off too easily.

Proponents of drug courts argue that they are effective because they reduce recidivism and save taxpayers money. Research generally supports these conclusions. Multiple studies and meta-analyses reveal that those in drug court programs and other similar criminal justice initiatives have lower rearrest rates and drug use than their counterparts who do not go through drug court, as well as reduced recidivism postgraduation (Anspach and Ferguson 2003; Belenko 1998; GAO 2005; Gottfredson and Exum 2000; Lowenkamp, Holsinger, and Latessa 2005; Marlowe 2010; Peters, Haas, and Hunt 2001; Sanford and Arrigo 2005; Turner et al. 2002; Wilson, Mitchell, and MacKenzie 2006; Zarkin et al. 2005). Still, there is much variation in the types and scale of outcomes between studies. In addition, there are no clear conclusions about which aspects of drug courts directly correlate to positive outcomes (NIJ 2006) or if drug courts have better outcomes than other initiatives that include drug treatment (Walsh 2011). Some studies suggest that higher-risk participants are more likely to benefit from drug courts (Fielding et al. 2002; Marlowe et al. 2007). It is important to note that the definition of "high risk" is relative across these studies; in some cases, just being younger is enough to designate the offender as "high risk." In addition, drug courts show significant cost savings, mainly due to reduced recidivism (Belenko

1998; Carey et al. 2006; King and Pasquarella 2009). Marlowe (2010) estimated that drug courts produce an average of $2.21 in benefits to the criminal justice system for every one dollar invested.

Not all research shows positive outcomes, however. Miethe, Lu, and Reese (2000), in an evaluation of Las Vegas's drug court, found that recidivism risks for drug court participants were significantly higher than for comparable offenders who did not go through drug court (26 percent versus 16 percent). In a study of Denver's drug court, Hoffman (2002: 76) found that the drug court was sentencing more drug defendants to prison than the traditional courts there ever did, by a factor greater than two. He also found no differences in recidivism between drug court participants and similar offenders before drug court started, a finding identical to the first drug court in Miami (Smith and American Bar Association 1991, cited in Hoffman 2002). A Government Accountability Office (GAO) study in 1997 looked at the existing drug court data and warned that there could be no firm conclusions regarding the impact of drug courts based on the limited information from evaluation studies (Terry 1999).

The benefits of drug court also are not evenly distributed among participants. Participants who are employed and have higher levels of education tend to have more positive outcomes in drug court, including graduating (Hartley and Phillips 2001; Schiff and Terry 1997). White drug court participants also have better outcomes, including graduation rates, than their black counterparts (Beckerman and Fontana 2001; Bowers 2008; Hartley and Phillips 2001; Sechrest and Shicor 2001; Wolfe, Guydish, and Termondt 2002). This discrepancy may actually exacerbate the already profound racial disparities in the incarceration rate for drug offenders considering that nongraduates are most likely sent to prison. In addition, studies have shown that the sentences nongraduates serve end up being longer than if they had never gone through the drug court program to start with (Bowers 2008; Miller 2004). Even the short-term jail sentences that drug court participants complete when sanctioned may add up to more time incarcerated than if they had gone through traditional criminal case processing (King and Pasquarella 2009).

Research studies on drug courts, especially early studies, are fraught with serious methodological problems, including the lack of appropriate comparison groups and statistical controls (Fischer 2003; GAO 2005; Hoffman 2002; Merrall and Bird 2009; Miethe, Lu, and Reese 2000; Turner et al. 2002; Wilson, Mitchell, and MacKenzie 2006). For instance, Belenko (1998) analyzed thirty drug court reports and found serious methodological problems, such as eliminating those who were evicted from drug court, which likely inflated the success rate. Many studies lack a comparable group to compare drug court participants to, and only compare graduates to nongraduates on recidivism rates (Finigan and Carey 2001). Also, most research follows up on participants in a relatively short period after graduation; few studies look at very long-term outcomes (Belenko 2002; Lowenkamp, Holsinger, and Latessa 2005). The individuals who are followed also determine how successful the drug court program appears; Wolfe, Guydish,

and Termondt (2002) found no significant differences between drug court participants and nonparticipants in rearrest at two-year follow-up, although there
was a large difference between nongraduates and graduates, with graduates
having much lower rearrest rates. Qualitative studies of drug courts show incon-
sistencies within the same court; for example, Paik (2011) studied three different
judges in a juvenile drug court and found that the outcomes differed depending
on which judge handled the case. She also found that the case managers' workload impacted results; those with fewer cases often had time to investigate before
applying sanctions. There is also apt to be more complexity when looking at cost
savings; a meta-analysis showed that drug courts were likely not cost-effective
for lower-risk offenders, those without prior records (Lowenkamp, Holsinger,
and Latessa 2005). Tiger (2013) pointed out an additional problem in evaluating
the success of drug courts: the main source of data collection and reporting
about graduates and nongraduates is also the national advocacy organization for
drug courts.

Critiques of drug courts and their evaluation studies focus on the bias of
who gets selected for drug court. O'Hear (2009) argued that there is racial bias
in the selection process (whites participate in drug courts at a higher rate than
blacks) because of the criteria that participants cannot have lengthy criminal
histories. Others have made similar arguments that drug courts essentially
"skim" the easier offenders to deal with, those who are more unlikely to re-
offend, even without drug court (Bowers 2008; Chriss 2002; Gross 2010; National
Association of Criminal Defense Lawyers 2009; O'Hear 2009). There are certainly more drug offenders arrested than there is room for them in drug courts,
allowing a selective labeling process for which individuals become "deserving"
addicts. This calls into question exactly why drug court participants show better
success rates than their counterparts; it might have nothing to do with the
intense supervision or coercion of drug courts, but instead the characteristics of
the individuals selected into drug court (Whiteacre 2008).

Other studies critique drug courts because of "net widening," where offenders who may have received probation or short-term jail sentences for their drug
offenses instead get pushed into the highly structured, intensive drug court program, where they also might spend more time than a potential jail sentence
(Drug Policy Alliance 2011; Gross 2010; Miller 2004; O'Hear 2009; Walsh 2011).
This could result in *more* individuals arrested for drug charges and therefore
under criminal justice supervision than if drug courts did not exist (King and
Pasquarella 2009; Tiger 2013).

There also is evidence suggesting that drug court participants do not always
meet the criteria for drug addiction yet are still permitted to participate in the
program (Bowers 2008; Miller 2004; Steen 2002). A study by the Urban Institute found that 80–90 percent of juveniles who were referred to drug courts
were *nondependent* users of alcohol and marijuana (Whiteacre 2008). If one
of the markers of "success" at follow-up is no illicit drug use, then those without
serious problems would be more likely to report not using drugs.

Regardless of the criticisms toward drug courts, they continue to have strong government and popular support, which has led to their rapid expansion. This explosion of drug courts has institutionalized the relationship between drug treatment and the criminal justice system. This chapter illustrates the tension between the medicalization and criminalization of drug problems. Policy has attempted to merge these perspectives through the parallel trend of increased federal funding for treatment *and* law enforcement. These seemingly contradictory aspects of drug policy actually overlap because both sides employ a medicalized view of addiction to achieve their goals. Unfortunately, this attempt to negotiate the multiple frameworks for labeling addiction into a coherent approach to "fighting" drug abuse ultimately leads to an ambiguous notion of what exactly the "disease" of addiction is and what should be done to deal with it. Does any other "disease" involve as many different institutions and individuals—doctors, psychologists, ministers, judges, parole officers, other addicts—as legitimate ways to treat it? This ambiguity is apparent in recent federal drug control strategies, where drug courts are named as a form of *treatment* despite their clear association with the criminal justice system. Reviewing these developments, it appears that supply-side tactics (like law enforcement) and demand-side tactics (like drug treatment) have converged in fighting the War on Drugs.

Conclusion

While the underlying philosophy of our drug policy might be confused and ambiguous, there is at least one concrete outcome: there has been a substantial increase in the number of people in treatment who are referred from the criminal justice system. As seen in Table 2.1, a 2007 report on treatment admissions nationally shows that 38 percent of all admissions were court mandated, the largest referral category (SAMHSA 2007). Looking at specific drugs that clients were in treatment for, the majority of those in treatment for marijuana problems (57 percent) were referred from the criminal justice system. This is not too surprising considering that arrests for marijuana sales and possession are the most common among illicit substances. Those in treatment for alcohol problems also had a high proportion that had been court mandated to treatment (43 percent). This is likely because treatment has been incorporated more into probation sentences for driving while intoxicated and in marijuana possession cases. The large proportion of marijuana users referred from the criminal justice system is also peculiar because marijuana has rates of admission similar to other substances like cocaine and heroin. Yet most of the admissions for cocaine and heroin are due to self-referrals or referrals from medical/treatment professionals. It appears that the criminal justice system is actually the primary one labeling marijuana addiction because so few individuals are entering treatment for marijuana use via their own assessment. These data suggest that the criminal justice system might actually be targeting marijuana users, or perhaps penalizing them more

TABLE 2.1. ADMISSIONS INTO A TREATMENT PROGRAM BY PRIMARY
SUBSTANCE OF ABUSE AND REFERRAL SOURCE, 2007

Source of Referral Treatment	PRIMARY SUBSTANCE OF ABUSE					
	Total Admissions	Alcohol	Marijuana	Heroin	Cocaine	Amphetamines*
Criminal Justice System	38%	42.5%	57%	14%	28%	57%
Self	33%	29%	15%	58%	36%	21%
Substance Abuse/ Health-Care Provider	17%	16%	10%	20%	22%	9%
Work/School	2%	2%	4%	0.3%	0.5%	0.6%
Other Community referral	10%	11%	14%	7%	13%	14%
Total (N)	1,817,577	732,925	287,933	246,871	234,772	143,024
Total Admissions by a Primary Substance		40%	16%	14%	13%	8%

*Includes methamphetamine.

Source: Office of Applied Studies, Substance Abuse and Mental Health Services Administration, Treatment Episode Data Set (TEDS).

harshly, in an effort to send a message about the seriousness of marijuana use in the context of the public's increasing push to decriminalize marijuana for medical and/or recreational purposes.

The main reason for this convergence centers around resources: as drug arrests and penalties increased, the court and prison systems became saturated with these cases. While recognizing this structural cause as a reason for the expansion of programs like drug courts, Nolan (2001) argued that the expansion was also due to a cultural shift in thinking about drugs as medical problems, a part of the larger therapeutic culture that emerged in the 1980s and early 1990s. As this and the previous chapter show, Americans do accept a medicalized notion of drug addiction to a certain extent and they have used it to advance reforms in drug policy (Reinarman 2005). However, medicalization is not the primary reason for the expansion of criminal justice initiatives that incorporate drug treatment. The primary reason is control: with increasing medicalization and overburdened courts and prisons, the criminal justice system was facing a crisis of institutional control over drug issues. If they failed to recognize that at least some of the drug offenders they were prosecuting needed treatment, then they would be viewed as too punitive and would lose institutional legitimacy. Hence, they created a model where treatment became firmly intertwined with punishment. This model not only reflects the public's perception that treatment on its own would not be punitive enough but also expands the criminal justice system's control over drug-related issues because it becomes the authority of not just punishment but treatment as well. As a result, drug courts, along with other similar strategies, actually increase the number of people under criminal justice supervision (King and Pasquarella 2009; Tiger 2013; Walsh 2011). Chapter 3 illustrates this expansion of control by looking at one city's drug court.

3

The Overlap of Clinical and Legal Authorities

Capital City's Drug Court

Though it was a blistery hot June afternoon, the courtroom's air condition-
ing made the city seem light-years away. Judge Gallo, a bearded white man
who appeared to be about sixty-five years old, sat at his bench; behind
him, a large banner proclaimed "Capital City Drug Court" in bright gold letters.[1]
A picture also appeared on the banner—the traditional scales of justice, modified by the addition of the medical symbol of two snakes around a staff in the
center. The judge began to lecture the six defendants before him, each of whom
had just entered a plea of nolo contendere (no contest) to their drug charges in
exchange for acceptance into the drug court program:

> To be in this program, we assume you have a problem with drugs and/
> or alcohol. . . . You all know the expression, "it's just the tip of the iceberg"?
> Well, if you understand that expression, then you get the point of this
> court. Only 10 percent of an iceberg is visible above the water. Well, the
> 10 percent above is the substance abuse. And the 90 percent below is
> the reason for it. If you have other problems, you need to recognize it.
> And we'll get you help. . . . You can get treatment, but you need to own
> up [*points to area in front of his bench*]. . . . You'll come here about once
> a month. You'll stand there in the middle. You'll have your case manager
> on one side and the treatment provider on the other. You know the Clint
> Eastwood movie *The Good, the Bad and the Ugly*? Well, we decide which
> you are. . . . I'm going to give you six words to memorize. If you memo-
> rize these six words and abide by them, you'll get through. There are
> three positive words and three negative ones. So, first, the positive ones:
> honesty—you have to be honest with the court and everyone else. There

can't be any denial. Second, be committed to doing this. It will take a year of your life, so you need to be committed. Third, be responsible. Maybe no one ever held you responsible for anything. Here, we'll hold you accountable. OK, now the three negative: [*says slowly*] people, places, and things. The vast majority of people fail the program because of these reasons. You can no longer after today be around people, places, or things. If you do, you'll fail.[2] . . . I'll leave you with a visual aid. There are three doors in this courtroom. The two doors behind you, that's where you come in and out, come and go as you please. The door to your left—that door goes to jail. So at the end, you will either go through one of those doors behind you, with a diploma under your arm, or you'll go through this side door and go to jail. It's up to you. Remember those six words: honesty, commitment, responsibility, people, places, and things. Back door graduate, side door terminate.

After finishing his speech, the judge exited the courtroom while the court coordinator, a petite white woman in her mid-forties, scheduled an appointment for each of the individuals to meet with the court evaluator; the court evaluator would, in turn, assign each of them to one of the court's approved community-based drug treatment programs. The six individuals had officially become "clients" of Capital City's drug court program.[3]

This chapter explores how a drug court program constructed and reinforced a "medicalized" understanding of drug addiction (that is, a disease that needs to be treated) in both its philosophy and daily operations. The analysis is based on fifteen months of observation of Capital City's drug court program, in-depth interviews with several of the court staff and program participants, and documents published both by Capital City's drug court and the National Association of Drug Court Professionals (NADCP).[4] While other criminal justice initiatives incorporate drug treatment, drug courts are the most heavily supervised of these initiatives, utilizing the threat of criminal sanctions while treating the "disease" of addiction.[5] Though the 2007 training manual of the NADCP conference asserted that "Drug courts strike a balance between 'hugging a thug' and 'locking them up and throwing away the key'" (NADCP 2007), the reality is that evoking two seemingly opposed perspectives—criminal and medical—in the same institutional setting actually created a great deal of ambiguity and tension when it came to labeling addiction and progressing through the program. While drug courts promote the idea that punishment and treatment are collaborative, these opposing approaches do not easily coexist. While the research for this chapter focused on one particular city's drug court program, the findings have a broader application to the larger movement of drug courts. While drug courts vary by locale, they have many components in common (Hora 2002). Thus, by examining one program in greater detail, we can better understand drug court programs as a whole, even if all of the findings are not representative of all drug court programs. Capital City's court also served as a "model court" for those who were planning drug courts in their own communities, indicating that its practices were promoted by the only national organization of drug courts.

In particular, three aspects of Capital City's drug court program reflected the tension inherent in marrying these two perspectives; the result was an ambiguous overlap of medical, legal, and moral frameworks in the labeling and managing of drug problems. These aspects were reflected in Judge Gallo's introductory remarks and form the basis for this chapter. The first aspect was that all members of the court had overlapping legal and clinical roles. As a result, they were charged with evaluating and monitoring both the client's clinical progress and legal issues. This created role conflict at times, especially for the public defender, who represented almost all of the drug court clients. While the traditional role of a public defender is to fully represent the client's *legal* interests, the court's emphasis on drug treatment meant that the public defender also became an advocate for the client's *clinical* needs. While this overlap of roles had the possibility of creating a more holistic approach to helping the client, it also created problems when there was a conflict between the client's clinical issues and legal rights.

The second aspect of the drug court program that exposed this tension between the medical and criminal perspectives was the way that the court program constructed addiction. The addict label was manipulated to either restrict or expand the number of clients eligible for the drug court program. In addition, court staff routinely reminded clients that they were not just addicted to using drugs, but that they also were addicted to the so-called "drug lifestyle"—the fast money of selling drugs and the lure of the criminal underworld associated with drug dealing. This framing resulted in the intertwining of addiction and criminality by labeling both as moral failures *and* clinical disorders. While all of the court staff and documents mentioned that addiction was a "disease," there was still a heavy moral overtone of the individual's responsibility for contracting the "disorder." This framing was found both in Capital City's drug court program and in training documents for the NADCP.

The third aspect was the drug court's overarching yet understated goal: to resocialize clients into responsible, dependable citizens. The court staff viewed the client's successful transformation into a healthy, productive citizen as the most important aspect of the program and, as an extension, saw their own roles somewhat as missionaries, leading lost souls to salvation. While the official requirements for moving through the drug court program focused on attending drug treatment and abstaining from drug use and additional crime, clients also had to prove to the court staff, especially the judge, that they were using the program's "tools" to become responsible citizens. Clients demonstrated this transformation by pursuing additional education, attending job training sessions, and providing evidence that they were supporting their families. Since addiction was perceived as a cause of criminality, the court used resocialization in an attempt to cure both. As such, an *individual's* transformation was enough evidence for the court staff that a drug court program was the best way to handle *society's* drug problems.

Overlapping Clinical and Legal Roles

The participant's handbook for Capital City's drug court program indicated that the program was "unique because it represents a much closer working union between treatment and the criminal justice system than is traditionally seen in the criminal courts." At the same time, however, this "union" between legal and clinical institutions was ambiguous in both theory and practice. Because the labeling and management of addiction took place in a courtroom setting and involved the court staff, it was difficult to disentangle the "treatment" part of the program from the other components. It also contributed to the ambiguity of whose authority (clinical or legal) it was to evaluate the extent of addiction and to provide treatment, since the court staff played such a large role in both the clinical and legal aspects of the program.

The Court Evaluator: Determining Who Is an Addict

Eligibility criteria for drug court programs vary by court; Capital City's program only accepted those who were arrested for a nonviolent offense and had no more than two prior convictions or juvenile adjudications. The Capital City program (through the district attorney's office) targeted individuals with first-time felony drug charges, mainly possession with intent to deliver, for entry into the program. As a result of this effort, almost all (96 percent) of the drug court participants faced a drug felony charge, according to an evaluation of the program between 1998 and 2000. That same report also indicated that the racial/ethnic breakdown of participants was 58 percent black, 28 percent Hispanic, and 13 percent white, which was very different from the racial/ethnic breakdown of the city where the program is located (43 percent black, 8 percent Hispanic, and 45 percent white, according to the 2000 census), although it may reflect the disproportionately higher arrest rate nationwide of African Americans and Latinos for drug-related crimes (King 2008). The median age at the start of the program was twenty-three years, and participants were almost exclusively male (83 percent). I witnessed a similar demographic breakdown during my own observations.

For those flagged as legally eligible for the program, the court determined the extent of each client's drug problem and appropriate level of treatment. The primary means for determining the level of treatment was a subjective questionnaire in which the client reported what types of drugs he or she used and how often. Thus, if a client admitted using *any* drugs and characterized it as a problem, the court evaluator, a white male in his twenties, labeled the client a drug addict in need of treatment. Further, the evaluator indicated that only serious mental health issues like schizophrenia would rule a client ineligible for the drug court program.

Using these criteria, the evaluator assigned most clients to outpatient drug treatment, often for "marijuana abuse."[6] The court evaluator also determined the type of treatment program a client needed based on how much structure the evaluator perceived the client had. Positive structure included having a job, going to school, or taking care of family responsibilities. Too little structure was seen as a symptom requiring a higher level of care. In an interview, the evaluator discussed his rationale:

> If you're twenty-eight and unemployed, playing PlayStation all day, chances are you're lit while you're doing it. And also if you're not *about* anything, then I'm gonna put you in treatment. I'm gonna make you about something. So a situation like that, I might put him in intensive outpatient just for a more healthy engagement. . . . More time in treatment is more access to making clients want more of themselves, you know what I mean? To want an education, or *want* a better job, or to *want* to do job training, anything like that.

In other words, the evaluator determined the appropriate drug treatment program not by the severity of the person's drug problem, but by the perceived severity of other individual or social problems like unemployment, undereducation, or the client's criminal history. In the above example, the evaluator assigned a client into intensive rather than ordinary outpatient treatment based on his unemployment. Intensive outpatient treatment typically involves eight to ten additional hours of treatment each week (in the form of group therapy), compared to ordinary outpatient treatment, and is typically reserved for those with more serious drug problems.

In his statement, the evaluator also revealed that part of the court's criteria for diagnosing the problem was an assessment of the client's *values*; the court evaluator emphasized that treatment could help transform a client into *wanting* education or a job. In order to assess these values, the evaluator gauged the client's own motivation for stopping drug use: "If two people are using the same amount [of drugs], I might make one outpatient and one residential [inpatient]. . . . What it really comes down to is, do I think this person is going to be able to become abstinent on their own? . . . I get a feel from the client . . . then I might try him at intensive outpatient, knowing I can always increase the level of care if I need to." These interview excerpts illustrate that while any drug use made a person clinically eligible for the drug court program, the evaluator also heavily relied on subjective judgments about motivation and values in his assessment of the severity of the "problem."

Funding restrictions also dictated the level of treatment the evaluator assigned because of the trend of reducing reimbursement rates for inpatient care. As a result, most people currently in treatment are in outpatient care. Similarly, the funding source for the court program had restrictions on inpatient care, which often was related to the client's own history of drug treatment. According to the court evaluator, "If someone has a couple of inpatients under their belt and I want inpatient, there's a very good chance that they're not gonna get it. [The funding agency] will say, 'Look, this isn't cost-effective. . . . They're just gonna have to stick this through at outpatient.'"

The funding agency's philosophy was to try a lower level of care before a higher one. This rationale was at odds with most medical treatments and also calls into question the whole point of assessment. If no client really "deserved" inpatient treatment, then why assess the drug severity at all? Similarly, the rationale that prior treatment excluded a client from future treatment was an affront to the belief that addiction is a "chronic disease" requiring repeated treatment episodes, which has been the perspective that many drug researchers and the National Institute on Drug Abuse (NIDA) emphasize (McLellan et al. 2000; Volkow and Li 2005).

This initial evaluation determined the client's course through treatment. Even if the treatment program evaluated the incoming client's drug problem differently, they had to follow the regimen the court sent them. The program supervisor for one of the treatment programs affiliated with the court mentioned to me in an interview that on occasion they had appealed the results of the court's evaluation, but that the court most times upheld the initial evaluation. The court makes the ultimate decision of what the client needs in terms of treatment. While the Capital City drug court staff embraced all forms of treatment, from inpatient to outpatient to methadone maintenance therapy, there have been other drug courts where the judge demanded that clients stop the use of methadone as a condition of participation in the court (Hora 2005). In those cases, the judge imposed his moral judgment about methadone as not a legitimate type of drug treatment despite its widespread acceptance and use among the treatment community. The NADCP supported these "no methadone" positions until recently (Hora 2005).

The Case Manager: Balancing Clinical and Legal Interventions

Once the client entered the program, the court evaluator assigned each of them a case manager. The case manager worked very closely with both parts of the drug court program—the clinical and the legal. As a result, case managers were in a very demanding position: they had to ensure that the client's clinical needs were being met while overseeing his or her progress through the program.

On the court side, the case managers were responsible for helping clients access the ancillary services that the court expected clients to utilize, such as general educational development (GED) or job training classes. Because of the individualized plans, this involved very different work for each client. For instance, the same case manager might help one client enroll in community college courses and then locate funding for transitional housing for another client. Case managers also carried a large caseload, about forty-five to fifty-five clients each at any given time, indicating that they likely spent very little time each month with each client. Still, case managers had mandatory monthly meetings with each client, so they undoubtedly had a very busy job.

At the same time, the case manager had to "ensure the client's current level of care is and remains appropriate" (from "Overview of Case Manager Responsibilities"). This involved monthly visits to the treatment programs and meetings with therapists to discuss the client's progress in treatment. Case managers were the only members of the drug court team that I ever witnessed visiting the treatment programs associated with the court. While the other court staff had roles that overlapped the clinical and legal aspects of the court program, the case manager position was deliberately constructed with overlapping roles.

The Public Defender and the Assistant District Attorney: Negotiating the Illness with the Crime

After an individual was deemed clinically and legally eligible for the drug court program, he or she met with the public defender, a white woman who appeared to be in her mid-forties. She was the only public defender who represented drug court clients, and by her own estimate was the appointed attorney for 75 percent of them. At the time of our interview, she had been working in this role for about eight years. Even the clients who hired private attorneys had frequent contact with the public defender since she often represented them at monthly court appearances. At the initial meeting, she went over the details of the client's case and made a recommendation about whether or not she thought the individual should enroll in the drug court.

In a traditional criminal court, the public defender's primary role is to offer the best possible legal counsel to the client to ensure that the client's due process rights are protected. In the drug court, the public defender often blended legal and clinical advice. For instance, the public defender's recommendation to the client to enter the drug court program was based not just on the evidence of the alleged crime but also on the evaluation of the client's drug problem:

> INTERVIEWER: If you think that someone, if they take the case to trial will get off, will you advise them that [the drug court] is probably not in their interest?
>
> PUBLIC DEFENDER: Not always, it's really a combination of factors . . . because the other thing that the drug court offers is very effective drug treatment and intense case management and referral to ancil-

lary services. So there are a lot of benefits to a client, so it's not strictly based on the [criminal charges].

The public defender explained that she sometimes considered other factors
besides the chances of success in a traditional criminal court when recommend-
ing the program, a practice found in other drug court research (Paik 2011). If
she thought that the client's drug problem was severe enough, or that the individual would benefit from "ancillary services," such as job training, individual
counseling for mental health problems, or access to further education, then she
might advise the client to enter the program. In other words, she advised clients
to enter drug court even if they had a good chance of "beating the case" in the
traditional criminal court system. Using both legal and clinical criteria to determine her recommendation repositioned the public defender as an advocate not
just for the client's legal rights but for clinical ones as well. While she appeared
to appreciate this overlap in roles because she felt that the drug court could
address the underlying problems associated with the client's criminal behavior,
her advocating the drug court program for reasons other than legal considerations
could be construed as a conflict with her assigned duty and could negatively
impact the clients' constitutional right of due process.

The court evaluator concurred with this analysis. He suggested that the
public defender recommended the program to everybody that he labeled an
addict: "[The public defender] really encourages *everybody* to take the program
and she has a million clients and not a lot of time, so they don't really get the
scope of the program necessarily. They kinda get the like, 'if you don't want this
on your record, take drug court.'" This description suggested that the public
defender did not clearly explain all of the client's legal options. At the same time,
she did not personally benefit from so many clients entering the program since
having more clients actually increased her own workload, so it appears that her
advice to the clients was based on a clinical judgment. Clients, however, may have
been more persuaded to enter the drug court program by the threat of prison and
a criminal record than by the desire for drug treatment or ancillary services.

One assistant district attorney, a white woman who appeared to be in her
late twenties, was assigned to the court and was present in almost every court
session I observed. For the most part, she remained quiet during monthly court
appearances and seemed to work together with the public defender and the
judge in making sure the clients were progressing through the program. Studies
of other drug courts across the United States reveal that one of the defining
characteristics of a drug court is that the judge, public defender, and district
attorney shed the typical adversarial roles associated with a criminal court and
instead work cooperatively on each client's case (Hora 2002; Mackinem and
Higgins 2008; Nolan 2001; Steen 2002; Terry 1999; Whiteacre 2008). While this
certainly also was the case in Capital City's program, conflict arose periodically,
and it was almost always related to the inherent tension of operating as both a
legal and a clinical authority.

One way that those who worked in the drug court, the "court team," attempted to balance clinical and legal elements in conflict was through successful manipulation of the "backstage" and "front stage" settings in the courtroom (Goffman 1959; Steen 2002). While the front stage was the courtroom floor where cases were publicly presented, the backstage was the judge's chambers, where the various court players discussed clients who had violated one or more of the program's rules. During these backstage meetings, which took place before the afternoon court session, the court staff discussed the day's "problem cases" and predetermined sanctions. The client was not present at those meetings, and likely did not even know that they took place. Here, the public defender described those meetings:

> PUBLIC DEFENDER: It's really collective decision making so everybody has a say, everyone asks questions, everybody tries to figure it out.
> INTERVIEWER: So is everything basically decided in that meeting, before the client appears in front of the judge?
> PUBLIC DEFENDER: Correct.

At the same time, as the evaluator explained in an interview, there was often disagreement in the backstage meetings: "The [problem cases] are addressed before court with the DA, the public defender, the judge, the case manager, and the case manager supervisor. So when it does come to the bar of the court, it's almost like it's scripted. Sanctions are usually decided back there. 'Cause the argument that takes place back there, nobody needs to see [that], certainly not the client." As the evaluator illustrated, conflict occurred at those meetings over what was considered an appropriate sanction, or whether or not the client should be terminated from the program. However, when it was time for the client to appear before the judge, and for the team to put on their "front stage" performance, the team created the appearance of unity, thus promoting the view that they were always in agreement over the client's clinical and legal progress. Other drug court studies suggest that these "backstage" meetings are a common practice (Lindquist et al. 2006).

Occasionally, disagreement between the court team occurred in the front stage view, on the courtroom floor. These situations, which were rare, most often involved the public defender arguing for leniency in sanctioning due to an unaddressed treatment need. The assistant district attorney, in those times of conflict, most often argued against any leniency and advocated for harsher punishment, regardless of the "clinical" case that the public defender made. The following is one such example from my field notes of a "show cause" hearing, the final hearing that determined if the client would be terminated from the drug court program:

> ASSISTANT DA: Your Honor, you know this case well. The client began the program in March of 2004 and she doesn't even have a phase 1 certificate yet. She went AWOL, relapsed. In September of 2004 she

was sentenced to a jury box . . . three days jail in October 2004. Tested positive for opiates and cocaine . . . was discharged from Recovery House for breaking rules. . . . Your Honor said it was her last chance. . . . We request that she be terminated from the program.

PUBLIC DEFENDER: Your Honor, the client is only twenty-four years old and she doesn't have a substantial criminal record. What she does have is an addiction. Her problem in the program has primarily been with relapsing. At [treatment program], there was some report of behavioral problems. The court ordered a psychiatric [evaluation] because it was felt that the client might be a dual-diagnosis. It's known that 60 percent of women addicts have a dually diagnosed mental health problem. The psychiatric didn't occur. It was finally done and she was diagnosed with a mood disorder and bipolar disorder. The dual diagnosis should have been identified earlier. I am asking the court for another chance because of this late diagnosis.

JUDGE GALLO [*addressing public defender*]: Tell me. What responsibility does *she* bear? What you're telling me is it's collectively all our fault. What's *her* responsibility? Second, you asked for all those things. *You're* the one.

PUBLIC DEFENDER: Judge, I missed this too. I didn't push for the psych evaluation. What's her responsibility? To be honest with what's going on with her, I don't know if someone can diagnose themselves. A lot of our clients give in to impulse and they don't know why. She's found out and now needs to deal with it.

JUDGE: But she's not even trying! I don't see any basis for letting her continue.

PUBLIC DEFENDER: Will the court hear from her?

JUDGE: Sure, go ahead.

CLIENT [*crying*]: I don't think I deserve another chance. . . . Nobody has any reason to believe me, including my mother, who is present here [*motions to back of courtroom*]. But, I'm just tired of using.

JUDGE [*angry*]: What are you *doing* about it? Now you're tired because you're going to jail?

CLIENT: No. I'm tired of everything. The lifestyle . . .

JUDGE: I hear this all the time: [*in a mocking tone*] "I'm an addict. I need help. But I won't stop using and I won't go to treatment!"

CLIENT: I had a hard time at some of the programs. . . . I didn't get along with the counselors. I don't know what else to say.

JUDGE: I don't see any effort. . . . The court finds you guilty of possession of OxyContin with intent to deliver. Guilty of conspiracy. November 15th, back here for sentencing.

This is a typical scenario of the type of conflict that occurred in the courtroom. In this situation, the public defender used addiction research as well as a personal appeal by the client to try to persuade the judge that the client needed more intense treatment and therefore should be allowed to stay in the program. The public defender justified the client's irresponsible behavior as a symptom of her "disease." The judge, however, did not give the client another chance because he perceived her as irresponsible, regardless of her mental health or addiction issues. The judge and the assistant district attorney did not dispute the evidence that she had mental health issues, but for them, a psychiatric diagnosis did not diminish the client's level of responsibility in any way. While these cases were relatively rare, they revealed that the public defender's role was to "defend" the client's addiction from those who pushed for more punitive outcomes. In that sense, she advocated both clinically and legally for her client's rights. The judge and the assistant district attorney, however, shed most of their clinical roles during times of conflict and pressed for legal consequences for what they touted was irresponsible behavior. The assistant district attorney never asked the court for leniency because of clinical issues.

Another way the public defender advocated for clinical treatment over punishment was by requesting a clinical reevaluation for a client facing termination. This appeared to be used mainly as a stall tactic. If the judge permitted the reevaluation, then the case was pushed back another month. The public defender advocated for reevaluations most often when the judge appeared undecided about what to do with a particular client, as though the extra month and more serious diagnosis would sway the judge to let the client have another chance in the program. The court evaluator mentioned that he might get sent some clients from the court to reevaluate if the public defender was "lookin' for an angle." In a sense, the public defender used clinical issues as "evidence" that the client should not be sent to prison, preserving her primary role as a defense attorney.

Similarly, the public defender pushed for clinical considerations during sentencing hearings. When a client was terminated from the program, the judge determined the final punishment. The following excerpt is from a case that was scheduled for a "show cause" hearing, but the client waived his right to the hearing and asked to proceed directly to sentencing:

> PUBLIC DEFENDER: I would like to ask the court to recognize that he did waive his right to a show cause hearing. He's taking responsibility. . . . He also made substantial progress on his recovery. . . . He did relapse and he didn't come back and ask for help. . . . He says he's learned a lot from the program. . . . Hopefully, once he finishes his sentence, he can put those tools to use . . . he can come out and be the person he's learned to be through treatment—a good husband and father.
>
> CLIENT: I accept my failure. Thank you for the opportunity. I learned a lot, but unfortunately I wasn't able to apply it. When I'm out, I'll try to apply it.

JUDGE GALLO: This is not pleasurable for the court, especially since you've been here for more than three years. And now you're being terminated and sent off to prison. You will be released from prison at some point, and if you don't change your ways, you'll be right back here. Either jail or death, that's it. I accept that you've learned a lot and the court recognizes that you completed phases 1 through 3. Sentence is as follows . . .

In this case, the assistant public defender's appeal appeared to result in leniency; while the maximum sentence for the client's two charges was thirty to sixty years, the judge ordered the client to jail for only eight and a half to twenty-four months for both charges concurrently. While there was no case in which the judge gave the maximum sentence, both by my observation and through his own admission to clients during court sessions, the sentence he gave in the previous case was particularly lenient (about one year) compared to the maximum sentence (sixty years). The image the public defender created—that the client took responsibility despite violating the program's rules—was enough evidence for the judge and led him to agree with the assessment.

The Judge: Holding both the Carrot and the Stick

Like other drug courts, Capital City's program used a "carrot and stick" approach, where the "carrot" symbolized an expunged criminal record and the "stick," prison. Judge Gallo discussed this during a radio interview:

The carrot is this: you're arrested for selling drugs, it's a felony offense, many people are facing five to ten years as a maximum sentence. What we're gonna do is give you all the treatment you need, all the ancillary services you need, and then at the end of this, if you graduate, your plea is withdrawn and your case is dismissed with prejudice. It's over forever. . . . And then a year later, if you're arrest-free and drug-free, we're gonna expunge your record. . . . Now that's the carrot. The stick is this: if you don't complete the program, you are going to jail, and the only question is how long.

This carrot and stick model implied that the client required *coerced* treatment. Access to high-quality treatment would not be enough to curb the client's drug and criminal problems. In the same radio interview, the judge emphasized that the clients eligible for drug court required intense supervision by the court staff through all phases of the program: "I'm not here to minimize treatment, 'cause treatment is a major component of this, but you have to have a carrot and stick. There are statistics out there that will tell you most voluntary treatment does not work. What works is coerced treatment. . . . This program, they come before me, we review everything . . . we hold them accountable for what they need to do." In a sense, Judge Gallo was saying that clients needed the court's supervision to adhere to a treatment program because they lacked the requisite responsibility to get "better" on their own. The "sicker" a client was, the more they needed the stick inherent in the drug court model.

Other court staff also mentioned that many drug court clients initially lacked motivation for the program. According to the court evaluator, "one of the things that drug court offers is the riding. Like, even if you don't want it, we're gonna ride you and make you want it." The carrot and stick model, then, was not just a passive symbol of the possible repercussions in the program. These interviews revealed that the court staff also took on paternalistic roles because they did not think clients knew what was best for them, either clinically or legally.

The drug court model puts judges in charge of both the client's treatment plan and his or her criminal record. In Capital City's drug court, Judge Gallo had the ultimate authority in assessing the client's legal and clinical progress; the judge's role has been referred to as a "moral authority" in other drug court research (Tiger 2013), a useful framing for the power the judge held in the drug court. While the court staff mostly functioned as a "team," they all acknowledged who the leader was. When the public defender was asked in an interview how she monitored her clients' progress in the program, she responded: "Well, I don't monitor their progress, the judge monitors their progress. The treatment team, we *evaluate* their progress." Considering the attack on judicial discretion through policies like mandatory minimum sentencing, it is not surprising that judges have embraced the drug court model; it puts them back at the forefront of determining the client's punishment and, in this institution, treatment.

Like a well-rehearsed play, the client's monthly appearance in the courtroom followed a script. The client appeared before the judge, standing in between the case manager and the drug treatment counselor, both of whom summarized the client's report. The judge then asked, "How are you doing?" and often congratulated the client on having a "good report" or said that he or she was "doing well." From these interactions, "doing well" meant that the client had attended all scheduled treatment sessions, had no positive urine drug screens, and had met with his or her case manager. In addition, if the client had been in the program for a significant length of time, then "doing well" also included achieving gainful employment or pursuing some educational goal, such as taking GED courses. The judge seemed genuinely pleased when clients were doing well, and often joked with them or asked about family members during these interactions. He also used these clients as examples of responsible behavior to the rest of the courtroom, where all of the clients scheduled that day had to sit and wait until they were called. The vast majority of cases I observed involved clients consistently "doing well." It also was always the judge who gave sanctions to those clients deemed not to be doing well.

The Drug Court: Both Part of and Distinct from the Criminal Justice System

The drug court team's overlapping clinical and legal roles is a fundamental aspect of the structure of drug courts. The NADCP explicitly stated in a training session that "every member of the drug court team is in a therapeutic relationship with the client." Drug courts promote the idea that punishment and treatment are collaborative, yet critics have argued that this setup could violate the client's due process rights and the true purpose of a court of law (Boldt 2002; Fischer 2003; Hoffman 2002; Mackinem and Higgins 2008; Quinn 2000; Spinak 2003). Still, drug court proponents argue that the law can be used as a "therapeutic tool" to help people, a principle known as therapeutic jurisprudence (Wexler and Winick 1996). Drug courts emerged around the same time as this perspective of therapeutic jurisprudence (Nolan 2001).

The structure of funding for drug courts also reveals their distinct position of being both clinical and legal entities. For instance, while drug courts are part of the criminal justice system (the "supply" side of the drug war), they are largely funded through state and local dollars earmarked for drug *treatment*, which places them on the "demand" side. The staff saw themselves on the treatment side of fighting the drug war, despite being an arm of the court system. For example, the public defender referred to drug court as a "treatment program" to potential clients at an orientation session. The judge also claimed in an interview that at an invited luncheon on national drug control policy he was the only one from the "demand side" (referring to treatment).

Because of this structure, drug courts are also political entities that require special funding in order to survive. A search of newspaper articles regarding Capital City's drug court showed that the court nearly shut down in 2003 due to lack of state funding; the state legislature restored its funding in early 2004. While criminal courts are considered essential to the criminal justice system, drug courts need to market themselves as effective alternatives for drug-related crime in order to maintain funding. One way that Capital City's drug court marketed its positive aspects was by inviting prominent politicians to graduation ceremonies where they witnessed successful clients earning their diplomas and publicly having their cases dismissed. At one particularly emotional graduation, I witnessed several members of the state legislature, including the Speaker of the House, observing the event from the jury box. The NADCP Web site showed that other drug courts across the United States went as far as to set themselves up as nonprofit organizations that hosted fund-raisers, including one drug court in the Midwest that held an annual golf tournament to raise funds for the court.

The court staff also viewed themselves as a distinct entity from the traditional criminal court and the rest of the criminal justice system. In many ways, they saw themselves as part of a new solution to the "drug problem." The court evaluator commented: "I have no problem with drugs being a criminal issue. I do have a problem with the incarceration around it, the fact that we're building prison-industrial complexes all over. Our whole drug court is about keeping people out of jail. And the case managers, the legal team, everyone has that same mentality." Everybody I interviewed had a similar view—that the drug court was a better way to handle these types of offenders than the typical court system; nobody advocated for drug legalization.

Related to their distinct position as being involved in both clinical and legal outcomes, members of the drug court team also monitored the drug treatment programs affiliated with the drug court. Through weekly reports and meetings with case managers, the therapists from the treatment programs had to demonstrate the extent to which the client was participating in the court-determined treatment plan. According to the public defender:

> The drug court is very involved in holding the treatment facilities accountable for providing effective treatment. The traditional criminal justice system is not usually involved. They usually assume that the treatment facility is providing adequate treatment without really knowing if they are or not. So that allows the client to get effective, real treatment.

The court staff emphasized that monitoring the treatment programs was another positive aspect of the drug court program; this monitoring also differentiated the drug court from the traditional criminal court system. In a sense, the court extended its carrot and stick model to the treatment programs: the carrot being a continued relationship with the program (and paying for the clients it sends there), the stick being the discontinued use of that particular facility, which could have negative financial consequences for the treatment program. The court was an active participant, then, in assessing how treatment services were delivered, rather than just monitoring the client's compliance with the program's rules.

Because of the staff's overlapping roles in managing the clinical, legal, and punitive components of the program, they ultimately chose which area to emphasize (that is, whether the client needs more treatment or the client needs prison). In the next section, I discuss situations in which the addict label was contracted to exclude clients from the program and when it was expanded to include broader drug-related activities. I also examined documents from the NADCP to understand how issues of addiction were framed and formally communicated to drug court staff.

Labeling Addiction in Drug Court

The Contraction and Expansion of the Addict Label

A potential client's criminal record initially determined eligibility for Capital City's drug court program; drug use was not the first consideration. Since the district attorney's office targeted drug felony cases and there were only enough resources to handle approximately four hundred cases a year, most individuals who qualified for the program never had the option of entering. Most eligible participants were probably not even aware of the program, since the DA's office only diverted the drug sale cases it deemed eligible into an orientation meeting where they explained the court program. Other research has estimated that about half of eligible cases do not get referred to drug courts (Goldkamp, White, and Robinson 2001). Some of these other cases did find their way into the program—perhaps the individual's lawyer knew about the program or the case was sent to the public defender's office and the attorneys decided to refer the case to the drug court. Still, almost all of the cases that ended up in drug court were from that targeted group of drug sale cases that the district attorney's office processed.

This classification led to two possible outcomes and, as a result, problems with the way the addict label was constructed. One possible outcome was that those with drug problems were not labeled "addicts" if the criminal offense was too serious to be eligible for the court program. For instance, individuals who committed violent offenses or offenses that carried mandatory minimum sentences were, for the most part, not eligible for the court program. They were not "deserving" of treatment. However, the implication by the district attorney's targeting system was that if you sold drugs then you likely also used drugs, making you eligible to be labeled an addict. But if you carried a gun when you sold drugs (a violent offense), possessed a large quantity of drugs when you were arrested (something that might trigger a mandatory minimum sentence), or had been arrested before, then you were not labeled a "deserving" addict and your case went through the traditional court system. Mackinem and Higgins (2008) observed three drug courts in the southeastern United States, and they also witnessed this distinction between criminals and addicts regarding who was considered appropriate for drug court. In one of their courts, someone went as far as to say that "criminals, not addicts, used guns" (73). These distinctions, while somewhat arbitrary, are related to how drug court workers frame addiction and who they consider deserving of the addict label. Admittedly, there are other criminal justice initiatives that such a person might be eligible for, including treatment in prison. However, most people with drug problems never receive treatment in prison and many prison-based drug treatment programs have been cut or eliminated.

More important, there was a conceptual problem in assuming that those who sold drugs also were addicted to using drugs, which was the underlying assumption of the district attorney's targeting scheme. Thus, the second possible outcome was that someone legally eligible for the drug court program based on the targeting might not actually have a serious drug problem. It is certainly not uncommon for heavy users to also sell drugs (Waldorf, Reinarman, and Murphy 1991), but that does not appear to be the typical drug court client. One research study found that about one-third of felony drug court participants across the United States did not meet the clinical criteria for having a significant substance use disorder (Marlowe, Festinger, and Lee 2004). In Capital City's program, evidence suggested that many of those labeled "addicts" never actually demonstrated a significant problem with drug use. Several staff members of a treatment program affiliated with the drug court revealed to me in interviews that they believed the majority of clients that the court sent to their treatment program did not have significant drug use problems. One of these staff members related the drug court's published success rate, as in the large number of clients who remained drug-free after graduating from the program, as "overinflated" because most of the drug court clients did not have a serious drug problem at the start of the program.

This mislabeling of drug addiction was largely because of three issues with the clinical evaluation. First, the evaluator assessed the severity of a potential client's drug problem solely on the client's self-report. As long as the client expressed drug use to be a problem, they were labeled an addict in need of treatment. This could be due to the use of a vague assessment tool and also to the evaluator's own view of the etiology of addiction, as he expressed in an interview:

> The idea of addiction that is laid out in twelve-step fellowships is the one that I subscribe to . . . that it is a *spiritual* problem, it comes from self-centeredness, obsession, compulsion, these kind of things. . . . Some people think it's too hokey to really talk about it that way. . . . They can't take it back to a gene or something or other. But I have noticed it to be the most true and that's good enough evidence for me.

The criteria of the *Diagnostic and Statistical Manual of Mental Disorders* (*DSM*) for drug abuse and dependence are loose enough that such a broad assessment of the client's problem is not surprising. In earlier versions of the *DSM*, a person would only need to exhibit one "symptom" of severity to be labeled as having a substance abuse problem.

The second and related issue was that any illicit drug *use* was conflated with drug *abuse*, a practice that occurred in other drug courts (Mackinem and Higgins 2008; Whiteacre 2008). In an interview, the judge expressed belief in the "gateway theory" of drug use, which proposes that those who use "softer" drugs like alcohol, tobacco, and marijuana, especially in adolescence, will progress to using "harder" drugs like cocaine or heroin (Yamaguchi and Kandel 1984). This theory is largely the foundation of current U.S. drug policy and helps explain the harsh penalties associated with marijuana possession (including the government's labeling of marijuana as a "Schedule I" drug, indicating very high potential for abuse and no medical value). Other research has shown the limitations of the gateway theory, including its lack of incorporating sociological aspects of drug use and the variations across birth cohorts in drug use progression (for example, Golub and Johnson 2002). In addition, data from the National Household Survey on Drug Abuse in the early 1990s showed that the vast majority of respondents who had used alcohol and marijuana very rarely became heavy drug users or abusers (Golub and Johnson 2002). Still, the theory has been widely promoted and helps to explain why those in the drug court program viewed marijuana use very seriously, even if it was infrequent. For instance, clients who used marijuana once or twice a week would be sent to outpatient treatment and labeled as clinically appropriate for drug court. Further evidence of this conflation of use and abuse was demonstrated during the formal entering of the client's plea of no contest. One of the court administrators would read the new client's name, what they were arrested for, their drug(s) of choice, and the assigned level of treatment. Often, the judge would then ask the client when his or her last drug use was. In one instance, I witnessed a new client who had been arrested for possession with intent to deliver heroin being assigned to outpatient treatment for marijuana use. When the judge asked him when he last used, he indicated "two months ago." That the illicit drug use occurred that long before the client was beginning treatment did not appear to be problematic. Several other clients assigned to treatment also reported past use but did not appear to be using drugs currently.

The third issue that contributed to potential mislabeling of addiction was that the clinical evaluation did not occur until after an initial orientation to the drug court program where clients learned that they already were *legally* eligible for the program and that the only other barrier to entering was being labeled a drug addict. The public defender told potential clients at the orientation to the drug court program that there were only two requirements for them to join drug court: that they were drug users, and that they plead no contest to their charges. An expunged record was a huge incentive for those facing a felony conviction, so undoubtedly some embellished or falsified their own drug use to become clinically eligible for the program. While other research questioned the validity of self-reports of drug use because respondents tend to deny or minimize drug use, as shown through the comparison with urinalysis tests (Harrison 1995), nobody in the court program seemed concerned with the opposite—embellishing a problem to get into the program.

While this subjective standard for labeling drug addiction might seem like a serious problem for the integrity of the drug court program, nobody on the court side ever articulated it as such. Further, the addict label itself was reconstructed within the drug court. That is, "addict" became a loose label for persons who engaged in any drug-related behavior, from occasional use to frequent use to selling drugs. This distinction was most apparent during the graduation ceremonies, where clients admitted to being addicts, but not necessarily addicted to *using* drugs. One former drug court client noted this in an address to a group of new graduates: "Let me start by saying that we have two kinds of addicts here—the drug user and the drug seller. One is addicted to drugs, the other addicted to money. I don't want you to think that if you don't use drugs that you're not an addict." In another graduation ceremony, one of the graduates expressed a similar perspective: "I wasn't addicted to the drug; I was addicted to *selling* the drug. . . . I would make a lot of money right on the spot and I could buy whatever I wanted, right then. Now I'm working and I make money, but it's different. I can't get things right when I want them. I have to wait for my paycheck."

All of the clients who graduated from drug court also completed a community-based drug treatment program. Most often, these clients attended sessions as scheduled and had few or no sanctions. The court staff defined the treatment experience as a success if the client attended sessions and tested negatively for drug use. However, if the client never really had a problem with using drugs, then abstaining would not be very difficult. Still, many clients appeared to embrace this broad label of addiction by self-identifying as addicts and reporting that the drug "lifestyle" was just as powerful an addiction to overcome. While other research has shown that drug sellers, especially those who began at a young age, were attracted to the job because of the fast way to make money (for example, Cohen and Stahler 1998; Daniels 2012), the drug court clients who defined their selling drugs as an *addiction* came from their interactions with the court and treatment staff. While my observations and interviews cannot verify whether or not the clients actually thought this or if it was something they voiced to come across as dedicated to the program, it shows the importance of the client publicly accepting the "addict" role in court. That is, the client learned through the actual drug treatment component and interactions with the judge how to appropriate the addict label. Proving to the court that the client had embraced and internalized the deviant role of addict was a necessary step in progressing through the drug court (Miller 2004; Nolan 2001; Steen 2002). Essentially, the clients had to adopt the addict role as their "master status" (Becker 1963). If clients refused to self-label as addicts, they were told they were in "denial," which became a symptom of their addiction problem, a practice found in other adult and juvenile drug courts (Burns and Peyrot 2003; Whiteacre 2008). Scheff (1999) wrote about a similar requirement for those in treatment for mental illness: there were rewards for conforming to the deviant role and punishments for not. The definition of "addict" and what the label referred to remained ambiguous, however, since the court staff approved of the client self-labeling as an "addict" for either selling or using any amount of drugs. The court throwing the widest possible net in defining drug addiction is evidence of the court operating as a medical authority in defining what is or is not a "disease" in need of treatment. By also determining legal eligibility, the court remains the legal authority in determining what type of offender can access a drug court.

The court staff also used examples of clients who could not complete the requirements of the program as evidence that those individuals must not have been true "addicts." This perspective gave the staff confidence that the court program correctly labeled addiction since those who made up having a drug problem would eventually be discovered, as was voiced by the court evaluator: "The reality is, if somebody comes here and says they have a drug problem, my role is to get them hooked up with the services that they then need . . . set them up [in treatment] and see if it works out. And if not, rest assured, that the judge will see what's going on." The evaluator emphasized that he operated under the assumption that the client was telling the truth, but that the judge could identify clients without actual drug problems. The fact that some clients clearly embellished their own addiction problems also was evidence for the evaluator that most people have "real" addictions:

> I mean, there's a lot of word on the street about how to handle this kinda thing. Like if you get caught dealing heroin, say you *use* it because you'll be a felony, delivery case. So a lot of guys come in here and sell me this whole story about the opiates they use and then they never pop hot for it. Maybe we put them in inpatient a week for no reason just because he didn't want to catch an F1 [felony charge].

These stories helped the staff feel confident that the structure of the program would discover those who initially lied about their drug use severity. Everybody I interviewed discussed cases like these as if there were never other clients who embellished their problems and were successful at hiding it. In a sense, the program was held together by the ambiguity of exactly what addiction was; by labeling the failures as "nonaddicts," they increased the credibility of the drug court and its targeting.

The judge also used examples of dishonesty to threaten clients when they entered their plea. He often told them about sellers without legitimate drug problems who had failed the program and had gone to jail. In addition to using these examples as threats to the new clients, the staff used these examples to preserve the program's credibility. They assumed that dishonest clients would inevitably be discovered and punished. The small number of terminated clients itself became a statistic used to show that the court was targeting the right type of offender. The court staff saw the intensity of the program—the frequent counseling sessions, monthly court appearances, and meetings with case managers— as an indication that only those who were "serious" about their addiction would be able to succeed. They often cited those who could not keep up with the demands of the program (and who were eventually terminated) as the few nonaddicts who had lied to get into the program.

Related to this ambiguous framing of addiction was the shift in the program's focus from treatment to education and employment once the client finished the community-based drug treatment program. At this point, the drug treatment part of the report became less important, and the judge focused almost exclusively on education and employment as indicators of the client's progress. Just as the court staff used "treatment" to add structure to the client's life, once treatment ended, they used education and employment to occupy the client's free time. The perception was that the client might return to drug use or other criminal behavior if work or school did not take up the time that had previously been used for treatment. In this sense, then, *any* activity was beneficial to the client; the problem was having a lack of "responsible" things to do during the day. This emphasis also related to the construction of a drug-selling lifestyle as itself an illness that needed treatment. Since drug use was not necessarily the chief problem for these clients, the court insisted on the completion of requirements that were related to extinguishing the "disorder" of the drug lifestyle.

This reconstruction of addiction to include the "drug lifestyle" implied that the client was also addicted to capitalism since the "lifestyle" was defined as the conspicuous consumption of material possessions, fast money, and the excitement of engaging in illegal activity. The labeling of these values as an illness was very much tied to the social class and race of most of the clients found in the court program (poor African Americans and Latinos). It is difficult to find examples of wealthy white CEOs who engage in large-scale fraud or embezzlement to be labeled "addicts" or sent to community-based treatment to occupy their free time. It also relates to sociologist Robert Merton's (1938) theory of criminal behavior in his classic work "Social Structure and Anomie." According to Merton, criminal behavior often was related to a mismatch of cultural goals and institutionalized means. While most people have the same life goals (such as financial success, a healthy family, and a feeling of self-importance), some lack the socially approved means of achieving them (such as access to quality education, affordable health care, and job skills). The result is that some people commit crimes (such as selling drugs) to achieve those goals. The drug court's assessment that a person who lacked education or a job was more "sick" (required more intense treatment) in some ways reflected this perspective, although they attributed problems at the individual level. The implication was that a client would resist future criminal activity if he or she had the "legitimate" means of achieving culturally approved goals.

Take the Bone Away from the Dog

Capital City's drug court program is part of a network of more than 2,700 drug courts nationwide (NADCP 2012). Each year, the NADCP holds an annual training conference for interested court staff. The organization also promotes the development of drug courts throughout the United States, so those who are interested in starting a drug court in their community can attend a special track of workshops at the annual conference to learn about the organizational aspects of drug courts. To better understand how this national association framed addiction, I examined online documents from both the 2006 and 2007 national conferences. In addition to the conference program, the NADCP Web site posted detailed PowerPoint slides from some of the sessions. I analyzed the descriptions and slides from these sessions to see how information about addiction and drug treatment was disseminated to the attendees, which was reported to be more than three thousand individuals at each conference (NADCP 2007).

The 2006 conference offered twenty-one different "tracks" that each contained multiple sessions on a given topic. Only four of the tracks appeared to be exclusively about drug effects or drug treatment. One of these tracks addressed the chemical properties of various drugs, and included separate sessions on marijuana, opiates, and cocaine and their physiological effects on the individual. Another track dealt primarily with developments in pharmaceutical drugs for treating alcohol/drug abuse. Two tracks were devoted to assessing clients and issues about treatment for alcohol/drug problems. The remaining seventeen tracks were devoted to program issues, such as starting a drug court, getting funding for the court program, clearing legal "hurdles" to implementing drug courts, issues with juvenile drug courts, evaluating rewards/sanctions, and the role of state government in drug court programs.

The 2007 conference was organized similarly to the one in 2006, with twenty-four total tracks. Four tracks discussed drug and treatment issues explicitly, while the remaining tracks covered programmatic issues. One of the differences between the two years' conferences was the sponsorship of two additional tracks by "commercial partners" in 2007. These tracks were almost exclusively made up of sessions on drug testing systems and pharmacological treatments for addiction; large corporations that provided either drug screening technology or pharmaceuticals sponsored the sessions. These sponsors were designated "gold" or "pioneer" corporate members in the program, indicating that they had paid an annual membership fee of either $10,500 (gold) or $25,000 (pioneer). While the program stated that the presenters' viewpoints were not meant to be seen as the NADCP's endorsement of these products, these corporations were prominently listed in the conference program, could place free advertisements in the program and NADCP newsletters, were given display booths at the conference, and received a list of all conference attendees. In addition, corporate members at these levels were invited to a yearly meeting where they served as members of the "Corporate Advisory Roundtable" to the NADCP's Board of Directors (NADCP 2007). Therefore, they likely had a great deal of influence on the organization and its members.

My purpose in researching the sessions at these annual meetings was to discover how the NADCP educated its members about issues of addiction and treatment. These conference materials reveal the institutional discourse promoted by the only national organization for drug courts and add to the generalizability of what occurred in the labeling of addiction at Capital City's drug court (Smith 2006a; DeVault and McCoy 2006). Both the 2006 and 2007 conferences had similar sessions on drug issues. In addition to organizing the annual conference, the NADCP produces and disseminates training materials and hosts regional training sessions throughout the year. The Web site boasts having trained more than 36,000 drug court professionals since 1997 (NADCP 2012).

One 2006 session entitled "Understanding Drug Abuse and Addiction" discussed the effects of drugs on the individual's neurochemistry and brain processes. This session emphasized that "addiction is a brain disease" and discussed evidence about how prolonged drug use could change the brain in fundamental and long-lasting ways. This is also the primary perspective of addiction that is promoted by NIDA, a federal government agency that provides millions of dollars each year to research about drug addiction and treatment. This conference session had slides discussing the particular effects of cocaine, opiates, methamphetamines, hallucinogens, marijuana, and alcohol. The same presentation also had a slide titled "Relapse Happens" that discussed how relapse was primarily due to "poor craving management," but that it was possible to "get the train back on the tracks." None of the slides in this session discussed treatment issues explicitly or indicated what the appropriate types of treatment would be for the "brain disease." In both 2006 and 2007, most sessions that focused on the effects of drugs neglected to discuss drug treatment.

Another session in 2006, "Substance Abuse Treatment: What Works?" consisted of forty-four PowerPoint slides for the hour-and-fifteen-minute presentation. One slide showed a picture of a dog with a bone in its mouth with large letters across the top that read, "Addiction is like . . . A Dog with a Bone." The same slide elaborated on the characteristics of addiction: *addiction/denial* is the dog not wanting to let go of the bone, *craving* is the dog getting excited when it thinks it is going to get its bone, and *loss of control* is the idea that the dog always wants more bones. The next slide had the same dog pictured, but without the bone in his mouth and proclaimed "Treatment is like . . . Obedience School for the Dog." According to this slide, "you teach the dog's owner to control the dog" and "you develop a variety of tools (relapse prevention) to help the dog be obedient." The slide also warned that "some dogs are harder to train," but that you can "try to motivate the dog to change." Further slides explained various approaches to drug treatment, such as counseling, cognitive behavioral approaches, and pharmacological methods.

Since there were so few presentations on the definition and treatment of drug addiction, this presentation carried a lot of weight in promoting a certain perspective. The presentation's stated purpose was to make the attendees aware of treatment issues so that they could better understand the clients they dealt with. However, the overtly judgmental metaphor used in the presentation (the client as a dog) was troubling since that was the only image the attendees were left with in trying to understand their clients' addiction. This metaphor also overlaps moral and medical perspectives. While the image of the dog is pejorative, it also employs the psychological foundations of the brain disease of addiction theory (craving and stimuli). This conceptualization of addiction is not very different from a pamphlet put out by the federal government's Public Health Service in 1951, entitled *What to Know about Drug Addiction*. In that pamphlet, addicts are described as "irresponsible, selfish, immature, thrill-seeking individuals who are constantly in trouble—the type of person who acts first and thinks afterward" (in Duster 1970: 20). This image of the addict as impulsive and irresponsible has continued for more than half a century, despite the medicalization of drug addiction.

While the metaphor of an addict as a dog was discussed in only one presentation at the national meeting, I found at least one instance where a drug court judge publicly used this metaphor in another setting. In a speech before students at a local college, district judge Andrew Puccinelli, the drug court judge for the Eastern Nevada Adult Drug Court Program, was quoted as saying, "Addiction is like a dog with a bone" (Kobak 2007). Further research into the pervasiveness of this dog metaphor revealed that the NADCP's framing of addiction in this way extended into other areas of the criminal justice system. For instance, I also found a PDF document of the exact PowerPoint slides from two of the sessions described above, including those of the dog and the bone, on the Web site for New York State's Unified Court System (NY COURTS 2010). It is not clear how the presentation made its way to New York's statewide court system, but it shows the pervasiveness of this image as an educational tool throughout the criminal justice system.

This perspective also related to the framing of addiction in Capital City's drug court, with the addition of the "drug lifestyle" as another one of the dog's "bones" that needed to be taken away. Both Capital City's drug court and the NADCP promoted an ambiguous definition of addiction that carried heavy moral overtones and associated addiction with a drug-selling lifestyle and poor values. These frameworks used to label and manage addiction also related to the ultimate goal of drug court programs: resocialization.

Drug Court's Ultimate Goal: Resocialization

> CLIENT [*addressing courtroom at graduation ceremony*]: What is drug court? A second chance at life!

There was a great deal of ambiguity between the clinical and the legal roles that the court staff had, as well as between the various frameworks the court used to label and manage addiction. However, the court staff did not necessarily see these ambiguities as problems because the implicit yet primary goal of the drug court was to transform the client into a responsible citizen with good moral values (Nolan 2001). The implication, of course, was that the client lacked responsibility and good values. The stated goal of drug courts is to get at the root "cause" of drug-related crime, which is often touted as addiction. However, the drug court program focused on much more than just drug treatment, revealing that the root "cause" was seen as something larger than just drug use: it was irresponsibility that came from poor values. The framing of the drug "lifestyle" as an addiction fit into this narrative; the client was sick because he or she had missed the necessary socialization to become a moral, productive member of society. In many ways, this mission of resocialization fits into the culture of poverty arguments popular in the 1960s, where researchers argued that certain groups living in poverty produced their own culture of adaptation that perpetuated their poverty, often because of misplaced values (see Katz 1989 and Leacock 1971 for excellent overviews and critiques of the culture or poverty thesis). Despite the plethora of research studies that have disproved this hypothesis, showing that those who grow up in poverty still hold a strong work ethic and family values (for example, Bourgois 1997; Dohan 2003; Jones and Luo 1999; Valentine 1971; Wilson 1996), culture of poverty arguments are still promoted today, although perhaps in slightly more disguised versions. The court staff believed that improved values and skills would enable the clients to live a life free from future criminal activity, which would benefit both the clients and society as a whole. The court staff emphasized the client's need for resocialization and often saw their most important job as facilitating that transformation. Throughout the program, staff members looked for evidence that the client was being transformed into a responsible citizen; positive evidence led to the court staff trusting clients more and eventually permitting them to graduate from the program. If clients could not convince the staff (mainly the judge) that they were embracing the resocialization process, they were terminated from the program and sent to prison.

The Need for Resocialization

Just as the court staff medicalized the "lifestyle" of drug-related crimes into an addiction that needed to be treated, the client's lack of moral values was a symptom of inadequate socialization. Court staff implied that most clients lacked values such as responsibility and honesty. They believed the lack of values came from the clients' upbringing, their neighborhood culture, and/or the lack of positive role models in their lives. Wendy, a drug treatment counselor, explained: "Dad's in jail, grandpop's in jail, brother's in jail. A lot of these clients expect to be in jail at some point. It's like a rite of passage." The source of the inadequacies was not important, however, since it ultimately was up to the individual client to make him or herself into a better person. As Judge Gallo commented in a radio interview, "Many of these clients are lacking in everyday living skills. They don't understand being on time, they don't understand picking up a phone and calling someone when you can't be there."

Similarly, the evaluator also assessed the client's lack of "skills" when determining what type of treatment to assign:

> If you clean him up but then return him back into [the same environment], he has the same skill set which is almost nothing. . . . The long-term facilities are much better about how to open a bank account; they'll move you to transitional housing, things like that. . . . The same thing with [younger] kids . . . if I have a nineteen-year-old who's been shootin' dope since he was sixteen, we have major impairment of character development, social development, so that's gonna take a little more [time in treatment].

Judge Gallo related this lack of skills to poor primary socialization that occurred in the family: "I tell them, at some point you may have to walk away from your family and your lifelong friends because if you don't, you'll never make it through here, you'll never break that cycle." The judge's belief that family was sometimes the underlying cause of the client's criminality was emphasized early in the drug court program. When clients officially began the drug court program, the judge almost always recited the story of a nineteen-year-old client who had been rearrested for selling drugs and continued testing positive for drug use. This client requested that the judge send him to a recovery house (a structured living environment). When the judge asked him why, the client told him how everyone in his house—his mother, his sister, his brother—used and sold drugs. The judge used this story to illustrate to new clients that in order to succeed in the program, they might have to give up what always had been very close to them. The story also illustrated the transformation that the court expected each client to undergo. It was not enough to stop using and selling drugs; the clients had to transform themselves into better people.

Some clients also promoted their own resocialization. One former client I interviewed was serving as the president of Capital City's Drug Court Alumni Association, which meant that he returned to court periodically on graduation days to address the graduates. In our interview, he discussed his own lack of social "tools" due to the drug-using lifestyle. Speaking about his Narcotics Anonymous (NA) sponsor, he said: "When I came out of incarceration . . . he took me around. He showed me it's like being a baby again. I never went to dinner and things like that. How to take a woman to dinner, he showed me! How to use a fork and things like this. And how to gain credit. He showed me."

These statements from clients, both inside and outside of the court, reinforced the staff's belief that clients needed to be resocialized, and that the client's transformation into a better person with good values was the drug court's most important goal. This focus on resocialization and accountability is found in other drug courts, including juvenile drug courts (Paik 2011).

Court Staff on a Mission

Because the court staff perceived the drug court to be a "second chance" at life for the client, they saw their own roles as almost missionary in nature. They saw themselves as necessary components of the resocialization process. For instance, the evaluator discussed the role of the case manager as "walking with the client" to help him or her to access resources like job training, GED classes, and mental health treatment. The staff also discussed their relationships with clients as going farther than just what the job required. One evaluator commented: "I have a certain attachment to some of the clients when they come in, so I'll make sure they hold my phone number. If there's a problem, I tell them to call me. . . . These are not parts of my evaluator position; this is just because I like the guys or whatever, so I want to be a little more involved." This evaluator also mentioned assigning certain types of clients to one case manager in particular if they appeared to be problem cases:

The knuckleheads, like real hardheaded guys . . . if I can see it from the door or if they come in for a reevaluation and I can see that this is not working, I'll put them at one of Stan's facilities, because he's like an icon in his community. He works with guys inside and outside of his job. He really knows what it's like and takes care of what needs to be done.

Stan was the only male African American case manager during the time I observed. The evaluator implied that Stan worked as a case manager for the drug court out of some greater calling to help his "community" rather than just as a job. Stan did appear to put in extra effort in his capacity as a case manager. In court sessions, I often observed him speaking with recent graduates, especially young African American men, about joining the court's alumni association. He appeared to be looking for other potential role models for existing clients.

In our interview, the evaluator commented on the enthusiasm and passion of the court staff, including Judge Gallo, the public defender, and many of the case managers: "There's definitely a spiritual alignment there. You don't do this for the paycheck [*laughs*]. So, I think that these [clients] are pretty lucky to walk into this." That he referred to a "spiritual" alignment showed how the court staff saw their work as *morally* important. They believed that in addition to helping clients become better people they were also possibly producing larger social changes. This gave them a sense of fulfillment in their work and also made them feel positively toward the drug court as an effective program for handling drug-related crime. Similarly, while talking about graduation ceremonies in a radio interview, Judge Gallo related a story that illustrated how clients and their families viewed the court staff as something larger than their job titles:

Another woman comes back and says, "Thank you for saving my son." And I say, "Well, I didn't really save your son. You did and he did." . . . And she says, "Well, he was in an apartment with two other young men and he got arrested and went to prison. And then you took him in your program. And two months into that program, those two young men were killed in that apartment. So, you literally saved his life." And I said, "Well, maybe someone higher, some higher authority was looking out for him."

In this case, the client's mother viewed the judge's influence in the program as some sort of divine intervention. Similarly, a former client expressed his appreciation for the judge during an interview: "I thank God for drug court because my life made a whole 360. . . . God gave me another chance, Judge Gallo, everybody in drug court gave me another chance to make that 360 and do the right thing." The judge was the most visible representation of drug court, both inside the courtroom and in the outside community. Almost all the clients thanked the judge during their graduation speeches for helping them to get through the program and turn their lives around. Clients rarely thanked any other court staff, showing how important symbolically the judge was for this transformation.

Tools for Positive Resocialization

How exactly the clients turned their lives around was not important, so the court offered a variety of tools to assist them, including drug treatment, family counseling, educational programs, job training, and therapy for mental health problems. These tools were all attempts to restructure the client's life into a more productive one. They also encouraged, and sometimes mandated, that clients attend twelve-step meetings. These meetings were seen as extensions of both therapy and resocialization; clients would be forced to engage with other "clean" individuals and start building new social networks.

The view that the court was really a positive resocialization program related to the staff's view that the client's criminal activity stemmed from various individual and social problems (which also led to drug use). This also explained why the addict label was morphed into having many different meanings within the court setting. The staff wanted to help these clients, and they used whatever tools they could to accomplish that. Here, in a radio interview, the judge explained the court's attempt to break down the individual so that resocialization could occur:

> INTERVIEWER: You said as you sat in criminal court you were unable to address really the underlying problem. Do you see [drug abuse] as a mental health problem primarily?
>
> JUDGE GALLO: No, it's a substance abuse problem. But it's like I tell them, what came first, the chicken or the egg? Did the drug abuse create these other issues they have or did these other issues lead to the drug abuse? Most people in the program do have other issues to deal with. And, they're emotional: anger, very low self-esteem, they're distrustful of everyone in the system. So again you have to break down, it's almost like, I guess, in boot camp. You know, you see these movies where they really strip down these people and then they try to build them up. But the principle's the same and we obviously don't do it exactly that way. But we try to break down all these barriers and then build it up from the beginning with the hope and the expectation that they really buy into this. Most people do this initially because they don't want to go to jail.

The judge's comparison of the court program to basic military training reinforced the idea that the court program's ultimate goal was to resocialize clients into responsible citizens, even if they were initially resistant to the idea. The judge also admitted that most clients initially chose the drug court program to avoid a criminal record or prison. Resocialization, then, was also necessary to show the clients that they *needed* the program to improve their whole lives, not just to avoid jail. Here, the evaluator explained how he would present the program to a potential client by emphasizing the importance of getting a job and going to school rather than focusing on the client's drug problem:

Over time I've learned, instead of making the pitch, "Hey, you can come in here and get clean" . . . what I'll say is, "Look, if you want to be *about* some things, and smoking weed all day is standing in the way of that, this might be a good idea. If you want to start a little business, if you want to start a little rap game, if you want to do whatever" . . . Because *that* message everybody's interested in. "Look, I can help you get a job, I can help you get an education." *That*, they wanna hear. But as far as, "I can offer you drug-free living" [*laughs*], unfortunately, it just doesn't really resonate with them.

The judge emphasized nonclinical components later in the program, like enrolling in a GED program or getting a job. It appeared that these actions were more significant markers of success than abstinence. Judge Gallo added that: "one of the goals is to have that person employed, supporting their family, and paying their taxes." The judge's comment about clients paying taxes illustrated the resocialization goal. For the judge, it was a symbol that the client was a productive and integrated member of society.

The court staff regarded evidence of positive resocialization as one of the "unquantifiable" benefits of the drug court program. In a follow-up question, Judge Gallo elaborated on his previous statement:

One of the things we need to look at is . . . the cost effectiveness of this. Our average cost per client is roughly $3,500 to complete the program. A year in custody, that's maybe $27,000. Beyond that, the major savings run the social service medical stuff. You have people paying taxes, they're buying homes, they have apartments, they're getting their children back . . . they're not using the emergency room at the hospital. . . . And, how they raise their children.

This uniform emphasis on resocialization reinforced two important viewpoints of the court: (1) that the client was individually responsible for becoming a better person, and (2) that these clients were not bad people; they just needed to learn better values and skills. The court staff saw themselves as missionaries offering tools for "salvation," but it was up to the client to take advantage of them.

At the same time, the court's emphasis on the client getting a job implied that the client did not really *want* a job, another indication that the culture of poverty thesis covertly existed in the drug court program. Framing the selling of drugs as an addiction to the "drug lifestyle" implied that the client sold drugs because of a sense of status and quick money, and not because it may have been the best option available or a job that required hard work and skill. For instance, Karen, one of the female drug court participants discussed how much effort she put into selling drugs: "It was like a job. I was up from sunup to sundown out there, competing with the fellas out there. Only female standing the grounds, winter, summer, spring, or fall. I was out there hounding my business. Strap up and we goin' to work!" This client doesn't mention money or material possessions as the motivating factor, but instead a sense of empowerment (especially as one of the few women in a male-dominated field). Similarly, the court never mentioned that the client's unemployment might be a result of structural conditions like the limitations that a criminal record puts on job prospects, or that minimum-wage jobs in a large city did not really offer enough income to support a family. Instead, the court emphasized a client's lack of skills or desire to work as the problem that needed to be fixed.

The existence of the program itself, and the perceived helpfulness of the court staff, also became evidence for the court staff that drug courts reduced the stigma associated with addiction. According to Judge Gallo,

[The district attorney] has been totally supportive of this program since day one. Every police commissioner we've had has been totally supportive of it. So I have not seen that [attitude] in terms of [these clients] are bad people or they have leprosy or something. No, I have not seen that at all. If it existed, we would not have this program.

According to the judge, drug courts were evidence of a shift in cultural thinking about drug addiction, from a punitive conceptualization to a therapeutic one. However, one of the few presentations about addiction at the national conference for drug court professionals portrayed drug addicts as dogs that needed better training, indicating a very pejorative view of drug addicts. Also, the fact that it was still an arm of the criminal justice system heavily monitoring clients' behavior (including their clinical progress) showed instead that these programs expanded the criminal justice system's control over drug-related issues, especially since the court's addiction label encompassed everything from infrequent use to selling drugs. Clients, then, were actually stigmatized twice: first, as criminal offenders (by pleading guilty) and second, as drug addicts (by accepting the label). As I show in Chapters 1 and 2, conceptualizing addiction as a "disease" does not take away the moral judgments associated with it.

The judge constantly reminded clients that they had to take responsibility for their own shortcomings and limitations. No individual or social problem was seen as an excuse for not progressing in the program. The judge always reminded clients starting the program that they might have psychological problems like depression or low self-esteem, but that they needed to acknowledge the problems and ask for help. In an initial court session, he once cited the example of a twenty-three-year-old female client who had been seriously abused as a child. The judge told the new clients that the court could provide help for those issues, but that since she could not address it, she ultimately failed the program and went to prison.

When the court staff believed clients were acting responsibly and engaging in the appropriate tools of resocialization, they were congratulated and moved through the phrases of the program toward graduation. While this progress took several months, the judge and other court staff also then trusted these clients more. Even when these clients appeared to have violated some program rule, such as using drugs or missing an appointment, the judge often believed their excuses and gave them the benefit of the doubt. Paik (2011), in her observations of a juvenile drug court, also observed a similar negotiation of how certain rules and sanctions were selectively applied. Clients who did not prove to the judge that they were acting responsibly did not garner the same level of trust and were sanctioned. Repeated sanctions led to expulsion from the program. Judge Gallo discussed this in a radio interview:

> JUDGE GALLO: I had a fella yesterday who had been in the program for over two years and has [missed court appointments]. And he comes in and says, "I have a job to take care of my family." And I said, "Well, that's very noble. Taking care of your family is your responsibility; it's not exclusive to going to treatment and doing what you have to do." So his point was, "I'm gonna lose my job if I go to jail." So I said, "Here's the mirror. Look in the mirror. And you tell me, whose problem is it?"
>
> INTERVIEWER: And you mean a real mirror?
>
> JUDGE GALLO: A real mirror, yeah. "Look in the mirror." And he says, "You're right, it's my problem." And I said, "Unfortunately, you're going back to jail. And I'll let you know next week if you're terminated."

While the court valued employment, and often required it before a client could graduate from the program, this client still violated the judge's trust because he had missed court appointments. At the same time, balancing a full-time job with frequent court appointments could prove difficult. In two qualitative studies of drug court graduates, several participants explicitly mentioned that the court meetings interfered with their maintenance of full-time work (Wolfer 2006; Wolfer and Roberts 2008).

Graduation ceremonies, which occurred once a month, were public displays of the drug court's successful resocialization program. Spirits often were very high at graduations, especially among the court staff, who enthusiastically congratulated clients, took their photos, and met their family members. The judge read each graduate's name and summarized the client's progress through the program, including the drug treatment program completed, whether the client was working or going to school, and other accomplishments that the judge deemed worth mentioning. The judge also cited examples of problems and sanctions that the client had in the program before making some sort of "turnaround." For example, when introducing a graduating client, he said: "You were sanctioned six times before you did the right thing. After that, it was clear sailing. . . . Now she is enrolled in GED classes . . . became a better mother." At graduation ceremonies, the judge often stressed initial difficulties that the client had in the program and the positive outcomes that occurred after some sort of wake-up call. He often emphasized these markers of becoming a better person as evidence that drug courts were transformative experiences.

After the judge's introduction, the client received a framed graduation diploma and addressed the crowd. Most of these speeches were short, sometimes just a quick "thank you" to the court or even a curt "I did what I had to do, now I'm outta here" type of remark. About half of the graduates prepared more in-depth speeches on index cards or paper. In the sessions leading up to their graduation, the judge frequently asked clients if they had prepared a speech, revealing how important he regarded their own discussion of their experiences in the program. Some graduates were quite emotional while addressing the crowd. Many clients reiterated their progress in achieving the ultimate goal of drug court—transformation into a better person. The following comments are from my field notes:

> GRADUATE: I came into this program as a little boy and I'm walking out as a man.
>
> GRADUATE (male): I want to thank drug court for this opportunity. It showed me who my real friends are . . . kept me out of trouble.
>
> GRADUATE (female) [*speaking in Spanish*]: I learned what drugs do to you. They make you lose your family, your house. . . . If you're not ready for the program, this is not a joke. You can lose a lot of opportunities. Take this opportunity.
>
> FORMER GRADUATE (female) [*addressing new graduates*]: In 1992, God answered my prayers. I was arrested. I thank God for the guard who arrested me. . . . To the clients who haven't graduated yet, take advantage of this program. It might be your last chance. . . . To Judge Gallo, I don't know how to thank you enough, so I'll give you a song [*sings a song for about two minutes; the song refers to "the Lord" many times. Afterward, there is loud applause in the courtroom and many give her a standing ovation*].

To conclude the graduation program, the judge asked family members of clients to stand up and be recognized for their support. He also offered the graduating clients some words of advice: "You're leaving a cocoon today. You will be challenged, tested. . . . Don't let your guard down. You have the tools . . . [*holds up Missouri license plate*]. You have shown me, and I'm proud of that. . . . You've been given a second chance. . . . Congratulations to all of you; I wish you well."

The Missouri license plate was another prop the judge used in court sessions (along with the mirror he discussed earlier). He referred to Missouri as the "show me" state, and would tell clients early in the program that they had to "show" him that they were taking responsibility in the program. The cocoon metaphor was likely used to represent two things: (1) the protective shelter that the court program provided to clients in the form of frequent court sessions and a network of "helping" people, and (2) a symbol of rebirth into a new person with positive values, prepared to become a productive citizen.

The court staff referred to these emotional speeches as further evidence that the drug court program was successful at accomplishing its goals, even though the majority of speeches were not emotional or particularly long. During an interview, the evaluator commented:

> I'll tell you, I came in here with a little bit of a bias. . . . You know, there's not enough money for drug [treatment] these days. So my attitude was, if you think I'm going to waste my money on dealers that are trying to beat a case, you're out of your mind. There are too many people dying out there for some little eighteen-year-old who got caught hustling three nick bags to take the money for treatment so that he doesn't have a felony on his record. . . . And then after making a couple of the graduations, boy, that will really open your mind up. . . . Guys talkin', "Look, you know, I found a wife, I pay child support now, I have a job." You know, *those* can be really moving. I mean, that's where this program excels, in taking not even really a spark of desire and turning it into something.

Judge Gallo explained in a radio interview: "You have others that come up and say, another young lady, that her mother never knew her sober after she was twelve years old. And her mother died like three months ago and missed her graduation and then she holds up her diploma and says, 'Mom, this is for you.' I mean, I could go on and on with the stories." The court staff offered these events at graduations as evidence that the program was the right way to handle these cases (regardless of the client's actual problem with using drugs); it was likely not a coincidence that the only time I saw state legislators observing court was on a graduation day.

Other court staff also articulated that the program was effective because of positive outcomes for the client, most of which were social markers, rather than becoming drug-free. According to Mario, manager of specialty courts:

> Most of our clients, I think 70 percent of our clients who graduate are doing very well—have obtained proper employment, have reengaged with family members, and, you know, have become productive members in our society. . . . instead of just giving them a prison sentence. And *if* the client does have a problem, it's a great way to get back on their feet. Ok, I messed up. They're given a second chance. (emphasis mine)

As the previous quote suggests, whether or not the client had an addiction to drugs was not the most important consideration for evaluating "success" in the program. The court evaluator also had a similar perspective:

> INTERVIEWER: Is [drug court] the best way to handle these kinds of cases?
>
> EVALUATOR: I'm *definitely* a fan. Because taking any kind of marginalized population that doesn't have a lot of access to resources and offering them resources, I'm a huge fan of. Which is what we do. . . . A lot of them one-parent households, no strong male influence in their life. So, offering them parenting classes, job training, things like that, that they really wouldn't have access to otherwise. I really think that's important.

All of the court staff I spoke with mentioned similar positive outcomes as evidence that drug courts "work." Nobody felt that any of the clients were mislabeled as "addicts," even if they did not have a significant drug use problem, because of the benefits the program offered. In a sense, the drug court selected clients who would most easily undergo this moral transformation: nonviolent offenders with short criminal records, many without serious drug use problems. Like other institutions that emphasize a client's moral transformation (such as the maternity homes studied by Rains 2007 or the incarcerated mothers in Haney's 2010 *Offending Women*), the clients selected for drug court were those who would not threaten the integrity of the process. This selection process was not at odds with the drug court program because the end result was much larger than just treating a possible addiction to drugs; the end result was that the client was transformed into a "better person." In interviews with drug court advocates across the country, Tiger (2011) found a similar theme in that these individuals saw themselves as saving both clients and communities.

It is impossible to ignore the racial and class implications of the court's emphasis on resocialization. All of the court staff was white, with the exception of two case managers. The court staff universally applied the assumption that these clients lacked middle-class values and skills, likely because of the race and class of most of the clients. The typical client in Capital City's drug court was also the typical violent criminal depicted on television and in films: a "dangerous" young black male. By transforming these individuals' lives, the drug court staff likely saw themselves as not just helping the individual client but also protecting society as a whole. The NADCP captures this sentiment well. The words, "Drug Courts Work—They Transform Lives" reads across the front page of their Web site, right next to a photograph of a middle-aged white judge hugging a young black man (NADCP 2012).

Conclusion: Ambiguity and Institutional Legitimacy

This chapter presents how one drug court program, within the context of the larger drug court movement, labeled and managed drug problems. From the targeting of individuals for eligibility into the program through the graduation ceremony, each stage of the program involved an ambiguous notion of "addiction" within a criminal justice framework. All of the court staff members had roles that overlapped the clinical and legal interventions of the program. This overlap produced ambiguity about what was actually the clinical part of the program since the court's supervision extended into areas outside of drug treatment, such as employment, schooling, and family life. While any drug use could be defined as addiction (as long as the client professed that it was a problem), "addiction" was extended to a broader range of behaviors than just drug use. Addiction was openly discussed in the courtroom as a problem of the drug "lifestyle," most often that of selling drugs. One possible reason for this is that many of the clients might not actually be addicted to using drugs, at least from a clinical perspective, and therefore the court needed to label some other aspect of the client as "diseased" in order to legitimize the program. In addition, through the initial speech he gave to new clients entering the court program (the iceberg metaphor), Judge Gallo implied that addiction meant something more than just using drugs. In that opening speech, he also articulated that clients had to admit that they had a drug "problem," but the problem was not defined specifically as *using* drugs.

This extension of addiction to other behaviors was also related to the court's focus on what it saw as other treatable problems, like unemployment and under-education. Once the treatment episode was over, the client continued to appear in the courtroom monthly, and the focus turned to the client becoming "responsible" in other areas. Of course, abstinence was still paramount in the client progressing through the program; a relapse at a later phase of the court program resulted in the client having to go back to the beginning of that phase. Still, once the client appeared to get the drug "problem" under control and completed treatment, the judge rarely brought up issues of drug addiction in the courtroom. He instead asked the client about employment, school, or family issues.

The court staff viewed the drug court program as helping an underserved population to access services that they needed to improve their life situation (and, by extension, their values). In interviews, the court staff framed the court program as a "second chance" at life. Clients also used similar language in describing the program at the graduation ceremony. Job-training programs, assistance with getting further education, parenting classes, and individual counseling are certainly much-needed services for those arrested (and for those in prison) if we want to reduce our recidivism rate. However, it is problematic that these programs are only available to individuals who agree to be labeled drug addicts and to be continually monitored by the criminal justice system. Ironically, we have seen major cuts in spending on employment and social service programs since the 1980s that could have eased the socioeconomic problems at the root of using and selling drugs (Waldorf, Reinarman, and Murphy 1991). This setup furthers the notion that the underlying problems that led to the initial arrest (such as lack of decent jobs, access to education programs, family problems) are individual problems with individual, not structural, solutions. The client's social environment was consistently minimized in the courtroom; everybody was seen as equally able to overcome any obstacles they had to leading a life free from drugs and crime.

Drug courts, because they incorporate drug treatment, often appear to be a more "therapeutic" response to drug crime. Researchers have analyzed the rapid growth in drug courts as evidence of a larger cultural shift in how Americans think about drug addiction (Nolan 2001). Certainly, Capital City's court staff and the NADCP embraced this perspective. At the same time, however, drug courts legitimize and expand the criminal justice system's authority and power over *all* drug-related issues. Others have commented on this increased surveillance because of the court's authority in managing all aspects of the client's progress through the program, including treatment issues (Bowers 2008; Burns and Peyrot 2003; Paik 2011; Tiger 2013; Whiteacre 2008). Drug courts successfully accomplish this by promoting the evidence that drug addiction is a "disease" that needs to be treated. However, they put treatment for it under the legal supervision of a judge and promote an ambiguous definition of "addiction" into which any problem could be placed.

Becker (1963) wrote about the "double problem" that law enforcers face: they must prove they are successful and at the same time demonstrate that they are still needed, or else they lose legitimacy. Drug court advocates effectively deal with the double problem by promoting drug courts as reducing recidivism while continuously widening the net of who "needs" treatment. The pool of potential clients for a drug court, or similarly structured "model" court, is endless. All drug use becomes conflated with drug abuse. Drug sellers are sent to the same treatment regimen as drug abusers. At the same time, the restriction to mostly nonviolent offenders who do not have extensive criminal histories means that drug courts are not including those who may actually benefit most from such a program (Walsh 2011). Including more serious offenders, however, could threaten the success rate and possibly the legitimacy of drug courts.

Drug court advocates have convinced the American public that we do not need to reform our drug laws; instead, we can just change how to deal with those arrested. The end result is that drug courts and similar criminal justice initiatives become the primary authorities (rather than medical professionals) for labeling and managing drug users in the United States. Such programs effectively silence the debate around alternatives to dealing with drugs, such as less harsh sentencing or the expansion of harm reduction techniques.

Ultimately, for somebody to succeed in Capital City's drug court program, they had to identify as an "addict." However, exactly what that addiction was to—whether it was marijuana, opiates, or the "lifestyle" of being a drug user—was not of prime importance. Further, while the drug treatment portion of the program typically lasted only three to six months, to "graduate" from the program took at least another six months to a year and required demonstration that the client had transformed into a better, more responsible person. In Chapter 4, I explore similar issues about the labeling and management of addiction in two outpatient drug treatment programs that were affiliated with the court program.

4

Labeling Addiction in Outpatient Treatment

Southside and Westview Programs

I sat in the employee workroom one morning at Westview's outpatient drug treatment program before the start of the group therapy session that I had been observing. A counselor (Betsy) for one of the other morning groups walked into the room holding a book and a file folder and began using the photocopier. Another counselor, Peter, walked into the room and said "good morning" to both of us.

> BETSY [*responding to Peter*]: Morning.
> PETER: What are you copying, Betsy?
> BETSY: It's from the book *Jekyll and Hyde*. I'm going to use it in group today. I think it's a good example of how they're good when they're not using, but then what happens when they do. Like how bad it can get.
> PETER: Oh, OK. Let me know how that goes. I might borrow it.
> BETSY: Sure.

In 2011, about 1.3 million Americans received treatment for drug abuse or addiction in a designated drug treatment facility (SAMHSA 2013). Most of these individuals (about 90 percent) attended an outpatient treatment program, which typically involves individual and/or group therapy for several months. This chapter focuses on the labeling and management of drug addiction in two outpatient drug treatment programs named Southside and Westview.[1] Just as in Capital City's drug court, the treatment programs promoted a definition of addiction that overlapped moral and medical frameworks. As illustrated in the previous observation, counselors communicated to the clients that drugs could make them into "bad people," yet at the same time emphasized that addiction is a disease that can be effectively treated. This example from *Dr. Jekyll and Mr. Hyde* was likely also used as a warning sign of what the clients could become if they returned to the drug "lifestyle." However, as in the drug court, the specifications of the disease were ambiguous and not precisely defined. In the treatment programs, the addiction label was also broadened to include aspects of the drug "lifestyle," like selling drugs, although this designation was more often for court-mandated clients who, the staff admitted, were not likely to have a drug use problem. All clients in treatment, however, had to embrace the addict identity to successfully progress through the program, just as they had to in the drug court.

This overlap of medical and moral frameworks was inherent in several aspects of the treatment programs. First, therapists promoted an ambiguous disease concept of addiction. Some of the vagueness in labeling addiction could have resulted from therapists being able to choose from a number of existing theories about why people become drug addicts. Most of the therapists I interviewed had elaborate explanations for how addiction fit into a "disease" framework, although their particular definitions varied and were not clearly communicated in group therapy sessions. The ambiguity could also be associated with the use of multiple treatment methods within one facility: methadone maintenance, twelve-step philosophy, and cognitive behavioral therapy. Therapists viewed multiple methods as a good thing because it allowed clients to choose what kind of treatment fit them best. However, such an array of choices also could muddle the framing of addiction as a disease, considering how differently each modality defines and treats it.

Second, even though therapists overwhelmingly promoted the idea that addiction is a disease, they were uneasy about the role of methadone maintenance in drug treatment. Despite methadone maintenance therapy being the most medicalized of the types of treatment offered, the programs advocated it as more of a "last resort" for opiate users and something that should only be used short-term. The program's intense regulations, many of them federally mandated, also created an institutional level of uneasiness about using methadone for drug treatment and contributed to the existing stigma around methadone maintenance therapy.

Finally, the ambiguity of the addiction label along with the social distance between clients and therapists led to intense mutual distrust between the clients and the staff. All clients, even those who had no affiliation with the criminal justice system, were perceived as potentially immoral or criminal. These treatment programs were located in an impoverished neighborhood that was mostly nonwhite, and the clientele reflected these demographics. The therapists, however, were all white, well-educated men and women. The mutual distrust also was a result of the moral messages about drug users in our wider society that have become ingrained in our subconsciousness, messages that those working in the drug treatment programs could not even completely shed in their daily interactions with clients. This distrust was a product of the stigma that drug users—even those who are in treatment—continue to face, and at the same time perpetuated that stigma. Only when we stop incorporating moral judgments into our labeling of drug addicts will drug treatment promote a truly medical view of addiction.

Overview of Southside and Westview Programs

The Southside and Westview programs were both state-licensed outpatient drug treatment programs affiliated with a university and hospital system in Capital City. The programs operated on different floors of the same facility, a two-story nondescript gray building; the only signs indicating that it housed treatment programs were 8 ½" x 11" paper printouts taped to the doors. Southside operated primarily as a methadone maintenance program with individual and group therapy sessions; Westview was classified as an "intensive" outpatient program (IOP), meaning that treatment required more group sessions each week than ordinary outpatient programs. Some of those who received methadone from Southside also participated in Westview's IOP.

The residential neighborhood where the facility was located was almost exclusively African American (94 percent), with the percentage of individuals living in poverty (32 percent) being considerably higher than the citywide rate (23 percent).[2] The median household income of the neighborhood also was much lower than that of the entire city ($21,800 versus $31,000). While I was unable to obtain the client demographics in each program, my own observations, as well as conversations with the clients, led me to conclude that nearly every client in the Westview program lived in the surrounding neighborhood. The Southside clinic, however, attracted clients from a wider geographical area, probably because there were fewer methadone maintenance programs in the city. This is typical for methadone maintenance therapy, where only about 11 percent of outpatient facilities nationwide offer it as a treatment option (SAMHSA 2010a). As a result, there was more racial diversity in the Southside program than in Westview's, which had predominantly African American clients.

Both clinics received most of their reimbursement for treatment services from government funding sources, primarily through Medical Assistance (Medicaid) and a state-funded program that allocated money for drug treatment to those who were low-income but did not qualify for Medicaid. Southside clinic had more clients pay out of pocket for treatment than Westview; the program supervisor estimated that about 25 percent of Southside's clients were "fee payers," who paid for services on a sliding scale. Neither program authorized services to get reimbursed directly from private insurance. The program supervisors in both clinics mentioned past problems in getting reimbursed from private insurance companies. If clients claimed that their insurance covered treatment, the programs required them to pay the clinic and then apply for reimbursement with their insurance company. This practice was not surprising since health-care advocates have pointed out the lack of insurance coverage for drug treatment and mental health services in general. For example, a 1999 national survey of managed care organizations revealed that only 56 percent of those surveyed covered outpatient methadone treatment ("Managed Care Not Stepping Up to Cover Methadone Treatment" 2000). Still, the same study found that 94 percent of managed care organizations covered general outpatient treatment. When I learned of that statistic, I asked an administrator at the Westview program for a further explanation of their policy. She explained that their location attracted so few people with private insurance that administratively they could not handle the separate billing requirements for each plan.

There was some fluidity of staff roles between the two programs. For instance, two of the therapists that I interviewed from Westview had previously worked as therapists in the Southside program. In addition, one of the group therapy facilitators at Southside also met individually with court-mandated clients in the Westview program. Both programs appeared to have high counselor turnover rates. This is consistent with studies that have shown substance abuse counselors to have a high rate of voluntary turnover (McLellan, Carise, and Kleber 2003; McNulty et al. 2007). One study estimated that the substance abuse counselor annual turnover rate was 18.5 percent, a much higher rate than other occupations considered to have high voluntary turnover, like teaching and nursing, which each average around 12 percent per year (McNulty et al. 2007). While I did not obtain official employment statistics at either treatment program, it is worth noting that among the six therapists that I interviewed in both programs, only the clinical supervisor at each program was still working there by the end of my study. All of the staff I interviewed expressed dissatisfaction with their salary; most also mentioned feeling emotionally exhausted by the job and the large caseload. The therapists in Southside's program also mentioned disagreements with the program coordinator and the general structure of the program as aspects of their job that they did not like. Emotional exhaustion has been found to be associated with greater intent to leave the job, even when controlling for counselor salary (Knudsen, Ducharme, and Roman 2006). Some research suggests that organizational structure, including counselor–management relations, is a much better predictor of counselor turnover than the types of clients counselors have to work with (McNulty et al. 2007).

Wendy, one Southside/Westview therapist, even foreshadowed her departure during our interview: "I have definitely been burnt out by this job. It hasn't affected the way I treat my clients, but I know that it's rapidly approaching, and I can't spend the rest of my life doing this." Wendy indicated that she was working on a nursing degree and planned on quitting once she found a job in that field. Two of the other therapists I interviewed also mentioned working on additional degrees or certifications. None of them expressed a long-term goal of remaining a drug treatment therapist, and almost all of them indicated that they were only "somewhat satisfied" with their job. Such a high therapist turnover rate undoubtedly had an effect on the quality of care that clients received in these programs.

The Language of Addiction

While all of those in the treatment programs were labeled addicts, the specific terminology the staff used to refer to a person in treatment varied. Most therapists referred to the individuals in treatment as "clients," suggesting a professional/service-oriented relationship like that found in other mental health services, rather than a more medicalized framework. There were some differences between the two programs, though. For example, at the program level, Southside attempted to label the individuals in treatment as "patients." The "Patient Handbook" that individuals received at the start of treatment consistently used the term "patient" to describe those in treatment. One of the Southside therapists who organized the pre-IOP group meetings, Jerry, also only referred to individuals in Southside as patients, either in speaking with me or during group sessions. In Westview, however, the label "client" was more consistently applied to those in treatment. Westview's handbook never referred to those in treatment as "patients," but only as clients. Similarly, Kevin, Westview's counseling supervisor (a white male who appeared to be in his late forties), always referred to those in both treatment programs as clients.

These labels were not consistently applied in each program, however. Some therapists referred to individuals in treatment as "clients" or "patients" interchangeably, with no apparent distinction between the two labels. While the use of "patient" more often in Southside suggests some program-level effort to "medicalize" those taking methadone, the lack of agreement about which term to use suggested that the staff did not necessarily view the different labels as meaning different things. For instance, Linda, Southside's program coordinator (a white, sixty-year-old female) used both terms interchangeably, despite working in the methadone maintenance program. This reluctance to consistently extend a medical term for the individual in treatment was another example of the ambiguity used around the labeling of addiction as a disease. The Substance Abuse and Mental Health Services Administration (SAMHSA) published a guide in 2004 aimed at those working in the treatment field. This guide explicitly advocated for the term "patient" rather than client and the term "medication-assisted recovery" rather than methadone maintenance. The SAMHSA favored these terms in treatment because they saw them as less stigmatizing. At the same time, publishing such a guide suggested that the less-stigmatizing terms might not be used often in treatment programs. For simplicity, I refer to those in treatment as "clients" in the rest of this chapter.

The use of interchangeable terms to describe addiction and those in drug treatment is common in treatment programs. Kelly, Dow, and Westerhoff (2010) found that the lack of precision and consistency for these terms is even seen at the highest scientific levels. Several studies have found that the terminology used to label those in treatment (substance abuser, addict, person with a substance disorder, and so forth) can impact how individuals are perceived; in an older study, subjects rated the term "drug dependence" more positively than "drug addiction" (Rippere 1978). More recently, Kelly, Dow, and Westerhoff (2010) found that people viewed someone with a "substance use disorder" as more deserving of treatment than a "substance abuser." The SAMHSA (2004) report urges those working in the treatment field to avoid certain words like "addict," "drug problem," and "user" because the terms are stigmatizing or unhelpful. Instead, they advocate the term "misuse" (rather than "abuse") and "disorder" or "disease" to reinforce a medical notion. That the *Diagnostic and Statistical Manual of Mental Disorders* (*DSM*-IV) and the International Statistical Classification of Diseases still use terms like "abuse" and "dependence" suggests that there is institutional conflict in how to refer to people in treatment that goes beyond individual treatment programs.

Program Structure

The lack of consistency in the labeling of addiction could also be related to the inconsistency in diagnosing it. The *DSM*, the chief resource for labeling drug problems, has undergone a number of changes in its five iterations (the *DSM*-V was published in May 2013). As Szasz (1994) pointed out, the *DSM* is decided by a task force of the American Psychological Association, and the inclusion of certain criteria can sometimes come down to a vote among a small number of clinicians. Even if specific criteria are agreed on, the actual application of *DSM* labels is still subjective and can vary by the race, gender, and class of the person being evaluated (Neighbors et al. 2003; Scheff 1999). Loring and Powell (1988) found that gender and race influenced how psychiatrists applied *DSM* categories; blacks were frequently diagnosed with more-serious conditions, while women received less-serious diagnoses. The application of "addiction" could be even more ambiguous for treatment professionals, considering the wide application that the term has in our society, where you can be "addicted" to anything, from work to Internet video games to sex.

On entering the program at Southside or Westview, clients responded to a series of oral and written questionnaires about their drug use history and other mental health issues. The Addiction Severity Index (ASI) was the chief mechanism used to evaluate the extent of the individual's drug problem. While the ASI is commonly used in drug treatment evaluations, it does not specifically score the individual for alcohol/drug "abuse" or "dependence" (*DSM*-IV labels) (Mack and Frances 2003). Thus, if clients indicated that drug use had caused them problems and they wanted to stop using, they were labeled addicts by the clinic and seen as appropriate for outpatient treatment.[3] Southside's clinic used additional evaluations to determine if the individual was appropriate for methadone maintenance treatment.

Westview's IOP typically lasted twelve to sixteen weeks and entailed six hours of group therapy each week in addition to one hour of individual counseling. Most therapists indicated that their individual therapy style was a variation of cognitive behavioral therapy (CBT), a common counseling style in drug treatment.[4] CBT aims "to help patients recognize, avoid, and cope with the situations in which they are most likely to abuse drugs" (NIDA 2006). Theories that guide the practice of CBT emphasize that drug misuse is a result of both cognitive and behavioral processes that are largely learned and, subsequently, can be modified (Gossop 2003). In addition, twelve-step ideology and practices were common in both the Westview and Southside programs.

In order to "graduate" from Westview's program, a client had to complete thirty-six sessions and test negative for all illicit drugs for at least one month. Westview also offered outpatient counseling services for those who were mandated to continue treatment after the IOP program (for instance, many court-mandated clients). Kevin, the counseling supervisor, indicated that the designated amount of time for treatment (twelve weeks) was based on a "research model" of what was deemed to be successful. He likely was referring to a number of research studies that showed that the longer somebody remained in treatment, the more positive outcomes they had at the end of treatment and at follow-up (NIDA 1999). Kevin also indicated that most funding sources refused to pay for treatment after sixteen weeks. Thus, not all clients graduated; some just had to end treatment after their authorized treatment episode.

There were many more clients at the Westview program who were court mandated to treatment compared to the Southside program. This likely occurred because most of the court-mandated clients were evaluated as needing treatment for marijuana abuse (and cocaine abuse to a lesser extent) rather than opiate abuse. Peter, one of the therapists, estimated that at any given time about one-third to one-half of the clients in his group session were court mandated to treatment. The associate director of the Substance Abuse Division of the university indicated that in 2006, about 50 percent of the clients in the Westview program were there because of involvement with the criminal justice system. He also indicated that this proportion had increased in recent years; he related that in 1997 only about 20–25 percent had been court mandated.

Wendy, a white female who appeared to be in her late twenties, ran one of the pre-IOP groups at Southside (the methadone maintenance program) each week and was also responsible for individual therapy in Westview for those referred from the criminal justice system. She also acted as the liaison to the various criminal justice initiatives, having frequent contact with the clients' parole officers and case managers. She also would appear in Capital City's drug court to give a monthly report for any of her clients in that program.[5]

The Southside clinic was primarily an adult methadone maintenance treatment program that offered outpatient group and individual therapy in addition to the prescription and distribution of methadone.[6] Most clients in the Southside clinic reported heroin as their main drug of use, although a substantial number reported using prescription medication (that is, OxyContin or Perco-cet). The program supervisor, Linda, estimated that about 90 percent of the Southside clients were self-referred, with the remaining 10 percent being referred from other sources, such as the criminal justice system.

New clients to Southside's program were mandated to attend a group therapy meeting twice a week for an hour each time. This group, named the "pre-IOP" group, was a recent implementation for those clients who were evaluated as need-ing intensive outpatient treatment. New clients spent about two weeks, on aver-age, in the pre-IOP group before being transferred into Westview's IOP program. Wendy created the pre-IOP group for methadone clients. The purpose of the group was to give the new clients a chance to "stabilize" on their methadone and learn some of the expectations of the intensive group sessions before they start-ed. All of the staff mentioned past problems with methadone clients "nodding off" in the IOP group as a result of not being fully adjusted to methadone's effects. After the client finished the IOP program, they continued individual counseling at Southside clinic for as long as they were taking daily doses of methadone, although those individual meetings would become less frequent over time.

Assigning the Right Treatment

The Westview program had four different IOP groups during my observations. The groups were divided into one group for those receiving methadone (all of whom were from the Southside clinic), one group for those not receiving meth-adone (named the "drug-free" group), and two "mixed" groups that consisted of both methadone users and those who were "drug-free." The program went back and forth about whether or not to have "mixed" groups, but ultimately decided to keep them because other factors, like clients' schedules, became more impor-tant determinants of which group someone was assigned to. The classification of the group not using methadone as "drug-free" implied that those taking methadone were still using an illicit substance, reinforcing the additional stigma that methadone users faced. There were many clients in the "drug-free" group taking prescription antidepressants and other medications; however, they were not labeled as drug users in the same way.

Being assigned to IOP treatment was supposed to reflect the need for a higher level of care than ordinary outpatient. However, the most critical factor used to decide whether a Southside client should attend IOP treatment was whether or not the client was working:

> INTERVIEWER: So when someone comes in and they are [on medical
> assistance], or fee paying, do they get evaluated differently?
> LINDA: No, but their treatment is different. If you're a fee payer, you are
> probably working; therefore, you don't go to IOP because it would
> interfere with work. If you are not [working], that means you don't

have anything to do with your day, so we make sure you do. And [medical assistance] will pay for it and pay much *more* for IOP.

The rationale was that IOP treatment helped structure the methadone clients' lives in a more positive way, implying that otherwise they would be more likely to use drugs or engage in criminal activity. Linda's response, however, suggested that there also was a financial benefit to the program since the cost of the treatment would be reimbursed by public insurance. Kevin also talked about this policy and defended it by arguing that those who were not working were actually "worse off":

In general, people that are not working are worse off on many levels. Because, you can't be that bad off and still work. You can be *pretty* bad off and still work, but there are limits. And, more often, some of the problems are less chronic among the people who are still working. The other thing, a very important component at least in my mind, is you need something constructive to do with your time. If you're working, that takes up a fair amount of time. If you're *not* working, well, being in nine hours of group and an hour of individual a week takes up at least some more of your time.

This rationale suggested that a person's employment status became a symptom of their drug problem. Those who were unemployed were more "sick" and therefore in need of more-intense treatment. There was no distinction made for those who might be actively looking for a job but had not yet found one or who may have recently lost their job not due to their own fault. Two clients I interviewed mentioned that even in the height of their addiction they were still able to work, although they were not working when they began Westview's program, indicating that work status might not be the best measure for what level of treatment somebody needs. Mandating a more intense level of treatment to occupy the client's "free time" also was common practice by the drug court evaluator, suggesting that this may be common practice among those who screen clients into drug programs.

Clients had a mixed reaction to this policy. Some liked the addition of group therapy. Christine (a white female in her mid-thirties,[7] who was with the South-side group) commented: "I was on this program like twelve years ago, but it wasn't anything like this. You just came and got your meds and that was it. There was no group like this. This is a lot better." Most clients, however, seemed to view the additional group therapy as punishment rather than an extension of therapy that would complement their methadone treatment. Jerry, a Southside therapist, discussed new clients: "And then they go to IOP and hear the mumbo jumbo from the older patients—that this doesn't mean anything. Just hang in there, don't make any waves, and this will be over soon." Other Southside clients expressed frustration with the policy of having to attend the Westview IOP program, especially if they began working after starting treatment at Southside:

> BRIAN (Southside group, white male, late twenties): So now I have a job and I want to keep it, but I don't know if I can because I have to come here.
>
> WENDY (Southside/Westview therapist): Well, this place is a lot better than jail. I mean, in jail they tell you what to do. Here, you get to dictate what you're going to do. The only thing we mandate is that you go to IOP, but the rest is on you.
>
> BRIAN: Yeah, but that could make me lose my job.
>
> WENDY: Well, what you could do is get a letter from your employer and show Linda. She'll then excuse you from IOP and you'll become a fee payer. It's like $75 a week, but I think there's a sliding scale. Because otherwise we think you're committing insurance fraud by working but having welfare pay for you to be here. . . . Look, if you're working and you're still using, you're going to end up spending like half of what you make on drugs. This way, you just give us three months for IOP. And in the long run, it's more profitable because you will be clean; then you can get a job and actually keep the money.

Wendy likely referred to jail as a possible consequence because Brian had recently spent ten months in jail. It is still interesting, though, that she made a comparison between jail and treatment. She also made a distinction between those who were perceived to be "legitimately" working and those, like Brian, who were working under the table. There was no discussion, however, about how difficult it likely was for Brian, a convicted criminal, to get a decent-paying job. Instead, Wendy suggested that those in Brian's situation were trying to commit insurance fraud. The policy, then, did not allow clients to begin a new job if it prevented them from attending IOP.

Just as the evaluation for IOP treatment relied on external circumstances and funding issues, other stages of the treatment programs were dictated more by funding than by clinical considerations. That is, when a person would complete treatment was often determined by his or her funding source. IOP treatment was designed to last twelve to sixteen weeks, although some funding programs extended that time for clinical reasons. However, those who could not continue being funded had to leave the treatment program, despite not actually being "better" by the clinic's standards. Many of Southside's and Westview's policies indicated that funding sources determined the organization of treatment more than clinical research.

Defining Addiction: Ambiguities and Contradictions

Institutional Frameworks

Both the Southside and Westview programs referred to drug addiction as a disease. However, the exact nature of the "disease" of addiction was not easily defined by the staff, and also was not clearly communicated to the clients during group sessions. Staff members and clients mostly agreed with the notion that addiction was a disease, but they had different ways to conceptualize how the disease worked. In addition, moral frameworks were promoted; clients were reminded often that drugs could make them do bad things. The prevailing definition of addiction also centered on the client accepting responsibility for his or her drug problem.

Staff in both programs mostly agreed with the notion that addiction was a disease, although they emphasized different disease theories in their conceptualization:

> INTERVIEWER: So do you think drug abuse is a disease?
> LINDA: I believe it's a disease, part physical and part mental.
> INTERVIEWER: What's the physical part, what's the mental part?
> LINDA: I don't separate the physical and mental. . . . Stress results in cortisol and other neurotransmitters being produced too much or too little, which leads to emotional reactions to those drugs. I believe that in some sense, genetics makes a difference. . . . THIQ, tetrahydroisoquinilone, it's been found in the brain of alcoholics when you dissect them . . . which is a by-product of metabolization of either alcohol or heroin. The fact that they make it and I don't leads me to believe for sure that it's a disease. . . . I don't make enough thyroxin. I take pills. I have a disease. They make too much of something else. They got a disease too.

In this interaction, Linda, Southside's program supervisor, used one of the genetic theories of alcoholism, the "THIQ Hypothesis," that was presented in David Ohlms's 1993 book, *The Disease Concept of Alcoholism*. While this theory has been controversial, it also has found much support in the addiction treatment community. Linda's use of it implied that she also attributed this characteristic to drug addicts, and not just alcoholics, since she never clearly differentiated drug addiction from alcoholism. Kevin, Westview's program supervisor, also defined addiction as a biological disease:

> INTERVIEWER: Would you say, then, that alcohol or drug abuse is a disease?
> KEVIN: Oh, sure, however one defines it.
> INTERVIEWER: And how would *you* define it as a disease?
> KEVIN: Ah! [*pretends to scream*] Probably that it is a . . . definable syndrome where you can specify the course and, um, predisposing factors and so on. The usual one they compare it to is diabetes. It's not a bad analogy.
> INTERVIEWER: Why do you think that's a good analogy?
> KEVIN: They are both affected by lifestyle behaviors. . . . Most people on a bad enough diet, lack of exercise and so on, you're going to become

diabetic; likewise for drugs and alcohol. There's an old AA [Alcoholics Anonymous] saying—once you become a pickle you can't go back to being a cucumber. And . . . there's good evidence that that is probably true. There are brain changes and physiological changes that come with long-term use of a substance that is the body's adaptation to that. . . . It never goes back to being like it was before. . . . I don't go with the idea that . . . nobody who drank alcoholically can ever go back to drinking socially. . . . I think it's a bad bet. But certainly some people can do it. And I've seen some people appear to do it. . . . You undergo changes in the substance abuse. So that means you're susceptible for the rest of your life, to some degree.

While Kevin also described addiction as a biological disease, his conceptualization was different than Linda's. Kevin employed a definition of addiction promoted by the National Institute on Drug Abuse (NIDA), which states that addiction is a "brain disease." On its Web site, NIDA's director, Nora Volkow, offered the following "Message to Medical and Health Professionals":

> Recognizing drug addiction as a chronic, relapsing disease characterized by compulsive drug seeking and use is critical to being able to identify and help those who have it. Drugs of abuse affect the brain by mimicking neurotransmitters (e.g., heroin or marijuana) or by altering their regulation and release (e.g., cocaine and amphetamine). In this way, they disrupt normal brain communication. Repeated disruptions in the brain's normal signaling processes can eventually lead to addiction—affecting the very circuits needed to exert good judgment and inhibitory control over actions. With these abilities "seized," the drug-addicted person will compulsively choose drugs, even in the face of devastating life consequences. (NIDA 2008)

Both Linda and Kevin articulated a definition of addiction that related to brain processes, although Kevin's statement was much closer to NIDA's definition of drug addiction. Kevin's conceptualization of addiction, and his comparison of drug addiction with diabetes, was also similar to a view that was published in the *Journal of the American Medical Association* in a 2000 article entitled "Drug Dependence: A Chronic Medical Illness" (McLellan et al. 2000). In this article, the authors suggested that drug addiction should be conceptualized as a chronic medical disorder rather than as an acute disease. They offered comparisons of addiction treatment outcomes with those from treatment for diabetes, hypertension, and asthma and concluded that adherence to medication and relapse rates were similar across all of these "chronic diseases" (McLellan et al. 2000). Linda, however, cited a genetic theory that was developed in the early 1990s. These two ideas are not mutually exclusive, as NIDA also promotes genetic factors as one of the reasons that some people become addicted to drugs and alcohol.

Neither Linda nor Kevin appeared to have been instructed as part of their job to adhere to one definition over another; each one preferred to emphasize either a biological or a genetic component.

The other therapists I interviewed emphasized different factors associated with addiction, and had varying notions of how it fit into a disease model, although all cited some biological or genetic explanation as one of the factors:

INTERVIEWER: Do you think that alcohol or drug abuse is a disease?

WENDY (Southside/Westview therapist): That's the million-dollar question. For some people I do believe it and others I don't. There's no cookie-cutter format that I can put each client into, 'cause they all have different backgrounds, they all have different reasons. I think that there are a lot of chemical imbalances, what you would be calling disease, that drive people to use, or drink, but in general, I think that everyone has choices, and people who are not being treated properly for whatever their symptoms are, are self-medicating and trying to make up for it.

INTERVIEWER: So, it sounds like they have some other kind of mental illness, but the drug abuse itself is *not* a mental illness. Is that what you're saying?

WENDY: Right.

INTERVIEWER: Like they're using that to medicate this other illness that they have.

WENDY: Right. And because of their lack of education or coping skills, they don't know what else is out there. . . . So, I don't believe that it's just one set thing. 'Cause you meet people, who you think, it's got to be a disease, it's got to be something like that, but once you get to the base of the problem, and you realize where they're coming from, it's a whole different story.

INTERVIEWER: What do you mean, at first you would think this has got to be . . .?

WENDY: I'm again going back to the methadone clinic. Like sometimes you think no one would actually say, "Let me stick this needle in my arm, that's a good idea," . . . So you think that it is some type of disease, but then when you work with them, and you find out the abuse that goes on in their families, the drug addiction in their families, the environment they live in, it's no surprise. A lot of the women, I'd say at least 50 percent of them, have been abused—verbally, physically, sexually . . . their histories reflect why they're self-medicating. If you come from a broken home and mom and dad beat you or disowned you, you'd have a lot to forget about. A lot of them are very successful with using benzos [benzodiazepines]. Benzos make these people into zombies, like you have no feelings left. Then when we start talking about feelings, and they're crying for a couple hours straight, like oh, you forgot what it feels like to have those, and they get really upset. . . . But I definitely think that there is some type of genetic trait, I guess, a characteristic or a weakness. That's my best guess.

Wendy explained addiction in multiple ways, but focused heavily on external circumstances that might lead one to abuse drugs (specifically, different types of abuse or social environment). She still also related a possible genetic component to addiction, however, indicating that it is perhaps some combination of these external factors along with a genetic "weakness" that leads to addiction. She did not cite any research studies, however, like Linda or Kevin did, to explain her perspective. Her initial reaction to the question ("that's the million-dollar question") indicated that she believed the disease concept was something to be debated, was controversial, and was a question with no easy answer. Tom, another therapist at Westview, disagreed with the idea that addiction was a disease:

> INTERVIEWER: Do you think drug abuse or alcohol abuse is a disease?
> TOM: No. [*laughs somewhat nervously*]
> INTERVIEWER: Could you elaborate a little bit?
> TOM: Well . . . a couple reasons. One, this idea that it's a brain disease and that once somebody uses a substance . . . that their brain is going to continue to need the substance, I just know that's not true given the amount of people who use and experimented with drugs and never end up having drug use problems. We can see a significant decline after [age] twenty-four/twenty-five, which is right about the end of college, of the people who are using at significant levels, it kinda drops off. And then there is the whole gateway theory which . . . you can't switch causality where the majority of marijuana users, even though the majority of cocaine and heroin users may have started with marijuana, alcohol, the majority of alcohol users and marijuana users never used harder drugs, so it's not this kind of progressive disease.

Tom argued against the "brain disease" and "gateway" theories of addiction. Like Linda and Kevin, he also used evidence from research studies. For instance, surveys about drug use consistently show that drug use goes down as age increases and that the majority of those who use drugs do not become compulsive drug users; many stop altogether on their own (a phenomenon often called "aging out"). While Tom quite clearly articulated evidence against the disease view of addiction, his own definition of addiction was not as straightforward:

> INTERVIEWER: Why do you think some people become alcoholics or drug addicts?

TOM: Um . . . multifactorial. I think for the large part it's a learned behavior; it's a skill they developed to give them either positive experiences or take away negative experiences that they learned. . . . either through modeling from parents or close friends or just their own experimentation and they find this just works for that . . . but each person it's gonna be different. I mean, you have the one person, they're an alcoholic, but they only keep drinking because there is a social aspect to it . . . and they don't want to give up that social life. . . . And then there is the one that just drinks all day and all night. Even isolated and gets completely . . . blacks out . . . or the one that needs to drink to avoid withdrawal. So there's many, there are economic reasons, availability of the substance in the community and their environment, social supports and, you know there is some genetic, biological component, but I think that all those other things bring that out.

While Tom initially articulated strong opposition to the idea that addiction was a disease, in the end, he explained the etiology of drug abuse similarly to Wendy. Tom used much of the same reasoning Wendy did, citing addiction as often the result of poor coping skills and environmental influences. He also indicated that there was not one definition that captured everybody, that there were multiple reasons, including genetic/biological factors that influenced whether somebody became addicted to drugs. While Tom initially dismissed the idea that addiction was a disease, he eventually cited genetic or biological components as possible reasons why somebody might become addicted to drugs. It was not clear how he negotiated those opposing perspectives. It is clear that in addition to different therapists having different understandings of addiction, even within an individual, multiple perspectives existed. Indeed, multiple perspectives about addiction were emphasized by each therapist:

INTERVIEWER: Why do you think some people become drug addicts?
KEVIN: I think there's a definite genetic component, and the research suggests as well that there is a significant genetic component. On the other hand, it's clearly related to social influences. . . . There's a book by Stanton Peele . . . from years ago. And one of the studies he cites is where there were a fair number of people who used heroin while in Vietnam and the greatest proportion of them came back to the U.S., stopped using, went on with their lives. They were physically dependent on it there, but didn't carry it over. Substance abuse, like almost any compulsive activity, serves to be an escape from self. And that can be a powerful thing. . . . The determinant is how it's affecting your life. Certainly, anybody using a physically addicting drug at sufficient quantities for long enough is going to be hooked, and may have a hard time getting off. And if you throw in other factors: socioeconomic, emotional, psychiatric, and so on, complicates the picture

and makes it less likely that they will be successful in doing that. So it's a lot of things.

Kevin adhered to the concept that addiction was a chronic disease with a genetic component. It was peculiar that he cited Stanton Peele and the well-known Vietnam study to illustrate possible social forces involved (that is, the stress of fighting in a war). Peele is a very outspoken critic of the biological disease concept of addiction and explicitly states that he uses a "distinctly nonmedical approach" to understanding and treating addiction (Peele 2008).[8] Kevin also agreed with Tom and Wendy's notions about social and environmental factors that can influence drug use. In fact, all of the therapists at Southside and Westview articulated social and environmental factors as major causes of drug addiction:

> PETER (Westview therapist): On a very basic level, doing drugs is a defense . . . needing to take a substance so I don't have to feel x, y, and z emotion. . . . It's like, I'm living in this poverty-stricken area, I have basically no options, I dropped out of school in the ninth grade . . . so there's a lot of hopelessness, especially with the socioeconomic level that we deal with here. And so they got to get away from that hopelessness and powerlessness for a while.
>
> JERRY (Southside therapist, white male, early fifties): I think part of it is genetic, I think part of it is the whole nature/nurture thing. . . . I think the genetic component could be overcome if the person is free from the stress that make people want to self-medicate.

The idea that addiction was largely the result of an individual "self-medicating" was another widespread notion articulated by the staff at both the Southside and Westview programs. It related to both the internal psychological problems (that is, a mental disorder like depression) and the external forces (that is, living in a poverty-stricken area) that were also cited as factors that could lead to addiction. Peter and Jerry were the two therapists I interviewed who also discussed having had their own problems with drugs and alcohol. Still, their definitions of addiction were quite similar to Wendy's and Tom's, even though they had a different personal experience with drugs.

The importance of social factors in the etiology of addiction has not been universally emphasized by treatment professionals in the literature. For instance, a survey of treatment providers in a Northern California county indicated the majority felt that drug addiction was social in origin (Gassman and Weisner 2005). However, in another study of drug treatment counselors, most viewed addiction as due to personality characteristics rather than social influences (Taxman and Bouffard 2003). The frequent reference to environmental and social factors by the counselors in Westview and Southside suggested that the therapists may have focused on circumstances that they observed in the neighborhood surrounding the facility. Unfortunately, I cannot say if this perspective would have been different if the therapists worked in a treatment facility that attracted mostly middle-class (and white) clients. It would be difficult to negotiate this definition, however, if the therapists worked in a different social environment. Perhaps they would emphasize the genetic component more in that type of setting. Jerry's elaboration that even some with the "addict" gene could avoid becoming drug addicts if they lacked stress suggested that a belief in the genetic component to addiction could help the therapists explain the variation in different communities.

The therapists' emphasis on how social/environmental factors contribute to drug addiction also was likely because clients themselves cited these factors as triggers for relapse. During group sessions, clients often discussed the high prevalence of drugs in their neighborhoods and their concern for their families' safety; one client made a point of saying that a crack dealer was closer to his house than the nearby deli for buying beer. Following is an interaction in a Southside group meeting when the counselor posed a question about what the clients could do to avoid relapse:

> LORETTA (black woman, age forty-three): What about when it's right in your neighborhood? Like two steps from your house and it's right there! Then what?
>
> KEVIN (counselor): Well, you know what they say: If you play in the tracks, you're gonna get hit by a train.

In this interaction, the counselor seemed to dismiss Loretta's concern about the high prevalence of drugs in her immediate surroundings. While therapists cited these issues as a reason for addiction, they were still not seen as a justification for avoiding future drug use.

Clients also agreed for the most part that addiction was a disease, although some were not initially comfortable with the idea:

> JERRY (Southside counselor): Lisa, do you realize that you have a disease?
>
> LISA: I'm not sure.
>
> JERRY: Do you think it's all willpower? If you had diabetes or epilepsy, would you tell yourself, "I don't need treatment, I'll just willpower this disease away"?
>
> LISA: No.
>
> JERRY: Well, addiction also needs to be treated medically. There are cures—therapy, IOP, inpatient. You need to get treatment, though.
>
> LISA: So you're saying it's the same?
>
> JERRY: Yes, it needs to be treated medically.
>
> LISA: My counselor is always saying that. I don't know what to think about that.

Lisa's uncertainty about the disease label is likely due to her exposure to the moral frameworks for labeling addiction. That both Jerry and her individual therapist have tried to help her identify with a disease instead reveals the institutional emphasis on the medical framework for labeling addiction. Still, clients viewed their problem as a disease mostly in a metaphorical way; they voiced ambiguous notions about how it was caused or why they were afflicted. In addition, clients did not have much interest in defining these aspects; discussions about the etiology of addiction were extremely rare in group sessions.

Only one group member ever vocalized the desire to have more time in group devoted to discussing the "disease of addiction" more explicitly. Still, not all of those in treatment agreed with the disease concept. Sam, a white twenty-six-year-old from the Westview program, commented: "I don't think it's a disease. I think it's a decision that we make and when we do it, we do it excessively. I don't like that word for some reason. Disease to me is something you have no control over." While Sam disagrees with the idea of addiction as a disease, he still refers to himself as an addict because of how central drugs were in his life. As he stated in our interview, "I lived to get high." That compulsion was how he defined addiction, although others cited the same compulsion as reason for why addiction was a disease. According to Karen (black female, forty-five years old, Westview program): "It's very much a disease . . . like I'm saying, you got to steal from your mother, out here selling your body, it's a disease. . . . When you got to go out of your whole characteristic of yourself to take, just to get one more, it's a disease."

NIDA's definition of addiction as a "brain disease" emphasizes this compulsive nature of doing drugs. Clients, however, interpreted that compulsion in different ways.

Responsibility and the Sick Role

The apparent widespread acceptance by the staff that addiction was a disease did not interfere with a concurrent notion that the client had to take responsibility for getting "well." This idea is central to many medical conditions, and is one of the characteristics of illness that Talcott Parsons (1975) described in his theory of the "sick role." Parsons contended that to be "sick" was to take on a new social role. One of the legitimizing criteria for being able to take on the "sick role" was a general notion by the population that it was not the person's fault that he or she was sick. However, to sustain that legitimacy, the person also must demonstrate an effort to get better, by visiting a doctor, taking medication, or seeking some other socially approved treatment method. If the person was perceived to be taking responsibility for the illness, then he or she would be granted the sick role status and would not generally receive any moral condemnation for contracting the illness (Parsons 1975). Addiction however, does not easily fit into Parsons's "sick role" concept. Even though the therapists viewed them as ill, clients were still at fault for "contracting" the disease of addiction since they chose to initially ingest drugs. That is, the treatment staff was more hesitant to extend the "sick role" to the clients at Southside and Westview because of the perception that the client in some ways created the problem. For instance, Linda, Southside's program supervisor, emphasized the responsibility that clients needed to take for the "disease": "I think too many professionals make excuses and enable. We don't set enough structure and enough expectations. . . . We say, 'Oh, you poor thing, you've got a disease.'"

While Linda was talking about the client's responsibility to adhere to treatment plans, other staff would fault the client for initially engaging in a behavior that could lead to drug addiction:

> INTERVIEWER: To what extent is a person's drug problem their own fault?
> WENDY: I'd say, 98 percent their fault. Because everyone has choices. No one stuck a needle in your arm; no one shoved the booze down your throat. Everything that they do is a choice in life. Once they're actually addicted to the physically addicting drugs—that could be different. Some people claim becoming addicted to the painkillers that were prescribed by a doctor. I believe that that happens. I know that people have chronic pain, and before you know it, you can't stop taking them. But, I'd say that majority of it is their choice.

Here, Wendy differentiated between those who become addicted unknowingly by becoming physically addicted to medications prescribed by a doctor, and those who took a drug initially just for pleasure. She ascribed different levels of responsibility to the two groups. In a sense, she was extending the "sick role" to those who unknowingly became drug addicts, but not for those who "chose" to become an addict.

For most therapists, however, adhering to a disease philosophy for addiction meant that they could not assign too much blame to the individual client:

> INTERVIEWER: To what extent is a person's drug problem their own fault?
> PETER: I would say not too much. . . . Well, if it's a disease, then would you say somebody is at fault for having tuberculosis, or is somebody at fault for having cancer? . . . Now, at certain points, a person assumes responsibility for dealing with the problems . . . and obviously part of the addiction characteristic is denial, not wanting to deal with it. So I would say it's probably nobody's fault for becoming an addict or an alcoholic, but . . . wanting to deal with it is their responsibility.

Defining addiction as a disease took some of the responsibility off the individual client. However, the therapists at Southside and Westview all emphasized that the client still had responsibility for dealing with addiction. Kevin made this distinction by separating the idea of "fault" from responsibility:

It's not their own fault, it's their own responsibility. . . . Fault, I think, is a bad way of looking at it. Responsibility, I think, is a good way of looking at it because . . . it doesn't matter how you got lost in the forest, it's up to *you* to find your way out. Blaming other people is pointless, blaming yourself is pointless . . . it's up to you to make the changes. Treatment, et cetera, are all there to try and assist you and encourage you. . . . It's still up to you.

The therapists did not equate responsibility and blame. At the same time, there was an implied view that clients often did not accept that responsibility, as in Peter's assertion that many clients were in "denial" of having a problem. Denial is a particular characteristic of addiction; it is not often associated with other diseases. It also has a strong moral connotation because the implication is that they are not being honest or responsible.

This notion of responsibility related to the therapists articulating to the clients in group sessions that they had control over their "illness." Here was a discussion in group about giving up control over obstacles in life:

WENDY (Southside/Westview therapist): What do you have no control over that you have to accept?

CATHY (white female, mid-forties): Using drugs.

WENDY: Well, you have control over that. What do you try to control, maybe with other people that you can't? Like my husband does such and such and it drives me nuts, but I have to step back and realize that I can't control that.

In this interaction, Wendy was quick to tell Cathy that she had control over using drugs, even though Cathy thought otherwise. With the notion of responsibility came this insistence to clients that while treatment could give them the tools to battle their addiction, it was ultimately their task to use them effectively. All of the clients I interviewed individually expressed agreement with the notion that addiction was the individual's fault. Unlike the treatment staff, they reiterated the use of "fault" rather than discussing it as responsibility.

The Ambivalence of Methadone

To be a state-licensed program that administers methadone, the program had to follow strict federal regulations, as well as additional state-level regulations. Federal regulations were first established in 1972 by the Food and Drug Administration (FDA) and are also managed by the Drug Enforcement Administration (DEA) since methadone is classified as a narcotic drug with potential for abuse (Rettig and Yarmolinsky 1995). In 2001, the regulations were updated and enforcement of them was shifted from the FDA to the SAMHSA. These regulations are very specific regarding how physicians may use methadone to treat opiate addiction. They also require practitioners who dispense methadone (or any other narcotic drug for maintenance purposes) to register with the DEA annually; the DEA then determines if the physician would be likely to comply with the security and record-keeping requirements. A 1995 report from the Institute of Medicine summarized these regulations by stating, "No other medication is so highly regulated" (28).

The federal regulations required a person to demonstrate that they had been addicted to opiates for at least one year. The Southside clinic typically verified this by making sure the client tested positive for opiates and exhibited physical signs of addiction (such as track marks from injecting drugs intravenously) or had a history of prior treatment episodes. If the individual reported using the opiate orally and had no previous treatment, then the clinic required them to bring in a letter from a family member or friend demonstrating that they had been using the substance for more than a year. In a sense, those seeking treatment had to make the case that they "deserved" treatment since the medical staff's own opinion about need was outweighed by federal regulations. These were the only criteria used to measure opiate addiction.

Federal regulations also restrict the distribution of methadone to hospital pharmacies and treatment programs, with additional regulations regarding "take-home" doses. Most clients, especially those new to Southside's program, had to visit the clinic daily to receive their methadone dose, which nurses administered in liquid form. Clients had to drink their prescribed dose in front of the nurses. They could qualify for weekend take-home doses after being on the program for three months. While concern over diversion is the primary reason for the restriction of take-home bottles,[9] research suggests the amount of diversion that occurs does not justify the extremely tight regulations (Rettig and Yarmolinsky 1995). While the federal regulations were changed in 2001 to permit more flexibility around take-home bottles, the Southside program's rules became stricter in the several years before my observations, possibly reflecting a higher level of distrust of their clients than in other programs.

Demand for methadone treatment often exceeds the supply. In the summer of 2005, when I conducted most of my observations at Southside, there was a three-week waiting list for the program. The program also emphasized methadone maintenance treatment as something of a "last resort" for individuals who wanted to stop using opiates. As Southside's brochure stated: "If you've been addicted to heroin or other opiates for many years, have tried a number of detoxes/rehabs and find yourself addicted again, or can't go into a hospital, methadone maintenance is probably right for you." Such a statement implied that a person should try other forms of treatment before enrolling in a methadone maintenance program. While on one level, this suggested that methadone maintenance was reserved for the most "severe" cases of opiate addiction, it also revealed the discomfort—even of those working in the program—with using methadone as a treatment. For instance, the following is from an interview with Kevin, Westview's program supervisor:

> INTERVIEWER: Do you think that methadone maintenance is the best way to treat opiate abusers?
>
> KEVIN: I think methadone maintenance is the best last resort for treating opiate users. I do not think it's the first choice for first-time treatment because if you don't have to go on methadone, you're better off not. . . . The problem is the proportion of people that successfully get off of it is small and it comes along with some negative baggage. . . . It throws in an extra step because with many clients they initially transfer their relationship with heroin to methadone. And they react in many of the same ways, in terms of protecting their source and being obsessed.

While Kevin elaborated on some of the difficulties of methadone treatment, such as the strict federal regulations, telling people in treatment that methadone should only be a "last resort" tells them that there may be something immoral or "bad" about methadone, a message also communicated by the twelve-step community and the criminal justice system.[10] Studies have shown that those taking methadone as part of treatment felt extra stigma from the wider addict community and from the drug treatment facility itself (Conner and Rosen 2008; Frank 2011; Gourlay, Ricciardelli, and Ridge 2005; Radcliffe and Stevens 2008). Others taking methadone report concern about becoming addicted to the substance, another message that they may be receiving from the treatment program or other drug users (Neale 1998).

Most of the therapists expressed dissatisfaction or ambivalence with methadone treatment. This appeared counterintuitive because methadone treatment is arguably the most "medicalized" way of dealing with addiction. That treatment providers who themselves adhered to a disease concept of addiction were often critical of methadone treatment could be due to a lack of knowledge about addiction science (Lawson et al. 2004), or the continuing stigma that surrounds methadone treatment (Newman 1987). It also might be due to their education and training being largely in the area of counseling, so they might be resistant to using medications when they believe more strongly in the power of talk therapy. One of Westview's therapists, Peter (a white male in his early forties), suggested that this could be the source of some of his resistance to methadone: "I sometimes get . . . a sense of . . . the methadone, it's a more primitive level of 'give me food.' And you're like a food dispenser or a food regulator, rather than, 'I'm here to work on problems.'" While Peter thought methadone could sometimes be an effective treatment, his general attitude was that it did not get at the underlying issues of addiction. This feeling was tied to his overall perspective on the medicalization of mental health problems:

And that's part of the medicalization thing . . . I think that sometimes the medical community uses things for a mechanistic view of the body and healing and it's like, there's more. I've been to some conferences for trainings on methadone and nobody said a word about alternative methods. . . . I think the basic orientation is, "let's deal with this chemically." And while it's successful in the short term, I don't know whether it does a person a service to just be limited to that. To make that your *only* thing in your toolbox that you go to, I don't think that's fair to people, or doing them a service.

Other therapists expressed a similar sentiment about how methadone could be a good tool, but that it should be used in conjunction with other treatment methods. They agreed that methadone could be effective at helping to alleviate some of the physiological symptoms of opiate withdrawal, but there were other factors that contributed to the drug problem that would not be addressed by medication alone. The development of methadone maintenance therapy was never designed to be an all-encompassing cure for addiction; the first programs using it incorporated nonpharmacological treatment as well and found that the best results were from those who used methadone in conjunction with other types of therapy (Gossop 2003).

This ambivalence about using methadone in treatment is related to the view that methadone might replace one drug with another that could also be harmful. Clients in Westview's program (those not in treatment for opiates) occasionally referred to the Southside clients as not "really clean," indicating that methadone was the equivalent of heroin or cocaine. Some clients in treatment for opiates concurred with this sentiment:

INTERVIEWER: You said one of your drugs of choice was heroin, but you've never considered methadone maintenance?

SAM: No, I don't want it because I feel that you're just substituting one drug for another. You're not clean. . . . To me, it's not recovering. If I'm going to do this, I'm going to do it right.

A study done almost thirty years ago found that those in the drug treatment community stigmatized methadone users as unclean "losers" (Hunt et al. 1986). That this stigma still exists reveals that attitudes toward the medicalization of drug problems are complex and at times contradictory. How can something be a disease if one shouldn't use medication to treat it?

Therapists who were critical of methadone often gave reasons that had more to do with the strict federal regulations over the distribution of methadone than the effects of the medication. One of these regulations required clients to visit the treatment facility daily to receive their dose. Take-home doses could be "earned" throughout the program, but nobody was ever given a very large supply, even those who had been on the program for years. Many of the therapists saw this as an unappealing aspect of methadone, in that clients were restricted in their daily activities because they had to go to the clinic. Clients also felt that these restrictions were problematic; they have been linked to high dropout rates in methadone programs in general (Hunt et al. 1986). Kevin, Westview's clinical supervisor, discussed some of his reservations about methadone treatment: "Having to get medicated early in the morning before they can do anything else . . . that's maybe where the Suboxone [buprenorphine] is a good choice because it's less confining. And less . . . what's the word? The word that came into mind is enslaving [*laughs*]." Kevin offered buprenorphine as a possible alternative to methadone since buprenorphine was dispensed as a take-home medication like most other prescriptions. It moves treatment for opiate abuse solely into a doctor–patient relationship. What Kevin did not mention, however, was that buprenorphine was very expensive and not covered by most (if any) insurance plans.

Research also suggests that drug treatment therapists have little knowledge about the effects of buprenorphine, so it seems unlikely they would offer it as a viable alternative (Knudsen et al. 2005). Peter also vocalized similar sentiments when describing the regulations of methadone treatment: "Some people are able to live pretty functional and worthwhile lives, and work. . . . But the fact is, they still have to come here like once a day for the rest of their life. It says to me, there's never full freedom. They're always enslaved to the substance at some level. That's a strong word to use, but . . ." That both Kevin and Peter used a variation of "enslavement" to describe methadone treatment was in part due to the federal regulations around its prescription. The term, however, also indicated their uneasiness about clients replacing one drug (such as heroin) with another (methadone). They made a clear distinction that it was not the "rules" that the client was enslaved to, it was the medication.

In addition, most of the staff was critical of the idea that clients would take methadone for "life" or for a very long time, even though in other scenarios, such as in a group sessions, they referred to it as a "life-saving" medicine, and compared it to other treatments like insulin. For instance, Linda, Southside's program coordinator, discussed a client who eventually left treatment: "One of my clients said to me, and I love it . . . He was approaching sixty, he worked for the school district, and he said, 'Look, I'm getting married, and I'm going to retire soon. . . . We want to travel. I want to get off. . . . I've been on for thirty years. Enough.' . . . He's fine." Linda was an advocate for methadone maintenance. In our interview, she indicated that her ideal treatment program would include methadone maintenance for those under the age of eighteen.[11] At the same time, however, she did not approve of its indefinite use. She spoke proudly of this client, who decided after thirty years that he did not want to take methadone anymore. She used him as the program's ultimate "success story." The staff's impressions of whether methadone was an appropriate treatment modality could be partly a result of the general ambiguity expressed about how addiction was a disease, but could also perpetuate that ambiguity within the treatment program since they were critical overall of a pharmacological approach to treating addiction while at the same time advising clients about medication issues. The therapists failed to recognize that their own ambivalence, as well as the strict program regulations, could have a negative impact on their relationship with clients in Southside. Other studies of those in methadone maintenance treatment have found that clients perceive the tight restrictions around methadone as not only inconvenient but also indicators of distrust and stigma (Holt 2007; Stancliff et al. 2002; Treloar, Fraser, and Valentine 2007).

Clients held a similar perspective about methadone; nobody that I encountered in Southside's program ever expressed interest in remaining on methadone for a very long period of time. They all viewed it more as a temporary medication for their problem rather than as a lifelong treatment. Many also felt that methadone was a drug they eventually would have to detox from once they were ready. As Drew commented, "I hope to get my take-home [bottles], and get clean from my other substances and successfully detox again. And get on with my life. Not be a lifetime on this clinic. That's my goal." Even though everyone I interviewed saw their addiction as lifelong, they did not want to be associated with a clinic for the rest of their lives. Similarly, the idea that addiction is a disease like diabetes would often come up in group settings. In these settings, methadone many times would be compared to insulin. Yet all of the respondents viewed methadone as a short-term medication. This has been found in other interview studies of methadone users, where recipients often cite very positive benefits from the medication yet ambivalence about using it long-term (Hunt et al. 1986; Stancliff et al. 2002). This uneasiness about using methadone is directly related to the strict regulations around it, as well as the staff's own ambivalence toward the medication.

The Equality of Addiction

The disease concept of addiction promoted ambiguity because of its impreciseness and multiple theories of causation surrounding it. Still, both treatment programs advocated the idea that addiction should be thought of as a disease, despite difficulty articulating exactly what caused the disease. As part of that notion, all "addictions" were discussed as equally devastating; those who injected heroin were the same kind of addict as someone who frequently smoked marijuana. This label of "addiction" also extended to other drug-related behaviors (as it did in the drug court); it was not restricted to only drug use.

Substances were not generally distinguished from one another, with the exception that methadone was used only to treat those using opiates. In the IOP program, groups tended to be mixed as far as what substances people reported having problems with. Additionally, in both program's group therapy sessions, strategies about how to avoid using drugs were often discussed. The strategies were discussed as if they universally applied to any mind-altering substance; they were never drug-specific. Jerry, a Southside therapist, addressed a group session: "That's what this group is about . . . you are all here to help each other. 'Cause we all have the same disease, so we can really help each other." Similarly, during another group session at Southside, where clients were in treatment for opiate use, Wendy handed out a work sheet entitled "Cravings to Use Cocaine or Other Drugs." Nobody raised the issue that the work sheet was designed for cocaine users.

One of the reasons that the general use of "addiction" did not apply differently to different drugs could be that clients reported using multiple drugs. Many of the clients taking methadone reported using drugs other than heroin. Similarly, the clients often discussed their drug-related problems in universal language, as if everybody had them:

> DREW (Southside clinic, black male, age twenty-five): I used to go to meetings and I didn't get anything from it because I just thought I was so different. Like, these other eighty-nine people got the same thing, but I'm so different, right?
>
> JOSH (white male, age late twenties): We all got the same disease.
>
> DREW: Right. And I don't think that anymore. But I used to. And then you'd hear some people, like looking down on heroin users.
>
> JOSH: Right. Like, "I only did OxyContin, so I'm not as bad as you, who did heroin." That's crazy. They're all opiates.
>
> DREW: Right. Or looking down on those who smoke. Like, I'm a snorter, so that's not as bad as you 'cause you're there smoking.
>
> CHARLOTTE (black female, age early thirties): Yeah. That shit don't make any sense.

Here, the clients discussed the hierarchy that was sometimes created among drugs users by differentiating the types of drugs used and the main route of administration. While most clients expressed the "we're all in this together" mentality, I observed clients in Westview's "drug free" (that is, no methadone maintenance clients) group on several occasions reflecting that they were not as "bad off" as the clients on methadone. Sociologists call this "deviance avowal" (Turner 1972), where those who are stigmatized try to minimize their own stigma by promoting themselves as less deviant than another group, in this case, the opiate users taking methadone. Deviance avowal is a common strategy among those labeled addicts because of moral frameworks for understanding addiction. It may have been the methadone clients, who faced the additional stigma of being heroin users, who more actively tried to promote the similarities among drug addicts. For instance, regarding twelve-step meetings, many of Southside's clients discussed going to meetings that were not necessarily named for their main drug of choice. That is, many of the opiate users discussed going to AA meetings because they liked them better than the Narcotics Anonymous (NA) meetings.

Addicted to the Lifestyle

The "disease" was not really about the substance itself, but more about the person who used the substance. This logic followed from those who discussed genetic predispositions as a major factor in developing an addiction to those who focused on neighborhood or family factors. While therapists discussed drugs as having chemical properties that promoted addiction, nobody relied on a theory that addiction was solely the result of using too much of a substance. All of the therapists included other factors as likely contributors to the "disease." Similarly, clients discussed other aspects of the drug-using subculture, not just the actual use of a substance, as being related to their own addiction. Billy, a white male in his early twenties at the Southside clinic, commented: "I've been clean from dope since October 27th of last year. That's the last time I used, right before I got locked up. But I think I'm addicted to the lifestyle. Like the whole copping, and going to cop and figuring out how you're gonna get the money." Clients spent a lot of time discussing this notion of being addicted to the *process* of obtaining drugs, often summed up as "the thrill of the chase":

> ANNIE (Southside clinic, white female, late thirties): I used to get up early. I would be out the door by like 6:00, 6:30. I used to take the bus up north. I just loved it. I mean, I loved the routine. I loved going to get it.
> KARL (black male, age thirty-five): The thrill of the chase!
> ANNIE: Yeah, I just loved it. I loved doing it too, but I even just loved the routine. Getting up early and going up there.
> KARL: [*chuckles*] You were getting there, and people were still there from the late shift!

Others described being "addicted" to other parts of the ritual of using drugs that they missed now that they were in treatment:

> LEE (Southside group, white male, early twenties): I think I was addicted to the needle. I just loved that feeling, that needle going in.
> JOE (white male, age twenty-three): Oh, me too. It got to the point where I would shoot water, just to have that feeling.
> LEE: I was the same way. I would shoot anything. The first time I was on methadone, I would take it and then shoot anything I could find in the kitchen. I would shoot baking soda . . . I shot crack.

Since addiction was related to the *behavior* that the person engaged in rather than the specific drug, other drug-related behaviors were identified and labeled as addictions. Most commonly, this occurred with the clients who were involved with the criminal justice system and had been court appointed to treatment. These clients, who overwhelmingly were arrested for selling drugs, were sent to

treatment as part of an initiative such as drug court. While they had been evaluated as having a drug problem, the staff felt that most of these clients were not
drug addicts in the classical sense:

> WENDY (Westview/Southside therapist): I would say that the majority of
> my [court-mandated] clients are not drug addicts. They have drug
> use histories, but not necessarily drug addicts.
> INTERVIEWER: So if you don't think that they're really addicts, why do
> they get referred to this program?
> WENDY: Marijuana will stay in your system for up to thirty days . . . so
> anybody who has a drug history and a drug background is presumed
> to have an addiction problem. And I do think that there is a type of
> addiction, but not necessarily to the drug. To the lifestyle, maybe.
> They're addicted to the lifestyle of selling drugs and making that
> quick money. The girls, the money, the cars, that's what they all tell
> me. So, it's the bling-bling.

Wendy reinforced the notion that one could be addicted to something about the
"lifestyle" of doing drugs. She further elaborated that she thought these clients
needed treatment, but not necessarily the type of drug treatment that the
Westview program offered. In a sense, their type of drug addiction required
a different form of therapy. Peter, a Westview therapist, also alluded to having a
similar perspective:

> So the focus sometimes is to help people see how even involvement with
> drugs led to criminality for them and how *that* impacted their life. . . .
> Even though they weren't addicted to using the drugs, some of them
> were . . . almost addicted to the drug world or the excitement. You can
> get a rush of excitement when you close a profitable deal. So that kind of
> *rush* is something that they were addicted to or found they were very
> drawn to repeatedly, despite the consequences, which definitely is a sign
> of addiction.

Despite the general agreement that these clients were not addicted to using
drugs, they still participated in the IOP group therapy sessions, even though I
noticed that they did not often speak about having a drug problem during group.
In addition, the clinic labeled them "addicts," although their disease was not
using drugs, but was instead the act of *selling* drugs or some other behavior. As
Wendy indicated, some of the clients might be labeled addicts simply because
marijuana metabolizes more slowly in the body and can be detected for a longer
time after use than other drugs like cocaine or heroin. This could also help
explain why so many referred to treatment from drug court reported their drug
of choice to be marijuana.

In the IOP group, those who were court mandated to treatment would occasionally mention being in the treatment program because of their criminal justice status:

MICHELLE (black female, mid-thirties): [to Karen] You were a dealer? That's why you're here?

KAREN (black female, mid-thirties): Yeah. Well, I also sniffed heroin, but that was a long time ago. . . . I kicked the monkey a long time ago. I had been clean on the street before I got locked up. I still had a habit 'cause I liked to sell the drugs. That was my habit, selling the drugs. So I had an addiction—my addiction was selling crack cocaine.

Michelle associated Karen's drug-selling status as the primary reason she was in the IOP treatment program. Karen agreed that her addiction to selling drugs created the need for treatment. This scenario revealed how the large number of court-mandated clients in Westview's program led to other clients also associating involvement with the criminal justice system as a reason to be in treatment.

The therapists generally still agreed that a drug treatment program was the appropriate place for these individuals, even though they did not have a significant drug use problem. They felt they were able to treat other problems that these individuals faced, which could help them stay "clean" from criminal activities:

KEVIN (Westview program coordinator): When you're working with a client like that, your main focus is not on abstinence from substance abuse because that's easily done. It's on, "OK, what the hell are you gonna do with your life? Do you like being in jail? Assuming you don't, OK, how you gonna get out of this stupid system so you don't *have* to put up with that crap?"

WENDY [referring to the court-mandated clients]: Because it's so hard to keep this program afloat, we've taken in the [court-mandated clients] to help generate money. And these guys definitely need treatment, but I think it's a different type of treatment than what is typically provided here. . . . I do like working with them. . . . Rather than going on and on about the drug addiction, I break it down to them in the beginning—like, "You're really not a drug addict, are you?" And we talk about what has happened *prior* to them getting arrested, their lifestyles, their behavior problems, their parents, family members who have been killed and shot. That's a very common thing. Dad's in jail, grandpop's in jail, brother's in jail. A lot of these clients expect to be in jail at some point. It's like a rite of passage. So, working on things and working with them to change the future.

From Kevin and Wendy's responses, there was some indication that they found working with the court-mandated clients rewarding because they were able to focus on issues outside of drug abuse. Wendy was the only one who mentioned financial benefits to the program, although most therapists rationalized that the court-mandated clients *needed* a form of treatment, even if they were not drug addicts. She also recognized, however, that the program's resources were at times disproportionately geared toward the criminal justice population and that others (such as those self-referred) who needed the program were not able to get admitted because of lack of space.

Kevin also extended this perspective into a critique of the "success rates" touted by programs like drug courts:

> [Criminal justice initiatives], I think, have an inflated success level because a significant proportion of clients never really had an addiction. If the guy doesn't *really* have an addiction, the fact that he stays clean isn't all that impressive. Does that mean it's a good reason *not* to do it? No, because I think it serves other purposes; they learn other skills. They get out of the life of selling and so on. But in terms of treatment of *addiction*, it's inflated.

Similarly, Tom, a Westview therapist, indicated that these clients likely belonged in some kind of program and that putting them into treatment was better than incarcerating them:

> If it was *legal* to use the substance, they probably wouldn't have any problems with it. . . . I guess putting them in treatment as opposed to jail would be the best option. . . . Honestly the system's not perfect, but I think a better assessment done when they get arrested, so that they get to a program or service. I mean it could just be they're just having financial problems. They don't need to come here for that.

Tom was the only one to raise the issue that the illegality of drugs was the primary reason these clients were in treatment; if they had not been arrested, they would have no reason to be there. This further complicates the addiction concept; how do you justify the disease label if it is really determined by criminal justice policy?

Other therapists, however, did not appear to agree with the addiction label being used for those with no drug use problem. Peter, a Westview therapist, commented while talking about his clients: "Some of them are court mandated and don't have a lot of true *interest* in making any changes in their life. . . . Some of them found that they could get a reduced sentence by saying, 'Oh, I'm an addict, and I'll go into treatment,' when the fact is they actually had no addictive problem whatsoever . . . But they still have to come here, so . . ." For most therapists (besides Peter), if the client self-labeled as an addict (to the lifestyle), that was enough evidence that they belonged in treatment.

The self-referred clients also did not see much utility in having court-mandated clients in treatment. In one interview, Barry, a black male in his late thirties and a self-referred Westview program client, discussed his disappointment with having court-mandated clients in treatment:

> Sometimes I'm outside [the facility] and other people be asking me, "You really have a problem?" Other people are like, "I don't have a problem." Well, I have a problem! I have an allergic reaction to certain substances. I'm not here because I'm made to come because of court or whatever; I'm here because I have a problem. . . . A lot of people here are not educated about the disease of addiction.

Barry was one of the only clients who openly expressed dissatisfaction with the group being largely composed of court-mandated clients. He suggested in several group sessions that he was not getting what he needed from Westview's program because of its inclusion of clients who did not have "real" drug problems. From his comments, it also appeared that he did not agree with the extension of a disease framework to those who did not have problems using drugs. While the therapists emphasized the positive aspects of having court-mandated clients, including economic benefits to the program, they did not often mention possible negative consequences for other clients.

I also observed differences during the group sessions between many of the court-mandated clients and those who were self-referred. The court-mandated clients often openly discussed with each other how many days they had left in the program and expressed excitement when they were close to graduating. Many of them projected an attitude that they were "doing time" while in treatment, a sentiment not normally shared by those who were self-referred (and could leave treatment at any time without consequence). Many of the court-mandated clients also were quieter during the parts of group sessions when people shared about their drug use and problems with stopping.

Treating the Disease

The moral and medical frameworks used for defining addiction resulted in a myriad of treatment methods that also had moral overtones, especially around the dispensing of methadone and the use of twelve-step ideology. Just as each therapist emphasized different causes of addiction, they used a variety of treatment strategies during individual and group sessions, including cognitive behavioral therapy and twelve-step philosophy. Having multiple treatment methods in one facility is often cited as a good thing for helping people engage in treatment and to stay longer (Hser et al. 1997; Stahler, Cohen, et al. 1993). At the same time, different treatment methods should not be just a buffet from which clients choose what they think fits them best; treatment programs need to be more purposeful in how they use different therapeutic approaches, especially considering that certain approaches might contradict one another (NIJ 2006).

The therapists who led the group meetings I observed had very different styles. Wendy, who also dealt individually with the court-mandated clients, emphasized formal learning strategies during group; she often had them read through and complete work sheets together in a school-like atmosphere (I even heard one of the clients refer to these group therapy sessions as "class"). Jerry, in contrast, posed very open-ended questions to group members to stimulate discussions that would often last the entire meeting. When he brought in educational materials, they were used as an impetus for discussion; rarely did the clients spend much time filling out work sheets. Perhaps because of Jerry's own participation in Alcoholics Anonymous, he protected the clients' confidentiality by only using their first names and always closing the door to the hallway. Wendy, however, frequently called the clients by their last names, preceded by "Mr." or "Miss." Despite the therapists' different styles and orientations, the programs emphasized four components of addiction: abstinence is the key goal; clients must recognize and assess their moral flaws; the benefits of twelve-step programs; and, particularly for the Southside clients, the effective use of methadone.

Promoting Abstinence

Abstinence from drugs and alcohol is usually an explicit goal of treatment programs in the United States; complete abstinence posttreatment is often constructed to be the most positive outcome in research studies (see, for example, Acharyya and Zhang 2003; Tiet et al. 2007). Both Southside and Westview programs emphasized abstinence as a goal, but also as a *requirement* of treatment. One of the forms that clients signed when beginning Westview was titled "Basic IOP Treatment Expectations." The fourth of ten points read: "I am expected to identify significant problems, set goals and actively work on significant personal change including *complete abstinence* from all psychoactive substances, including alcohol and marijuana" (emphasis mine). Abstinence was monitored in both programs by weekly urine tests. However, while the programs explicitly included alcohol as one of the drugs one must abstain from, I never witnessed anybody being tested for alcohol use (that is, through a Breathalyzer test). That the form highlighted alcohol and marijuana as psychoactive substances implied that clients might not consider these substances to be "drugs," as they would cocaine or heroin. In general, there was confusion among group members about whether alcohol and prescription drugs were, in fact, drugs. During one group meeting at Westview, I witnessed one client claim to be abstinent from drugs for almost a year, but then later in group he mentioned that he still "did some Xanax here and there."

The Westview program emphasized abstinence by requiring group members to introduce themselves at the beginning of each group session, list what drug(s) they were in treatment for, and how much "clean time" they had (that is, how many days they had not used drugs). Abstinence from drugs for at least four weeks at the end of treatment also was a requirement for "graduating" from the Westview program; those who had not achieved abstinence by the end of the allotted treatment time were said to have "completed" the treatment program, but were distinguished from those who graduated. Referring to the length of abstinence as "clean time" is common language within the addict community (both in treatment programs and twelve-step meetings) (Weinberg 2000). At the same time, the implication of not being "clean" is that one is *dirty*, a rather moralistic way of viewing drug use.

While the Southside program (methadone maintenance) also emphasized abstinence, they did so differently. The pre-IOP group in the Southside clinic did not focus in a similar way on counting the days that the client had not used, although the program itself did monitor client drug use. While clients were not told to report their "clean time" during group meetings in the Southside program, whether or not the client used drugs was attached to various privileges and sanctions in the program. There appeared to be an expectation in the Southside clinic that a new client would take several days or weeks to accomplish abstinence while their methadone dose was stabilizing. Some clients also expressed confusion about whether they could consume other drugs, including alcohol, while in treatment:

JOE (Southside clinic, white male, age twenty-three): Do you think it's a relapse if you go out and have a couple of beers, in a social situation? I mean, not to get drunk, but if I was out and just wanted to feel not so anxious, so I have a couple of beers to relax?

VINCE (white male, probably mid-thirties): Yeah, that's a relapse!

JOE: I mean, it's not hard liquor or anything. It's just a couple of beers.

AL (white male, probably mid-fifties): Yeah, I think that's all right. Like I have older kids. And my one son, he'll bring a pizza and a six-pack and we'll have a beer and watch the game. I don't see what the problem with that is.

JOE: I mean, there's drinking wine at events, like Hanukkah or Passover. Is that bad, taking a drink of wine then?

VINCE: Well, that's a religious ceremony, so that's OK.

KEVIN:[12] As long as Hanukkah is not every day, right?

JOE: But even just having like two beers? I mean, it's not to get drunk, just to be more comfortable socially. And it's only like twice a month.

VINCE: So you're saying you can't relax *without* drinking a couple of beers?

JOE: No, just that it helps. Like, it helps me to be more social. It doesn't make me want to go get high or anything.

KEVIN: OK, well, is alcohol a drug?

VINCE: Yep. Alcohol is a drug.

JOE: I think alcohol is a drug. But not beer, cause it's not hard liquor.

[*Kevin looks half amused, half astonished.*]

KEVIN: Karl, do you think alcohol is a drug?

KARL (black male, age thirty-five): Yes. Alcohol is a drug. . . . It's a gateway drug!

KEVIN: That's true . . . alcohol is an inhibitor, right? So it lowers your inhibitions. And a lot of people have found alcohol to be their downfall. Like they start drinking, and then maybe find themselves using again. Or maybe they try replacing alcohol or some other drug for their drug of choice. . . . You should be careful. Why take the chance?

AL: That's true. Why take the chance? Next time my son comes over, I'm gonna tell him, "Bring a six-pack of Pepsi or I'm not letting you up the stairs!" [laughs]

JOE: Yeah, I guess I see what you're saying.

KEVIN: And if you use alcohol to feel less anxious, then you're never learning how to act in those situations. Some addicts have used for so long and they never learned how to act in certain situations. But it does also lower your inhibitions, so you might find yourself wanting to use. But, hey, you're an adult so you need to make that decision.

In this pre-IOP group session at Southside, clients debated whether or not alcohol was a drug and whether or not it was acceptable to use it. Interestingly, Kevin did not explicitly tell them that using alcohol would be a violation of the rules of the clinic. Instead, he let them come to their own conclusion about whether or not they should use alcohol. The confusion could be due to alcohol being a "legal" drug or that the clinic did not test explicitly for alcohol, even though it tested for every major illicit substance. The confusion also might be related to the clients in Southside taking methadone as part of their treatment. Perhaps they questioned whether all drugs were "bad" to use, since they were using an illicit substance as part of treatment. Southside clients who were more vocal about total abstinence tended to be those who also attended twelve-step meetings like AA and NA. They were often the ones who "educated" the other group members that alcohol was as bad a drug as heroin.

The expression of "clean time" was a central component to the group meeting at Westview, yet there were no major repercussions for those who recently used drugs or who did not achieve long-term abstinence even after being in treatment for several weeks. Clients were given the option of "sharing" something that was bothering them with the rest of the group, but were never required to talk about their recent drug use. During the group sessions I observed, no therapist ever reprimanded a client for relapsing or not maintaining abstinence. I also did not witness extensive verbal praise for those who abstained for an extended amount of time, except in several group sessions where other group members would begin clapping for those who reported "clean time" of *any* duration. The program's rules stated that three consecutive positive urines would result in being placed on a "contract," which implied that continued use would lead to termination from the program (and possibly a referral to inpatient treatment).

Most therapists agreed with the policy that clients should abstain from drugs and alcohol and used sobriety as a marker of whether or not a client was doing well after leaving treatment. Only Tom, a therapist at Westview, explicitly stated that he did not agree with abstinence being a requirement for treatment or as the best measure of success: "No. There might be certain individuals [who should not use] again. . . . But there are people that smoke marijuana once a month, or two or three times a year they use cocaine . . . there is the whole moderation drinking . . . so abstinence isn't really a requirement." Tom did not see abstinence as the ultimate goal for all of his clients. However, he never brought up an alternative perspective to clients during group meetings, probably because it would either violate their own feelings about the importance of abstinence or contradict the facility's rules about abstinence.

Abstinence was tied to the idea that there was no cure for addiction, but that eliminating drug use could put the disease into a form of "remission." This notion overlaps both the disease view of addiction promoted by NIDA and a twelve-step view of addiction; both perspectives view addiction as a lifelong/ chronic disease. Clients and therapists shared this philosophy. Wendy, a Westview/ Southside therapist, addressed a group: "Dealing with your drug dependence is a lifetime thing. You may get to the point where you don't have to think about it every day, but it never goes away. It's the gift that keeps on giving. It's like, you won the steak knives, but you got the juicer too."[13] Most clients I encountered agreed with the notion that addiction was a lifelong issue they would have to deal with. Robert, a fifty-one-year-old black Westview client, summed up this perspective during our interview: "Once you're an addict, you're an addict. It just takes one slip; one slipup and you're right back." Occasionally, group members disagreed with this sentiment, but due to the program's emphasis on abstinence and the lifelong nature of the disease, I suspect those who felt differently rarely said so, especially if they were completing treatment as a condition of drug court, probation, or parole.

While the narrative of addiction as a chronic, lifelong condition is pervasive, studies suggest that this view might be overly simplistic. Heavy drug users have been shown to be able to monitor their use and self-regulate to control drug use when it became problematic, suggesting that abstinence and addiction are not the only outcomes of heavy drug use (Blackwell 1983; Waldorf, Reinarman, and Murphy 1991; Zinberg 1984).

While most clients abstained from drug use at some point during treatment, all of the therapists had a rather pessimistic view of the clients' future prognosis, largely because of the focus on abstinence as the most significant marker of treatment success. Wendy estimated that only 25 percent of her clients that graduated would meet her criteria of "doing well" in the future: not using drugs, no criminal justice system involvement, and positive engagement in employment or school. Wendy also mentioned that "most" of her court-mandated clients went back to using drugs (often smoking marijuana) immediately after completing treatment. Other therapists also gave low estimates for the number of clients they expected to still be abstaining from drugs after treatment.

Therapists related this low success rate back to the original factors that led to the client's drug addiction—namely, neighborhood, criminal, and family problems. According to Wendy: "I think that what's available outside for them is limited. . . . Try to find an ex-criminal a job today, it's insane, like it is so hard to find them employment. . . . And how can I talk these kids into working at McDonalds when there's bling-bling that you get from selling drugs quicker and easier?" Failing to abstain from drugs while in treatment was seen as evidence that a client was not adequately progressing through the program. In the Westview clinic, these clients often would be referred to a higher level of care, such as inpatient treatment. Southside clients, however, remained in the methadone program even if they continued to use other drugs, as long as the therapist perceived them as *trying* to abstain. In the pre-IOP group I observed, there was one client, Karl, who had been in the methadone program continuously for about two years despite Wendy's claim that he had *never* tested negative for drug use. Some of this contradiction in policy could be related to funding restrictions since Karl was also a fee payer, and therefore not limited in the amount of treatment he could receive, like those on medical assistance.

Feeling Ashamed

Within the programs, especially during group meetings, there also was constant reinforcement that drug users were "bad people" and that those in treatment needed to come to terms with the bad things they did while they were on drugs. The disease view of addiction emphasizes that an addict continues to use drugs despite negative consequences; in the treatment programs, these negative consequences were typically framed as something the client should feel ashamed of. During one Southside group meeting, the therapist asked the group to reflect on the "turning point" that led them to go to treatment. When she confronted Joe about this, he replied that he was not sure, so she pushed him further:

> WENDY: Was there something you did? Like something you said, 'I'll never do that' and then you found yourself doing that?
>
> JOE: I ended up doing everything I said I wouldn't do. Well, I never like held a gun up to someone, but I did everything else. Sold all my stuff, stole a lot.
>
> WENDY: Karl, what about you? What did you end up doing that you never thought you would?

> KARL: I don't think it was like one thing happened. I mean, I always had money. I never robbed, never sold my stuff. It was never like that. I mean, I never had unprotected sex with like a hundred women!
>
> WENDY: Right. Well, you've been married to the same woman for like forever, right? What about doing stuff that hurt your family? Like to your wife or kids?
>
> KARL: Yeah . . .

In this exchange, Wendy pushes clients to reveal something "bad" about themselves, even when some initially cannot think of anything. The assumption was that everyone must have something bad to report.

Having clients reflect on the bad things they did while using drugs also suggests that feeling ashamed or guilty is a necessary part of treatment. This notion was reinforced by program materials; a handout about handling cravings that Wendy used during a group session indicated that one strategy is to "think of how I'll disappoint myself and my kids." Another workbook frequently used during Southside meetings (the "Surviving Addiction Workbook") asks participants to "evaluate the effects of your addiction" by writing down all of the ways that using drugs/alcohol hurt their family and social relationships, including causing suffering for family members, financial neglect, and ruined holidays or special occasions. Other studies suggest that drug treatment programs and twelve-step groups can be stigmatizing and shaming (Bourgois 2000; Frank 2011; Radcliffe and Stevens 2008; Semple, Grant, and Patterson 2005).

Clients reinforced the importance of recognizing personality flaws and bad things they did in the past as part of treatment. According to Billy (white, early twenties, Southside clinic): "When you first figure out [that you're an addict], man that's . . . [*sighs*]. It's like you just feel the weight of the world come right on you. Damn, I'm a piece of shit." These moments of self-deprecation occurred during group meetings as well as individual interviews. During a Southside group meeting, Jerry asked why the clients started treatment and one responded, "I was sick of lying."

Another common practice was reinforcing the idea of having a "split personality" between their drug-using and sober selves:

> MIKE: I feel like I have sort of a split personality. Like I'm pretty quiet, but when I'm using, I'm a different person. It's like the drugs let out this other person.
>
> JERRY: Do you feel like it's kind of a *Dr. Jekyll and Mr. Hyde*?
>
> MIKE: Yeah.

At the beginning of this chapter is an observation in Westview's program of a therapist copying a section of *Dr. Jekyll and Mr. Hyde* to use during group therapy. The previous interaction occurred in the Southside clinic, so it is not clear why the two different programs would make reference to the same book. Most likely, it reveals the pervasiveness of the split-personality metaphor for addiction. While drugs obviously have a powerful effect on the brain, this metaphor is not merely about drug chemistry; it is about reinforcing the moral message that drug users are bad people.

Using Twelve-Step Methods

The use of twelve-step methods in state-licensed drug treatment programs is commonplace. A survey of substance abuse treatment services found that more than 81 percent of programs used twelve-step methods in treatment (SAMHSA 2010a). While twelve-step methods are common, there is actually little research on their efficacy as a treatment modality (Sered and Norton-Hawk 2011). Both Southside and Westview programs explicitly and implicitly used twelve-step philosophy and methods in their treatment programs. They did so in three ways: by integrating twelve-step practices and philosophy into group meetings, by encouraging or mandating that clients attend twelve-step meetings in addition to treatment, and by using twelve-step methods individually during counseling sessions. While the use of twelve-step methods as part of treatment is common, it also adds to the ambiguous definition of addiction that was promoted in both treatment programs since twelve-step philosophy includes the idea that addiction is a disease, but more so as a metaphor without reference to specific research on the causes of addiction. The twelve-step view of addiction really has not changed since its inception in 1935, despite major changes to drug treatment and new theories about drug addiction.

Group meetings in Southside and Westview often incorporated twelve-step practices. Westview's client manual explicitly stated the program's relationship with twelve-step methods: "Twelve-step ideology is incorporated into treatment. Twelve-step meetings are available on-site and participation is strongly encouraged as an invaluable source of support and path to a new way of living." One of the ways that the ideology was incorporated into treatment was that at the conclusion of every group meeting in Westview's IOP program, clients would stand up, put their arms around each other, and recite the serenity prayer.[14] Therapists in both the Southside and Westview programs also incorporated handouts from books and publications that used twelve-step language and practices into group sessions. For example, therapists sometimes started group sessions with short meditations from "Just for Today," a resource for those in twelve-step groups. Wendy and Jerry frequently used the "Surviving Addiction Workbook" in the pre-IOP group at Southside clinic. The workbook was overtly twelve-step oriented. For instance, in the beginning of the workbook, it read: "Twelve step programs can help you gain or maintain sobriety, and regain your self-esteem." Use of these materials promoted ambiguity in defining addiction because they often incorporated a moral framework in defining drug abuse. Some of the materials implied that those who used drugs did so because of other personality flaws. For instance, a work sheet in the "Surviving Addiction Workbook" asked the client to "describe how alcohol/drugs affected your personality, and any of your *character defects* that could interfere with your recovery" (emphasis in original). Is there any other disorder, even another mental health problem, where treatment demands that a person do a moral assessment of his or her own defects and weaknesses?

Two of the therapists, Jerry and Peter, were open about their own past addictions to drugs and alcohol. Both were also proponents of AA/NA's treatment philosophy and used such materials in their group meetings. In one group meeting, Peter passed out an excerpt from a twelve-step text that emphasized the need to accept a higher power, and commented: "Until 1933, when AA started, there was no cure for addiction. You ended up in a sanitarium or in jail. Or dead in the gutter." Twelve-step texts frequently mention that "jails, institutions, and death" are the three possible outcomes of addiction if one does not stop using. Again, there is no mention of the many heavy drug users who end up controlling drug use on their own.

Tom was the only therapist who expressed resistance to using twelve-step methods during the group meetings. In one group session, he announced that the group was no longer going to close with the serenity prayer, but that instead each person would say what they found most useful about group that day. His suggestion was met with vociferous resistance from the group members. One member said that she liked using the serenity prayer because it reminded her of an NA meeting. Ultimately, Tom backed down and let the group continue using the prayer. In an interview, I asked him about that event:

> INTERVIEWER: Why did you want to change that?
>
> TOM: Two reasons. One, because of the mention of God in there and being respectful to other people that might not believe or feel that is a necessary part of their treatment. And two, just to try and move treatment programs away from the twelve-step model, which hasn't been shown to be any more effective than running laps around the track.
>
> INTERVIEWER: Has there been anything else you tried to change to push the group away from the twelve-step type stuff?
>
> TOM: I come from a CBT [cognitive behavioral therapy] approach, so some of the [twelve-step] stuff, I'll work that in if it fits in. . . . But yeah, I do more behavioral and skills-type stuff during the activities and looking at how people think about their drug use, as opposed to talking about powerlessness and getting a sponsor.

Tom related his attempt to eliminate the prayer from the group session with the ineffectiveness of twelve-step methods. While research on AA/NA's effectiveness is difficult because of the group's insistence on protecting its members' anonymity, some conclude that its "success rate" is probably quite low (for example, Bufe 1998). While Tom attempted to focus the group away from twelve-step components, he admitted that he used some of the "sayings," if they fit in with what he was trying to accomplish therapeutically. He also mentioned that if he were creating his "ideal treatment program," he would include twelve-step meetings as an option, but also would include other kinds of group meetings as an alternative. Additionally, during group meetings, I never witnessed Tom discourage any of the group members from discussing the benefits of twelve-step meetings because he saw value in them, mostly for group support. Most therapists viewed twelve-step meetings as Tom did—a positive addition to treatment. Since the goal was abstinence, most therapists were not really concerned with *how* clients achieved "clean time." So even if therapists personally disagreed with the twelve-step philosophy, they encouraged their clients to use it. For instance, Linda, Southside's clinical supervisor, said in our interview: "[Twelve-step methods are] not my cup of tea. But the more different options you have, the more patients you can reach. I'm in favor of anything if it will work." All of the counselors viewed twelve-step meetings as one of the many tools that a client had in trying to achieve abstinence. The therapists viewed twelve-step meetings as providing a support system for the clients, that they could meet others living in their high-poverty, drug-infested neighborhoods and learn how to handle the "triggers" around them. Their encouragement also revealed that the therapists recognized their own social distance from the clients; by suggesting that clients needed to make connections to people in their neighborhood, they were essentially admitting that the treatment program was incapable of providing everything the client needed to get better.

Peter, the therapist (in addition to Jerry) who mentioned using Alcoholics Anonymous for his own drug problem, saw AA as central to his own ability to remain abstinent from drugs and alcohol. In our interview, he used phrases and concepts from AA to illustrate why some people might not overcome their "disease": "In AA, there's a slogan: 'Some don't make it.' Some people die of their addiction. Part of their will is so strong that it doesn't want to surrender to some sort of treatment or higher power or whatever." Peter's use of this AA slogan also may have helped him cope with the emotional difficulties of his job and the high relapse rate that did occur for Westview's clients. At the same time, his use of the "will" indicated a moral view of addiction, that some had character flaws that treatment could not overcome.

Some therapists were explicit in their support of twelve-step philosophy and actively encouraged clients to attend meetings outside of treatment. For instance, during a Southside group session:

WENDY: If being bored can be a trigger, what can you do?
JOE: I go to NA meetings with my brother.
WENDY: Meetings. That's a good one. Karl, there's a meeting right on the corner from your house. When was the last time you went to a meeting?

KARL [*thinking*]: I went . . . yesterday! I go to meetings four times a
   week!

WENDY [*seems surprised*]: Really?

KARL: Yeah. After I did my ninety in ninety . . . I think I did like 120
   straight.

WENDY: Did you get a sponsor?

KARL: No, not yet. I'm working on that.

In this exchange, Wendy supported clients attending AA/NA meetings. Karl's
response that he did "ninety in ninety" (ninety meetings in ninety days) suggested that somebody at the program may have told him to follow that schedule,
especially since at the same time he indicated not yet having a sponsor.[15] While
drug court participants were sometimes mandated to attend twelve-step meetings, I never observed a therapist at Southside or Westview demand that a client
attend them, although they often encouraged it. In addition, clients often
encouraged each other to attend twelve-step meetings. It appeared that many of
them attended meetings outside of treatment:

CHARLOTTE (Westview clinic, black female, late thirties): What do you
   mean you don't have support? Do you go to meetings?

RAY (black male, mid-thirties): Yeah, I go.

CHARLOTTE: Do you have a sponsor?

RAY: No. I can't find anyone that I could ask to be my sponsor.

CHARLOTTE: You should go more.

They also shared their twelve-step knowledge with others in the group who were
unaware:

PATRICIA (Westview clinic, black female, mid-forties): I was told to get
   a sponsor. I went and asked this woman and she said no. [*Asking
   Tom, the therapist leading the group*] What's a sponsor for anyway?

BARRY (black male, late thirties): A sponsor guides you through the
   steps. You call that person if you want to use and they talk to you.

Clearly, Patricia was not familiar with twelve-step meetings, but had been mandated by the criminal justice system to go as part of her probation. Another
group member explained the purpose of a sponsor to her; clients often educated
each other about twelve-step meetings and other treatment options. While therapists encouraged clients to attend twelve-step meetings outside of treatment for
additional social support, clients appeared to value twelve-step meetings most
for the sense of identity they provided. Twelve-step meetings, through their discourse and narrative techniques, are designed to construct a sense of shared
experiences among alcoholics/addicts by the use of certain phrases, themes, and

reminders about nobody being unique (O'Halloran 2008). The Southside and Westview clients who attended AA and NA meetings embraced the addict identity the most vocally. There is some indication, however, that those who are forced to attend such meetings might resist the totality of the addict identity. In a study of women court mandated to attend twelve-step meetings, Sered and Norton-Hawk (2011) found that the women they interviewed did not like the all-encompassing addict identity promoted by twelve-step programs; they preferred to view their drug addiction as a temporary problem to overcome.

While I did not observe any individual counseling sessions, there were some indications that at least some of the therapists would work on the "steps" of AA or NA with clients individually during sessions, or at least talk about twelve-step philosophy during individual meetings, as Wendy did while talking to the Southside group: "I have a client who's very much anti-NA. He said, 'There is no way I'm going to those meetings.' So, I do the steps with him as part of treatment. I'm not a sponsor, so I don't know all the things, but he works on the steps as part of treatment." Working on the steps and then discussing them with a therapist also was recommended by the "surviving addiction workbook" that was used in the Southside pre-IOP meetings. In Wendy's example, it was not clear whether she offered her client such assistance or whether the client approached her. Her clarification that she was "not a sponsor," also told the clients that she did not have a drug problem or use twelve-step meetings herself.

While many clients attended twelve-step meetings, a substantial number, especially those taking methadone, expressed reservations about attending meetings:

LORETTA (Southside clinic, black female, age forty-three): Oh, I hate those NA meetings! I won't go to those anymore.

DREW (black male, age twenty-five): Yeah, I can't stand them . . . like there was this one guy who was always speaking and leading meetings and all that. And then I see him copping on the street. I see him buy a big bag of dope! And then he gets up there in that meeting and is talking about not using and . . . that just really got me mad. And, you know, I didn't say anything. But one time, he was talking and then he saw me sitting there. And he was then like, "Oh, shit, is this guy gonna say something?" But I don't say anything. I figure, God knows you're full of shit. You know you're full of shit. I don't have to tell all these people.

LORETTA: Yeah, I couldn't stand those NA meetings anymore. Everyone's getting high outside of the meetings. Or all the guys will be checking out the ladies. I mean, it's all about getting high and having sex.

MATT (white male, probably late twenties): And don't dare tell them you're on methadone!

LORETTA: Oh, yeah.

One of the reasons group members gave for not wanting to attend twelve-step meetings was that they perceived many of the people in the meeting to be inauthentic in some way, most often because they continued to use drugs despite declaring their abstinence to others in the meeting. Most criticisms of twelve-step meetings by those in Southside, however, had to do with the hostility they reported feeling from others at the meetings:

> JOE (Southside group, white male, age twenty-three): I don't like some meetings, like people look at you 'cause you're on methadone. My brother says something, so people know he's on methadone and at this one meeting, they just started barreling him!
> WENDY (therapist): Does he say that he's on lifesaving medication?
> JOE: No, but then they just get all on people about that.
> KARL (black male, age thirty-five): It sounds like there's nothing good going on at *that* meeting!
> WENDY: Right. I mean, what would they say to someone on insulin? That you shouldn't be taking insulin?
> CATHY (white female, mid-thirties): Some of them are really against any medications whatsoever. Like I'm on antidepressants and there are people who would look down on that. So I don't tell them.

Here, the group members discussed how judgmental they perceived many people at NA and AA meetings. This exchange also illustrated a paradox about twelve-step meetings in general: they advocate for the acceptance that addiction is a "disease," yet members are often resistant toward any medications that could help with treating the disease. Some Westview group members who were not taking methadone also perceived methadone to be substituting one drug for another, that the methadone recipients were not really "clean." As Joe commented, "I go to NA meetings and I'll say I'm in a methadone program just to weed the people out. Like most people will give me looks and stay away from me, but there will be one or two who'll come up and say 'Yeah, I know what you're going through.'" During several group sessions, Joe mentioned the hostility he received at twelve-step meetings. However, his persistence in attending them revealed that he still valued the twelve-step philosophy. His strategy allowed him to meet others who were taking methadone but were hesitant to let those at the meeting know.

Accepting the spiritual component of AA/NA was also discussed as an impediment to attending twelve-step meetings or agreeing with the philosophy.

> JERRY: What do you think about the saying that addiction is a three-prong disease? There's the physical disease, the mental part, and the spiritual component. What do you think about that?
> PHIL (Southside client, white, mid-twenties): I don't think it's spiritual at all. I mean, to me it's all mental.

While AA texts try to distinguish religion from "spirituality" (a more ambiguous concept), O'Halloran (2008) found that the "Big Book" of AA still used the word "God" 269 times and "higher power" only eighteen. The Westview and Southside clients I encountered who were strong advocates of twelve-step meetings also frequently made references to Jesus and God. They also confronted those in group who were resistant to such ideas, and promoted the use of prayer.

The Westview program held NA meetings every week. At some point around the time I began my observations, they also started holding "Methadone Anonymous" meetings once a week. Methadone Anonymous began in 1991 by Gary Sweeney, an Education Coordinator at a methadone maintenance program in Baltimore. It is modeled after the twelve-step program of AA, but tailored for opiate addicts who also are using a physician-prescribed medication like methadone as part of treatment. Their initial formation was in direct response to the hostility that many reported receiving from other attendees at NA meetings. However, the organization's Web site also explains that medication issues should not be discussed at meetings: "There is no need at meetings for patients to discuss their medications, including methadone or other prescribed drugs" (www .methadone-anonymous.org). Rather, the primary goal of the meeting is to discuss the twelve steps and how to achieve abstinence from alcohol and drugs, just as AA or NA meetings. Southside clients expressed enthusiasm when they were told that these meetings existed in the facility; however, no members ever mentioned their experience attending these meetings in any of the groups I observed.[16]

The use of twelve-step ideology in the programs contributed to the general ambiguity that surrounded the disease concept of addiction. The main purpose of using twelve-step methods was to communicate to the clients at both Southside and Westview that their problem was a lifelong one that would require consistent monitoring. It also seemed to be advocated as a resource for meeting other people from their neighborhoods who might offer support, support that the therapists at Southside and Westview could not. Because AA/NA promotes the notion that addiction is a "disease," incorporating these methods into the treatment programs did not contradict other messages about addiction that the therapists were trying to convey. At the same time, however, promoting twelve-step philosophy did not help the client understand what addiction was. In the end, rather than clearly articulating how addiction should be considered a disease and what the appropriate treatment for it was, the two overarching concepts of abstinence and individual responsibility prevailed as the central concerns communicated to clients.

Monitoring the Medication

Group sessions also tended to focus on individual-level problems that clients were having, from finding a job to trying to regain custody of their children. In the Southside clinic, many of the group members and much of the group's time focused on the medication of methadone itself and whether the person was receiving the correct dose to prevent withdrawal symptoms. This was likely due to the Southside clients in the pre-IOP group being new to the treatment program and often new to taking methadone. What was not typically discussed, however, was the science behind methadone and the psychopharmacology of the substance. The chief complaint among clients was that they were not on a large enough dosage, and mentioned still craving and using heroin to avoid withdrawal symptoms like nausea:

> MIKE (Southside clinic, white male, early thirties): Well, if I had enough, then it would last and I wouldn't get sick at night.
> WENDY (therapist): You're getting sick at night?
> MIKE: Yeah, like around midnight. I get the sweats, I start shaking. Get sick, shitting. So last night, I went out at 2:30 and copped.
> WENDY: So you're high right now?
> MIKE [says defensively]: No. I mean I used, but I'm not high.

Wendy often told clients who complained about their dosage to make an appointment to see the medical director (a psychiatrist). Other group members sometimes shared their knowledge and personal experience with achieving the correct dose of methadone. For instance, in this observation, one of the other group members offered insights into Mike's situation:

> JACKIE (Southside group, white female, mid-thirties): Maybe he needs a split dose.
> MIKE: They keep raising it by ten milligrams, but it doesn't seem to do anything.
> WENDY: You should talk to the doctor. We're only allowed to raise it ten milligrams, but the doctor can see you and raise it more in just one time.[17]
> JACKIE: Maybe it's not working because of his metabolism.
> WENDY: Well, that happens sometimes, but . . . [says as if trying not to offend Mike] . . . usually the person is really thin.

Jackie, another group member, offered her knowledge of methadone and "split doses," where a client takes half of his or her dose every twelve hours. She also relayed her knowledge about the effects that one's metabolism has on the processing of methadone. Rarely did I observe any of the therapists in the Southside Clinic discussing such details about methadone with the clients in the group meetings. The "educational" component of the group never focused specifically on methadone on any day that I observed. Therapists occasionally offered advice to group members about methadone issues, but most often just referred them to the doctor at the clinic, sometimes citing their own ignorance about methadone's effects to the clients.

Clients in the groups seemed to have a general understanding of how methadone worked, and were acutely aware of how much they were taking, but did not often seem to know about the side effects of methadone, such as feeling nauseous when taking it. This lack of knowledge about methadone's effects often led to the more-experienced group members educating the lesser-experienced ones about how to negotiate medication issues within the program:

> [*Southside group, several weeks after the previous group meeting where Mike complained about not having a high enough dosage.*]
> KARL [*to Mike*]: How you doin'?
> MIKE: I'm OK. It's still not holding me, though. I'm still getting sick in the morning.
> KARL: Really? Did you talk to the doctor?
> MIKE: Yeah, but I need to get more. They only increased me ten milligrams. That's not enough.
> KARL: You just gotta keep going and making a big deal about it.
> MIKE: Yeah, I'm going to try to make another appointment.

Clients often relied on one another for information about the effects of methadone and how to achieve the "correct" dose. Karl's advice about "making a big deal about it" suggested that clients had to pester the therapists and medical doctor in order to have their medication adjusted. The minimization of specific discussions about methadone during group sessions also reflected the general ambivalence toward methadone expressed by all of the therapists. It also implied that it was separate from the "treatment" that occurred during group, resulting in clients having to figure out medication issues on their own.

Social Distance and Mutual Distrust

The overlap of moral and medical frameworks for labeling and treating drug addiction, along with the social distance between the treatment staff and the clients, created immense distrust in the programs. The staff members that I encountered in both programs were very different from the clients in terms of race and class. All of the counseling staff that I observed and interviewed were middle-class whites, who lived in predominantly white, middle-class neighborhoods. All of them had college degrees; all but one additionally had a master's degree. These demographic differences led to a social distance between the clients and the staff. This social distance resulted in the therapists and the clients poorly communicating with each other and led each to suspect the other of not being completely honest. While the therapists often minimized the effect that social distance had, to some clients it was an impediment to their treatment. Wendy, a Southside/Westview therapist, explained:

At first they give me that attitude like, "You don't know what I'm talking about, you don't know what I'm going through," and then we get past that because, really, what does that have to do with your addiction? And sooner or later, if I keep redirecting them, they get over it. But one woman I did have a lot of trouble with because she kept going, "Do you have any kids? You ever smoke crack?" I'm like, "No." "You can't relate to me, I'm not talking to you." And it got to the point where we weren't making any progress. She would sit in my office for an hour and not say a word . . . I'm like, "Well, you're required to be here for an hour a week and you will sit here for an hour." She'd say, "That is fucked up, I'm not sitting here." I'm like, "Well, then you're in violation." And, we did eventually change her therapist because there is no sense in pulling teeth. That's not constructive. So we eventually transferred her, but other than that, most of them, they get over it quickly.

Wendy indicated that some clients felt that she—a young, middle-class, white, single woman—was unable to understand their problems. Indeed, some studies suggest that "matching" clients with therapists by race, gender, age, or substance-abuse history could have positive outcomes for clients (Conner et al. 2010; Horwitz 1982; Hser et al. 1997). One such positive outcome is that clients perceive counselors who are more similar demographically to them to be more empathetic, and are they able to trust them more (Fiorentine and Hillhouse 1999). In the previous instance, Wendy described an encounter with a client referred from the criminal justice system, indicated by her comment that not attending the individual therapy session would put her "in violation." Wendy minimized this client's claim that she could not relate to Wendy, perhaps because she viewed herself as having the necessary professional credentials to treat this woman. The client, however, wanted to meet with someone who had more awareness of her background and situation. This social distance may have contributed to the negative aspects therapists reported about their job. It also resulted in a general distrust that occurred between the therapists and the clients.

Several of the rules in the Southside and Westview programs implied that at some level the treatment staff did not fully trust the clients. For instance, clients were not allowed to wait inside the clinic before being medicated or after group therapy; there were signs placed throughout the facility reminding the clients that the clinic was not somewhere for them to "hang out." In addition, there were video cameras in the areas where clients gave urine drug tests, as a reminder that they would be caught if they falsified a test. Therapists also frequently reminded clients about the various program "rules." Clients who perceive a program as too authoritarian and strict have been found to leave treatment early (Stahler, Cohen, et al. 1993). While the clients often complained about the program being too strict, therapists saw the rules as completely necessary to maintain order and offer them security in performing their job.

Therapists admitted to me that they did not fully trust their clients. They defined the distrust in terms of manipulation; they perceived their clients as not telling the truth or as trying to put something over on them. Wendy commented in an interview: "[The criminal justice clients] manipulate a lot, but it's a lot different manipulation than the methadone clinic clients. These guys are a lot more clever. They have a lot more stories, a lot more excuses." Other studies have found that drug treatment therapists do not always fully trust their clients, especially those referred from the criminal justice system (Paik 2006b). Being an addict referred from the criminal justice system creates a double stigma for the client, resulting in even greater distrust. Wendy worked with both the Southside and Westview clients, and she found both groups manipulating. What was surprising, however, was that the other therapists appeared to find the methadone (Southside) clients the most untrustworthy and difficult to deal with, despite there being far more court-mandated clients in Westview's program. Therapists often labeled the Southside clients "whiny" or "childlike":

TOM [*talking about working with Southside versus Westview clients*]: There are differences. But of course that's my own biases coming out . . . I definitely see the heroin addicts as more needy, more whiny, less functional. They're in constant need of something or complaining about something that I think the other clients just are able to do and take care of.

WENDY: Those clients [in Southside] are just exhausting. It's every day, they're very needy. There's very little progress that gets made. It's exhausting.

Interestingly, both Tom and Wendy had worked as full-time Southside therapists before moving into positions in Westview's program (Wendy still led the pre-IOP group at Southside). By the end of my study, Tom had moved from his position as a therapist to becoming the intake coordinator for Westview, a position where he would not have to have sustained contact with any particular client for a long period of time.

Treatment providers also occasionally suggested that the clients were irresponsible or untrustworthy during group meetings:

WENDY (*Southside counselor telling a group member to see the physician about his methadone dose*): I can make you an appointment, but you have to convince me you're going to go. Can you do that? 'Cause I'm not going to make the appointment with the doctor for you if you're just not going to show up.

MIKE: What's that?! Why wouldn't I?! Yeah, forget it. [*He says sarcastically*] Right, I won't show up.

JACKIE [*to Wendy*]: Why are you saying that? He just said he'd go and you're giving him a hard time.

MIKE: They're always giving you a hard time here. You're always doing something wrong.

It is not clear if Wendy confronted Mike during group because he had missed appointments in the past; she does not cite any specific violations he has made other than showing up to group late. Interacting this way, however, suggests that she views him as irresponsible and communicates that feeling to the rest of the group. Therapists also communicated a level of distrust to the clients:

JERRY: Josh, if you could hack into the computer system and see when you were going to be tested, would you use when you knew you wouldn't get caught?

JOSH: No.

In this exchange, Jerry implied that Josh would continue to use drugs if he knew that he would not get caught by the program's random drug testing. Such a question revealed that the client's own therapist suspected him of lacking moral principles. A similar interaction occurred between Wendy and another Southside client, Karl:

WENDY [*discussing strategies for handling the desire to use drugs*]: Do you ever call someone if you feel like using? Who do you call, Karl?

KARL: I call ... what's their name?

WENDY: Your drug dealer?

KARL: No! Oh, man.

In a private conversation, Wendy mentioned to me that Karl consistently tested positive for opiates and cocaine. Her frustration with his inability to abstain appeared to come out during this group meeting. Ironically, in a previous meeting, Wendy informed new clients to the group that they were not allowed to confront one another about their drug use.

Distrust was a two-way street in these programs; clients also openly expressed distrust toward the program and staff. For instance, in a Southside group meeting, the clients discussed their lack of confidence that the facility was giving them the correct methadone dose:

JACKIE (white female, early thirties): Well, you know what could be going on? I notice sometimes [the methadone] just tastes like water. Sometimes it tastes normal, but sometimes it tastes like water and then I'm feeling sick by the end of the day. It's not like it would be that hard to dump out half the bottle and fill it with water. I heard there was a nurse who was doing that and they got fired. And then like a week later they got hired back again.

WENDY (therapist): That wouldn't happen. I can say that that's definitely not true.

KARL (black male, age thirty-five): I can agree with what she's sayin'. 'Cause I notice the same thing sometimes. And they have the cups piled up and you can't even see what they're pouring out.

JACKIE: Yeah, and sometimes they already have the cup there, even before you get up to the window.

KARL: Yeah!

WENDY: All of the medicine comes out of the same machine.

JACKIE: But, you know it wouldn't be that hard to take some. I think you should put up one of those cameras in there to watch them. You have them in the bathrooms watching us, so why not watch them?

WENDY: OK. I'll bring it up at the next staff meeting. I can tell them what you're telling me, but I don't know what they'll do.

JACKIE: They won't do anything.

Wendy commented to me after this group about how ridiculous the clients' claim was and I doubt that she brought the concern up to any administrator. While it was a rather far-fetched concern, it demonstrated the level of distrust that the clients had of the facility and staff in general. Their expression that the nurses also should be under surveillance could be an attempt to defray some of the judgment they felt from the facility. At the same time, Jackie's conclusion that "they won't do anything" showed how little confidence clients had that the facility would actually address their concerns.

The clients' distrust also was manifested by questioning the therapists about information they were given:

STEVEN (Southside clinic, black male, late thirties): I need an increase [in methadone dosage]. But they said you didn't put it in for me, Jerry.

JERRY: The way it works is, I put the increase request in your chart, then the doctor looks at it. He signs off on it and then it gets put into the system. So if it's not there, maybe the doctor hasn't looked at it yet. You were with me when I wrote it up. I put it in the chart. So, I'll have to see if the doctor got it.

In this situation, Steven was concerned that Jerry did not put in a request for an increase in methadone, despite witnessing Jerry fill out the form during their individual session. Again, this suggested a rather intense level of distrust between the client and his therapist. Similarly, Jerry referred to the mutual distrust between clients and therapists: "And in this program, I see that 'us versus them' mentality, therapists versus patients." These comments suggest that this level of distrust was a barrier to treatment. In the previous interview, Jerry lamented this distance and distrust. At the same time, none of the therapists, including Jerry, saw themselves as part of the problem in any way.

Much of the client's distrust seemed to be attached to a general distrust of public institutions, like the criminal justice system or the Department of Human Services. Other research shows that marginalized groups tend to feel dehumanized from agencies that are supposed to help them access needed resources (Dohan 2003; Hoffman and Coffey 2008; Sterk, Elifson, and Theall 2000). Research also shows that black people in particular have a higher level of distrust of institutions like the police, the legal system, and the medical profession than whites (Kennedy, Mathis, and Woods 2007; Marschall and Shah 2007). In Westview, many of the clients who had been arrested for drug-related offenses expressed resentment toward the police and the criminal justice system. One member claimed that he was framed by a police officer, while two group members recounted stories that the police tried to set up a situation to make it seem like they were snitching on their dealers when they were arrested for drug possession. Others talked about corruption in the prison system:

STEVEN: I've seen them, guys I know, go in and get tested. And if they had methadone in their system, they'd get sent right back. Right back to [prison]! That's because it's all about the money.
GEORGE: That's right. It's a big moneymaker up there. They just want to get you back in. That's all they care about, is the money.

These clients felt that the main motive behind incarceration was profit making. Wendy also mentioned this distrust from the court-mandated clients during our interview: "They're oppositional about anybody who is authority. So, if they think that I am working for the [drug court], then they don't want to tell me anything." In addition to the criminal justice system, clients often expressed distrust of the Department of Human Services (DHS), which had removed their children from their custody. Amanda, a new group member, spoke about getting out of prison and wanting to get back custody of her seven-year-old son, who was living with Amanda's older daughter. Her daughter would not give up custody:

AMANDA: I just want to go get him.
KAREN: No, don't do that! That's kidnapping. You'll go right back to jail.
AMANDA: Yeah, maybe I should go to DHS.
KAREN [*expressing excited concern*]: No! You don't want to go there! DHS . . . They'll take him away from you *and* her.
RUBY: And then they'll take the grandson while they're at it!

Considering their level of distrust of government institutions, it was not very surprising that these clients also were distrustful of the treatment program. However, it was unfortunate that they drew such comparisons between the police and the counseling staff.

This distrust, then, was likely not merely from participating in these treatment programs, but rather an extension of clients' distrust with public institutions in general. At the same time, certain program policies, like having cameras in the bathrooms, reinforced that distrust. Similarly, the therapists' distrust was related to the stigma associated with drug addiction and their stereotyping of those living in poor, largely black, neighborhoods. Therapists admitted that they often did not fully "understand" clients because of their different class backgrounds; one therapist compared running her group to teaching in an inner-city high school.

This distrust was detrimental to the quality of treatment because it placed a wall between the therapists and the clients. Both made moral judgments about the other, although the therapists' moral judgments had deeper consequences because they were authority figures. They had the power to alter the client's medication, impose sanctions, and determine progress. Wendy described this moral judgment that the treatment programs would make: "We don't teach them about addiction. We say, 'good,' 'bad,' 'no,' 'yes,' and we treat them like they're in kindergarten instead of educating them about the consequences of it and the damage that it does." While Wendy placed some of the criticism on herself for these moral judgments, she also admitted to lacking a true understanding of what her clients were going through. The constant reference to the client's "lifestyle" as a problem in itself also was a moral judgment that the client was not living up to some objective standard.

Conclusion

Drug treatment has been shown to have powerful individual and social benefits, including improved health and reduced crime. However, decades of drug treatment in its variety of forms actually has not reduced the number of individuals with significant drug problems in our country (Reuter and Pollack 2006). In addition, the majority of those who enter drug treatment do not successfully complete treatment (SAMHSA 2010a). While some individuals may leave treatment when they feel they've met their own goals (Stahler, Shipley, et al. 1993), most view the high dropout rate as an indicator that one treatment episode may not yield very positive results and that most addicts require multiple treatment attempts (Hser et al. 1997; McLellan et al. 2000). While it is important to continue studying how the frequency of treatment episodes and the length of time in treatment can positively impact results, this chapter suggests that we also need to better examine the quality of treatment programs and the barriers that exist to effective treatment. One barrier appears to be institutional ambiguity about the nature of addiction, as can be seen in the organization of the programs at Westview and Southside. While the two programs differed in their primary treatment methods (intensive outpatient versus methadone maintenance), they used similar therapeutic techniques and relied heavily on a twelve-step approach for treating addiction. In the more "medicalized" program (Southside), there was no clear evidence that their approach to treatment was actually based on a more medicalized notion of addiction. On the contrary, treatment staff viewed the Southside clients as *more* untrustworthy, stigmatizing them further. The view that methadone was a "last resort" type of treatment also communicated uneasiness with a medical perspective of addiction.

Despite the different methods used, the staff in each program had very similar conceptualizations of addiction. Both programs used the "disease" concept for similar purposes: as a way to minimize the differences between individual clients (such as drug seller versus drug user) and in an attempt to convince the clients that they needed the programs to "heal" them. The differences in race and class between the staff and the clients also appeared to be related to how the staff defined addiction since they often named social and environmental factors as causes. These differences led to social distance and mutual distrust between clients and therapists, intensifying the stigma those in drug treatment already faced, and acted as an additional barrier to effective treatment. As this and the previous chapter show, in both the drug court and treatment settings, the labeling of addiction overlapped medical and moral frameworks. In Chapter 5, I discuss the consequences of this ambiguity in the labeling of addiction as both a disease and a moral disorder and how it resulted in the use of both therapeutic and punitive methods for managing those labeled addicts.

5

Managing Illness and Deviance

Therapeutic Punishment

I also have different leverage, like here [in Westview] you have the court
system as leverage; [in the Southside clinic], you just have their
methadone as leverage.

—WENDY, Southside/Westview therapist

Chapters 3 and 4 illustrate the ambiguous labeling of "addiction" in both a
drug court and two outpatient drug treatment programs. In both settings,
drug addiction was characterized as a disease, although individual staff
members had difficulty articulating the exact components of the disease and the
most appropriate treatment modality. While they also recognized addiction as
a social problem stemming from poverty, inadequate socialization, and jobless-
ness, both institutions promoted an increase in individual responsibility as the
best way to deal with it. The "addict" label also was reconstructed in both the
drug court and in the treatment programs to include a broad set of behaviors
associated with the "lifestyle" of using and selling drugs. This chapter elaborates
further on the ambiguities within these settings and discusses the consequences of those ambiguities. In particular, I illustrate how this ambiguity resulted in
the use of what I term "therapeutic punishment," a technique used in all of the
settings that resulted from the hybrid notion of addiction as both a disease that
needed to be treated and a symbol of irresponsibility and criminality. Therapeutic punishment, as I use the concept, relates to the punishment of clients in a
way that is characterized as an extension of the clinical "treatment" offered
in each setting. Thus, those working in these programs perceived what the
clients often viewed as punitive methods to be therapeutic in their execution
and goal.

Labeling Disease and the Diseased

While both the court and the treatment programs used the "disease" concept of
addiction to frame their organizational philosophy and practices, the concept

was ambiguous. It also suggested that there was either conflict around the use of the disease concept or at least a lack of agreement on exactly how addiction should be characterized as a disease.

What Is "Clinical" Progress?

The court proceedings and the examination of the roles of individual court staff members illustrated the complex overlap of the "medical" and the "legal" realms in the drug treatment court program. Rather than the clinical side of the program being distinct from the legal proceedings and monitoring (since it operated in a separate location), there was instead an ambiguity of who the authority was for both clinical and legal interventions.

This ambiguity of how the disease of addiction was articulated was found in the judge's differentiation between the "clinical" part of a client's monthly report and the rest of it. While he made a point of emphasizing whether or not the client was doing "clinically" well, at the same time, it never was clearly articulated what was clinical and what was not. One case involved a young black male client, who appeared to be in his late twenties. During his monthly appearance, the court staff reported that he was recently arrested at a concert:

> JUDGE GALLO: You're a mixed bag. Clinically, you're doing well. You
>   have all negative urines, you attend your sessions, go to NA [Narcot-
>   ics Anonymous] meetings. The downside is you were arrested
>   again. . . . You did an essay for today. What did you learn?
> CLIENT: I learned that addiction is a disease and recovery is the cure. As
>   long as I stick with my recovery, I'll be fine.
> ASSISTANT PUBLIC DEFENDER: Your Honor, the client completed phase
>   1 as of July 15th.
> JUDGE: Congratulations. [*Applause from the courtroom.*]

During this interaction, the client admitted that he was at a concert with his friends who were smoking marijuana. Still, the judge emphasized that "clinically" he was doing well (despite not avoiding the "people, places, and things" that could trigger a relapse). Additionally, the judge did not give him another sanction (he was already sentenced to community service through community court) and instead rewarded him for completing phase 1 (thirty days abstinent). This case presented a rather confusing message to this client and the others in the courtroom. While the client tested negative for drug use, he was still engaging in behaviors that in other situations the court viewed as a "disease" (selling drugs). The following was a similar case where a client was arrested in the previous month for drug possession:

> JUDGE GALLO: Let's start with the good stuff. You're going to sessions,
>   you have clean urines. But now you picked up a new arrest. . . .

Clinically, you're doing well. . . . Are you still working with your
grandfather?

CLIENT: Yes.

Again, the judge determined the client to be doing "clinically" well, even though
he was arrested for possession of drugs. From these two instances, doing well
"clinically" seemed to mean that the client attended treatment sessions and had
negative urine drug screens. At the same time, engaging in further illegal behavior involving drugs did not seem to impact the judge's perception of how the
client was progressing clinically through the program.

On the flip side, a client who was *not* doing well "clinically" meant that he
or she had missed treatment sessions and/or was continuing to use drugs. For
example:

THERAPIST: He has positive urines. He missed one session and made it up.

JUDGE GALLO: You relapsed. . . . This is a mixed report because you continue to use.

CLIENT: I just started the program. It's hard for me.

JUDGE: You'll have to write a two-hundred-word essay on relapse.

The judge referred to it being a "mixed report" because the client was not meeting expectations clinically, yet was doing well in other areas of the program.
Implied in this example was that the client would not have a mixed report if he
stopped using drugs. From other interactions, it became clear that missing
meetings with the client's case manager was not part of the "clinical" monitoring:

JUDGE GALLO: Clinically, this is an excellent report. The only negative
thing is that you haven't been staying in touch with your case
manager.

CLIENT: My grandfather passed. I've been goin' down South a lot.

JUDGE: Like I said, clinically, you're doing excellent. You're working.
Doing everything right. But you need to stay in touch with your case
manager.

That the judge mentioned working as one of the reasons the client was doing
"clinically" well added to the ambiguity of what the judge exactly meant by
clinical or nonclinical parts of the drug court program.

Also, as the client progressed in the program, the drug treatment part of the
report became less important, as if at some point the client moved beyond the
"clinical" portion of the program. Once clients had completed the specific drug
treatment program that they had been assigned to, they only had to meet with
the therapist at the facility about once a week. When clients were this far along
in the program, the judge focused almost completely on "nonclinical" issues
during their monthly court appearances. Issues of education and employment

became the major determinants of whether or not a client was "doing well." In one case, the client had recently finished the drug treatment portion of the program:

> THERAPIST: The client successfully completed IOP [intensive outpatient program]. Urines are all negative.
> JUDGE GALLO [to client]: Take your hands out of your pocket. This is a good report. Make sure you stay in touch with your case manager. Now you're in outpatient. . . . Why haven't you started GED [general educational development] classes?
> CASE MANAGER: We'll follow up on that.
> JUDGE: OK.

The judge recognized that the client was progressing through the program by finishing the treatment program and stepping down to individual sessions with a therapist. He also took the opportunity to remind the client that he was now expected to complete a GED to keep progressing in the program. At times, the judge also emphasized the importance of working once a client finished drug treatment:

> THERAPIST: Client attended all sessions and all urines were negative.
> JUDGE GALLO: This is a very good report. How you doing? Now the only thing you need is to get some work.

Most of the time, the judge did not specify whether the client needed to complete an education program or whether he or she needed to get a job; either one seemed to provide enough evidence that the client was acting responsibly and therefore progressing through the court program. At the same time, the transfer of focus from drug treatment issues (most often referred to as "clinical" by the judge) to issues of working and education added to the ambiguity of exactly what the court was "treating." While these social issues (like undereducation and unemployment) might be viewed as related to the causes of addiction (both to using drugs and the "lifestyle" of drug selling), they were not explicitly linked to the client's drug problem during the court sessions.

If a client did not pursue further education or employment, and was physically capable of doing so, he or she was reprimanded for halting progress in the program. It was never clearly articulated exactly at what point the client had to be enrolled in an education program or working, but it was implied that if clients were not pursuing either of those things, they risked negative repercussions. Still, I never witnessed a client getting sanctioned for not yet working or pursuing further education. For instance, the judge interacted with a client who had just completed the first two phases of the program:

> JUDGE: How come you haven't started GED classes?
> CLIENT: I'm going to as soon as possible.

JUDGE: What's holding you back?
CLIENT: I slacked off.
JUDGE: You don't want to slack off. Go get your GED or go get a job.
Congratulations on completing phases 1 and 2 [*applause*].

This movement in the program's focus from treatment to education and employment occurred once the client finished the drug treatment portion of the program. The evaluator, Patrick, explained one possible reason why this shift
occurred: "If they're in [outpatient treatment] and are unemployed, I mean, they
absolutely need to be enrolled in a GED program or community college or
something; you know, instead of just idle time, which we've found over and over
again in this program to really be a killer." As in the Southside and Westview
programs, court staff had a perception that the client's life was not structured
enough, and that the lack of structure would lead to problems. The reasoning
was that the client might revert back to drug use or other criminal behavior if
work or school did not fill the time that had been occupied by treatment. In this
sense, then, any activity was beneficial to the client; the problem was having a
lack of "responsible" things to do during the day.

This ambiguity over what exactly was "clinical" in the drug treatment program also related to the construction of a drug-selling lifestyle as itself an illness
that needed to be treated. Since drug use was not necessarily the chief problem
for these clients, the court insisted on the completion of requirements that were
extraneous to drug treatment, like getting a job or further education. The drug
court program was designed to take a year to complete, although most took
longer to get through the various phases. The frequent drug treatment sessions,
however, usually ended long before the client completed the court program.
Thus, the client often spent just as much time being monitored by the court
while they were supposed to be completing GED classes or getting a job, as they
had been while attending drug treatment sessions.

The Persistence of Stigma

Erving Goffman (1963) defined stigma as "an attribute that is deeply discredit-
ing" in that it prevents an individual from being fully accepted by the rest of
society (3). He elaborated on three different types of stigma. The one that best
relates to those labeled as drug addicts and criminals is the stigma that results
from being perceived as "weak-willed." All of the individuals in the drug court
and the treatment programs fit into this category. Even those in treatment who
were not court mandated (those who were self-referrals) were in some ways
treated as "criminals" since they had been engaging in an illegal behavior (drug
use). This was most evident when the staff had difficulty conceptualizing addiction as a disease and their tendency to ascribe some blame to the individual for
"choosing" to use drugs in the first place. Both the drug court and the outpatient

drug treatment programs used the disease concept of addiction in an attempt to shed the stigma associated with substance abuse. However, neither was successful, and instead promoted further stigma.

Drug abuse still carries a stigma despite its medicalization. If anything, the Southside clients who received the most "medicalized" treatment—methadone maintenance—were *more* stigmatized for their drug problem, based on the interactions they had with individuals at twelve-step meetings and even others in the same treatment facility (at the Westview program). The organization of dispensing methadone promoted this stigma and the clients recognized it. For instance, clients had to wait outside the clinic for their daily dose of methadone, as Joe explained: "I mean, the stigma of methadone, like standing out on the corner waiting for the clinic to let you in to get medicated. Where's the anonymity in that? When I was working at the store, my manager drove by and saw me standing outside of a methadone clinic. So now he knows about my problem!" Here, a methadone maintenance client recognized that there was a stigma associated with methadone treatment. He expressed concern about his employer knowing that he was taking methadone, suggesting that he might be treated negatively (or at least differently) because of it. The facility could have adopted strategies to help alleviate that stigma by creating a waiting area inside or by staggering medication times for a longer period throughout the day; however, no staff member I interviewed acknowledged problems with this system or linked it to stigma.

The organization of the drug court also promoted further stigma. It appeared that by conceptualizing addiction (including selling drugs) as a disease that could be treated, they were attempting to offer a more therapeutic method of dealing with these offenders instead of putting them through the typical criminal court proceedings. However, by attaching the "disease" label, since it is a "disease" that itself still carries a heavy stigma, they were in effect doubling the stigma that these clients already had as criminals. Thus, they were stigmatized twice: first, in the courtroom, where they were labeled criminals because they had to plead guilty to the charges against them in order to enter the court program; and second, in the drug treatment program, where they were labeled as diseased because they either were addicted to using drugs or addicted to the lifestyle of selling drugs. Both stigmas create discredited identities that the individual has to carry indefinitely.

Therapeutic Punishment

I use the concept "therapeutic punishment" to describe the response by the staff in both the drug court program and in the Southside and Westview treatment programs when the client did not follow a set rule. This technique resulted because of the belief that addiction is a "treatable" disease, but at the same time carried with it an unusual level of responsibility compared to other named diseases. In both settings, staff members described how this practice was necessary if the client was going to succeed.[1]

While I did not coin the phrase therapeutic punishment, I am using it in a different capacity than how other researchers have. "Therapeutic punishment" has been used to refer to a behavior-modification technique for individuals with severe mental deficiencies, such as autism or retardation (Rolider, Cummings, and Van Houten 1991; Simmons and Reed 1969). In this method, pain and punishment are used as treatment modalities in an attempt to change undesired behavior that is usually violent and/or self-destructive in nature. It is a punishment of the body in that it involves the restricting of movement, contingent exercise, and in earlier forms, the administration of electric shocks. While it is a controversial method, many researchers conclude that it can be effective. My use of the concept "therapeutic punishment" refers to a broader set of practices that both the drug court and the outpatient treatment programs used in an effort to extinguish the undesirable behaviors of the clients, usually after they had violated an established rule. The punishment in these settings was most often of the mind, although in the Southside program (the methadone maintenance program), therapeutic punishment techniques often revolved around the prescription of medication, and therefore were punitive to the body as well.

While nobody working in either program referred to their techniques as therapeutic punishment (or any form of punishment), I use the term because it conveys what the staff appeared to believe was the benefit of such a practice. That is, they often viewed the drug-using population as irresponsible and unmotivated for treatment ("in denial"). These techniques, then, became a way to punish what the staff viewed as irresponsibility, while at the same time preserved their role as therapists and treatment providers by rationalizing that the punishment was just another form of therapy. The best metaphor used in both settings that summarizes the main components of therapeutic punishment was "the carrot and the stick," which referred to the rewards and punishment system that existed because of the various rules in each setting.

Therapeutic Punishment in Drug Court

In Chapter 3, I describe the types of sanctions that the treatment court used. A number of sanctions that were given in the program seemed purely punitive—such as short-term jail sentences, writing an essay, or spending a day watching the court proceedings from the jury box. However, it was not always clear whether they were assigned for punitive or clinical reasons. Ordering a client to write an essay, usually of about two hundred words, was most often used as a sanction for relapse. The judge almost always emphasized that the topic of the essay would be relapse itself. Thus, since relapse was considered a likely "symptom" of addiction, this sanction had clinical overtones to it. There was a suggestion that writing this essay could be therapeutic for the clients and perhaps help them think more deeply about their drug problem. The court took such a sanction seriously; the judge asked the client for the essay during the next session and read it to himself while the client stood in front of his bench. He then usually commented on the content of the essay, most often a short approval, such as "good essay," and occasionally asked the client a clarifying question about what they wrote. While the clients who had to write an essay did not overtly object to the harshness of the punishment in the same way they did for other sanctions, many of them lacked a high school diploma, so it was likely still an arduous task for them to complete. At the same time, the judge ordered a client to write an essay for violating other components of the program besides abstinence. For instance, I witnessed the essay being used as a sanction for missing treatment sessions, where the client had to write on the topic of "responsibility." Whether this sanction was punitive or clinical, then, was ambiguous and appeared to be used as both.

The most ambiguous sanction used for both clinical and punitive purposes was the ordering of a recovery house. A recovery house, also known as a "halfway house," is a structured living environment where clients live with other individuals who have problems with drugs or alcohol. There was often an initial "blackout" period, where the individual could not leave the house for any reason, including work. Throughout their time in the recovery house, a client's whereabouts were heavily monitored and controlled. Typically, a person resided in a recovery house for three months to a year. When the judge ordered a recovery house, it was usually after repeated problems, such as missed treatment sessions and positive urine tests. The following is one example:

ASSISTANT DISTRICT ATTORNEY: This case was discussed in the back. He missed three more sessions and continues to be positive for marijuana.

CLIENT: I missed because I moved. I called them and told them.

ASSISTANT PUBLIC DEFENDER, LIZ: He admits he was using again. Says urine should be negative as of now. He was told about this previously and that the court would order a recovery house.

JUDGE GALLO: He's going to a recovery house.

CLIENT: Can the court please give me another chance? I need to go to work.

JUDGE: There's no reason you can't work while you live in a recovery house.

ASSISTANT PUBLIC DEFENDER: Well, there will be a thirty-day blackout.

JUDGE: [holds up a mirror to the client and speaks angrily] Don't blame me, blame you! If you lose your job, it's not my problem.

CLIENT: Please just give me another week.

CASE MANAGER: A recovery house is recommended.

JUDGE: That's where you're going.

Even though he viewed working as a positive sign of "responsibility," the judge was not concerned with the possibility that the client would lose his job because of the initial blackout period. Abstinence and making scheduled appointments (including treatment sessions) were always constructed as the most important signs of responsibility. While this sanction was meant to be punitive, the judge seemed to think that the added structure also would give the client more assistance clinically.

At times, however, sanctioning a client to live in a recovery house was not a direct response to his or her continued drug use and seemed to be used as punishment for other violations. For instance:

> ASSISTANT PUBLIC DEFENDER: The client missed five treatment sessions. . . . [Judge Gallo] sentenced him to community service and he has not done any of it. He was even given tokens to get there.
>
> JUDGE MALLOY: Where are the tokens?
>
> CLIENT: I live in Southwest. I used one to do some of my business.
>
> JUDGE: So all of this prevented you from doing your community service?
>
> CLIENT: I live far away.
>
> ASSISTANT PUBLIC DEFENDER: You should put it on the calendar.
>
> JUDGE: I order another recovery house. I'm not pleased with the reasons you give. When you're in front of a court and the judge tells you to do something, it's not a request. You need to do it. . . . judges are a cranky bunch when they order something and it doesn't get done. I will order a recovery house and order you to spend five days in jail. If you made an effort and fell short, I would have taken it into consideration. But you didn't even make an effort.

In this example, Judge Malloy (substituting for Judge Gallo)[2] ordered a recovery house as punishment for not completing another sanction. There was never any mention of continued drug use in this case, suggesting that a recovery house also was used purely as punishment for other program violations. Similarly, Patrick, the evaluator, indicated that a recovery house could be ordered in response to the client not attending treatment sessions, and not necessarily because of drug use: "If it's really just bad attendance, not so much hot urines, but really just poor attendance, then a case manager will just put 'em in [a recovery house] because that's just a lack of structure." Apparently, a case manager also could place the client in a recovery house for missing sessions; in these instances, ordering a recovery house was not really used for "clinical" purposes since drug use was not the issue.

The assistant public defender, Liz, often suggested that a client go to a recovery house because she saw it as a necessary part of treatment rather than as a punishment. There was one case of a young male client who tested positive for drugs in the past month, but would not admit to using drugs. He also had missed appointments with his case manager, who reported that he had not given her an accurate address or phone number:

> ASSISTANT PUBLIC DEFENDER: Will the court reorder the recovery house?
> CLIENT: Why do I need that?
> JUDGE: Because the court ordered it.

The assistant public defender requested a recovery house because she thought it would help the client clinically. Interestingly, the judge did not explain why he agreed with ordering the client to move into a recovery house, suggesting that the client should follow his orders without question.

Those working in the drug court program emphasized the clinical necessity of sending somebody to a recovery house. Mario, the manager of specialty courts, emphasized that recovery houses were sometimes necessary for clients who had more serious drug problems. He talked about conditions that might make the evaluator recommend a recovery house at the start of the drug court program:

> We don't just refer clients to a recovery house because we want to send them to a recovery house. Recovery house is a serious . . . you know, it's a recovery house. People reside, have drug problems. And if a client doesn't have a stable home environment, then we'll recommend. . . . If the client is residing with a friend who is using, we'll also recommend. There's certain red flags that will click with case managers, to refer clients to a recovery house. We don't just refer clients because we don't like them.

Mario emphasized that the evaluators would recommend that clients move into a recovery house if they perceive their current living situation to be an impediment to succeeding in the program. He probably emphasized this because the clients most often had negative impressions of recovery houses. Patrick, the clinical evaluator for the drug court, also echoed that recovery houses were *not* a form of punishment, even if the client thought they were:

> A recovery house is not a sanction; it's a clinical intervention. Like, you can't stop using, so we're gonna put you in a more disciplined structure where you can. But the client sees it as a sanction . . . being told when to sit, when to eat . . . and a lot of times that's the turning point because, to some effect, it's worse than jail because you can be in a recovery house for two or three months.

Patrick emphasized that a recovery house was a clinical intervention, not a sanction, despite previously mentioning that a case manager could order a recovery house for missed sessions. That he also framed it as a possible "turning point" because it was "worse than jail," alluded to the punitive aspects of a recovery house rather than the clinical ones. The reality was that, in the court setting, it was used as both a clinical intervention *and* a sanction. If the evaluator recommended a recovery house at the initial evaluation, he described it solely as a clinical intervention. However, it also clearly had punitive elements that the court staff recognized but refused to label as such.

Recovery houses fit into the program's model that *all* sanctions were clinical tools to help the client. Those working in the drug court program emphasized the use of recovery houses and other sanctions as a "wake-up call" for the client. According to Patrick:

> Sometimes those sanctions or the recovery house or whatever is the necessary wake-up call. I know a lot of people in recovery and a lot of people got clean in jail, period. Being in jail was the bottom they needed to hit to realize that I don't want to live like this anymore. . . . Sometimes I advocate for the two-week-long jail sanction. Let him wake up! Let him see; let him really get a taste of this. 'Cause right now he thinks this is glamorous. And jail will certainly take the glamour out of the game for most guys. But, you know, just letting people rot in jail is another thing entirely.

Commonly found in the addict community, especially in twelve-step groups, is the idea that individuals have to "hit bottom" in order to begin recovering from their drug problem. A similar idea was present in the drug court, although the key difference was that the court actively sanctioned individuals. That is, clients did not "hit bottom" on their own; the court attempted to force them to the bottom. In the previous interview, the evaluator distinguished between jail as a short-term sanction and putting somebody in prison for a long time. He did not see much utility in the lengthy prison sentence that many of the drug court clients were facing. Still, his statement implied that those who did not take the sanctions as "wake-up calls" were deserving of the strict punishment they received if they were dismissed from the drug court program. Many of the court staff held this perspective and at times even communicated it directly to clients:

Assistant District Attorney: The client has positive urines, he was discharged from two recovery houses, he has missed sessions.

Judge: What do you have to say for yourself?

Client: [*Talks for a while about getting into a fight at one of the recovery houses.*]

Judge: You're going to spend five days in jail. This is too serious to give you a nonjail sentence. Don't think of it as punishment, think of it as a wake-up call. You have three cases with us. You can possibly go to prison for a long time. . . . We can't tolerate people who get thrown out of two recovery houses. If you relapse, we're not happy about it, but we can tolerate it.

The judge told the client that the short-term jail sentence was not a punishment, but instead was a wake-up call, a foreshadowing of what the future could look like. The client likely viewed it as a harsh punishment. The judge also communicated that the jail sentence was a result of getting evicted from multiple recovery houses, not for relapsing. These sanctions operated similarly to "scared straight" types of programs, although getting "straight" meant discontinued drug use as well as criminal activity.

Short-term jail sentences were often a sanction for major violations or repeated problems. Even though they seemed like purely punitive sanctions, the court staff viewed them as having clinical benefits. Burns and Peyrot (2003) found a similar sentiment among drug court judges they interviewed who discussed incarceration in positive terms, as an extension of recovery. In one case, a young male client had missed several treatment sessions. He claimed that he had to go to work, although he did not provide any proof of employment. There also was some discrepancy about sessions that he attended and signed in for, that the therapist claimed he missed. Judge Gallo commented: "All these things start to add up. . . . You tell us you're doing one thing, you do another. We now have the book. We're going to check the signatures. You're going to do a day at CHOICES because of all of this unnecessary work we had to put into this case." "CHOICES" (not its real name) was a drug treatment program in a Capital City prison designed for inmates who would soon be released from prison. In the previous drug court case, there was no clinical reason for the client to go to CHOICES; he did not test positive for drug use. The sanction was used as a punishment for missed sessions and general signs of irresponsibility. Still, he was ordered to go to this prison-based drug treatment program for a day. The court staff also referred to this program as a possible "wake-up call" for the clients because they spent time in a prison environment.

The court staff never expressed concern that this simultaneous use of sanctions as both clinical interventions and punishment might be problematic in that it sent a confusing message to clients about the nature of their "disease." The court staff referred to the use of sanctions as an effort to always "help" the client. In a sense, they also were constructing who were "worthy" clients who may actually benefit from the intervention (Mackinem and Higgins 2008). As an extension, the staff often saw their job as helping clients in various ways. Judge Gallo explained in a radio interview: "I cannot be effective if I don't communicate to [the clients], to let them know that this program is only here to help them." The judge emphasized that the drug court program was a form of "help." Certainly, the program's organization promoted this philosophy because clients had multiple people to link them with services (including drug treatment, job training programs, and so forth). Clients also stayed in the program even if they violated the rules, and had an opportunity to correct many of their mistakes. The staff may have emphasized their role as "helpers" to help shift any responsibility for progress onto the client. If their job is to help and the client violated a rule, then it was the client's fault for not taking advantage of the things the program had to offer. Help, however, was enforced. For instance, the judge referred to himself as an enforcer of some sort when describing the program as "the carrot and the stick":

> INTERVIEWER: But do you think of yourself as the stick?
> JUDGE GALLO: Sure.
> INTERVIEWER: Because you're the judge, you make the final determination.
> JUDGE GALLO: Absolutely. The final call is always mine.

Similarly, the public defender discussed sanctions as a form of clinical help for a client:

> INTERVIEWER: So when a person is having trouble—on the report they're missing sessions or they have a positive urine result for using drugs—how does the team decide what the appropriate sanction should be?
> PUBLIC DEFENDER: Basically, we decide on a sanction by figuring out what will advance the client's treatment, what will help the client's treatment.

Sanctions, according to the public defender, were always used as clinical interventions. The judge also implied that everything about the program, including the sanctions, was an effort to help the client. The reality of when and how sanctions were imposed, however, resulted in a much more ambiguous overlap of clinical and punitive responses to clients' behavior.

Therapeutic Punishment in Treatment

Just as there were incentives and sanctions in the drug court setting, the Southside and Westview programs operated a form of the "carrot and stick" approach in treatment. Again, I use the term "therapeutic punishment" to describe these incentives and sanctions to illustrate what I perceived the program's philosophy to be around their use. In the treatment programs, therapeutic punishment operated in conjunction with the rules set by each program. Violating these rules at times resulted in serious sanctions.

In the treatment programs, therapists communicated the rules of the IOP to the clients, orally and in writing. Wendy, a therapist for Westview's program as well as one of the group therapists at Southside, educated the clients in Southside's pre-IOP group about these rules before the client started Westview's IOP. Every so often, she would hand out a four-page document that described the various rules, including one page describing the attendance and makeup policy that clients had to sign before beginning IOP treatment. Of all the rules, attendance was taken the most seriously, even above abstinence. Wendy described the rules of IOP treatment to the pre-IOP group one day at Westview: "And they want to start like a three strikes and you're out policy up there. Like if you're late to group three times, then you're kicked out. Because if you're going to just blow it off, why should we hold your spot? Why can't someone else from here take it?" Westview included tardiness in its rule of attendance, not permitting those arriving past a certain time (usually fifteen minutes past the start time) to join the group. I never saw a client dismissed permanently from group for being consistently late; it appeared there was some negotiation that occurred between the therapist and the client. While one could view the attendance policy cynically as the treatment program's insurance of getting reimbursed for services, a lateness policy being enforced suggested that the policy was at least related to the attempt to make clients more responsible. At the time of my observations, there was also a waiting list for clients to start at Southside. The idea behind the "three strikes" rule could have been related to the abundance of potential clients, given that the majority of Southside's clients were mandated to also enroll in the IOP at Westview.

Attendance was heavily monitored for clients who were referred from the criminal justice system. In many ways, the threat of returning to court or to jail was the "stick" that the treatment program used to make the clients follow the established rules. Abstinence also was enforced with this same threat. Therapists who worked with the court-mandated clients frequently met with the client's parole officer or case manager, depending on the program. This led to multiple facets of supervision over the clients. Therapists reported any attendance issues or drug use to the parole officer or case manager, and that person likely exercised some sort of punishment in return. Similarly, Peter, a therapist at Westview, mentioned the threat of sanctions from the criminal justice system: "There's the pressure of their parole officer saying you gotta do this or we're going to put you back in prison." In general, the therapists referred to this setup positively; they seemed to enjoy having more power because of the possible punishment that clients would face if they did not follow the program's rules. They did not see themselves as part of the criminal justice system, but they liked the extra authority that it gave them. Being perceived as an extension of the criminal justice system, however, could also be a serious impediment to establishing a trusting counselor–client relationship. It is not likely that the client would report any negative behavior to a counselor who had links to probation officers or the drug court judge, even though that honesty might help with his or her treatment.

As I describe in Chapter 4, court-mandated clients often publicly acted in the group meetings as if they were "doing time" by attending treatment. They frequently looked at the sign-in book to count the number of days of treatment they had remaining, and reminded others in the group that they were forced to be there:

MICHELLE (Westview group, black female, probably early forties): We have consequences if we don't show up. You don't.

BARRY (Westview group, black male, probably mid-thirties): I have consequences.

SEAN (Westview group, black male, age twenty): Yeah, but they're not as serious.

BARRY: They are consequences for *myself*!

In this exchange, Barry appeared offended that two of the court-mandated group members suggested that they faced more-serious consequences for missing treatment than he did. Certainly, their consequences were serious in that they could possibly be sent back to prison; however, their comments also suggested an inability to comprehend why somebody would feel an internal motivation to attend treatment. The different referral source (criminal justice versus self) led to some minor conflicts between group members, although not all court-mandated clients blatantly resisted group therapy. There seemed to be a tipping point where if there were a large number of clients referred from the criminal justice system in the IOP group (or several outspoken ones), then the group tended to focus on criminal justice–related issues and clients felt more comfortable openly challenging the idea that they needed group therapy or other forms of treatment, like twelve-step meetings. When the court-mandated clients were in the minority, they tended not to say much during group sessions.

In the Southside clinic, methadone served as the "carrot" and the "stick" to control clients. As Wendy mentioned in an earlier example, methadone could be used as "leverage" in the therapist–client relationship. There were a number of rules set up by the Southside clinic around the dispensing of methadone; clients were sanctioned if they did not follow these rules. For instance, the program designated a particular time each day that clients could receive their medication (there were three different medication times daily). Clients could only visit the clinic at their designated time. An incentive (or "carrot") in the Southside clinic was that clients could earn the ability to take home bottles of methadone so they did not have to visit the clinic daily. While federal regulations were relaxed in 2001 to allow methadone clinics to distribute a month's supply for clients, Southside's own policy was more restrictive around the number of take-home bottles permitted. When I inquired about Southside's policy on take-home bottles of methadone, the facility's "coordinator of treatment" indicated to me that they would never permit a client to take home as much as a month's supply because of the possibility that the client would sell the substance or use it not as directed. Southside's procedure manual for therapists indicated that it was possible for clients to earn up to six take-home bottles at a time (permitting them to visit just once each week), but this was only after three years of near-perfect attendance and complete abstinence.

The patient manual stated that "permanent THBs [take-home bottles] are a privilege and not a right." In addition, the clinic considered THBs as an "attempt to inspire more self-reliance and responsibility." Most clients ever earned only one take-home bottle per week (usually used for Sunday). A client only would be considered eligible for a take-home bottle after completing at least ninety days of treatment with regular attendance of counseling sessions, continuous abstinence from drugs for three months, and no reported behavioral problems. Furthermore, the patient manual indicated that "the treatment team must be able to justify that the benefits to your recovery of earning THBs outweigh the risks of diversion of the methadone." Southside's intense regulations (more strict than the federal requirements) implied that the clinic did not fully trust its own clients with the medication prescribed. Clients could easily feel this distrust when reading the patient manual and interacting with treatment staff.

While these were the program's written criteria around THB privileges, there were indications that the previous medical director did not always follow them:

> LINDA (Southside program director): I like the *new* medical director. I liked the old one, I just didn't like the way he ran the place.
> INTERVIEWER: What didn't you like about the way the old medical director ran things? What did he do?
> LINDA: "Benzo-Bill" gave everybody take-home [bottles] . . . even when they didn't deserve them. He made excuses for them and enabled them. . . . He put into place a set of principles which he quickly ignored. The principles were good. His ignoring them just taught people to try harder, beg harder, and reinforced everything wrong. . . . I like the man; I just didn't like what he did. He was trying to be too kind and too kind is not good. It doesn't help the people to change. He tried to please everybody, but that wasn't right. You don't please them. [*Imitating client*] "Well, I feel better when I take drugs." [*Imitating doctor*] "OK, take drugs."

After further probing, and speaking to other therapists, I learned that this nickname for the previous doctor, "Benzo Bill," was rather widespread through the clinic. The name was a reference to clients continuing to use benzodiazepines (such as Xanax) while taking methadone and not being reprimanded for it. Linda suggested that the doctor was too lenient with THBs and that led to the clients abusing other drugs, like benzodiazepines, with no real consequences. Other therapists mentioned to me that the use of benzodiazepines by their clients was quite common, even if they did not earn THBs, because the mixture of benzodiazepines and methadone produced a feeling very similar to heroin. Jerry, a Southside therapist, estimated that as many as 40 percent of Southside's clients used benzodiazepines, either by prescription or by purchasing them illegally: "We have this tiny window of opportunity to try to talk to them before the street just pulls them right back. And, I told you, like with the benzos [benzodiazepine]. I would say 40 percent of our patients are using benzos with the methadone. But I'm glad to see [the new medical director] is trying to take it out of here." Jerry referred to the new medical director, as Linda did, as attempting to change the culture of

Southside by being stricter around the client's benzodiazepine use. Jerry's comment about having a "tiny window of opportunity" to reach clients before "the street" pulled them back related to most of the staff's conceptualization of addiction as largely a result of the client's social environment and the negative influences prevalent in their neighborhoods. The metaphor also emphasized clients' own responsibility for their recovery and the importance of resisting triggers.

There were additional rules set up around the return of empty take-home containers. If clients failed to return an empty container at their next visit, they would lose THB privileges for one week and be placed on a late-day medication time for one to two weeks. The bottle also would be inspected to make sure that the label had not been removed or tampered with. One encounter during the pre-IOP group I observed suggested that clients also might be refused medication all together for not bringing back a THB:

> LEONARD (Southside clinic, white male, late twenties): I'm not feeling too good today because I didn't get medicated.
> KEVIN (therapist): Why not?
> LEONARD: I forgot my take-home bottle. So they won't medicate me.
> KARL: Can you get it and bring it back?
> LEONARD: Yeah, they said if I bring it back I have to wait until five.
> KARL: Five?! Why not when you bring it back?
> LEONARD: I don't know. I guess I'm being punished. I don't want to wait around all afternoon. I mean, if I don't get medicated, then I want to get high. And I got this money in my pocket now. And I'm thinking of leaving here and getting high!

While the program's manual described the restrictions around take-home bottles as an attempt to "inspire more self-reliance and responsibility," the clients instead characterized them as punishment.

Another way that methadone distribution was used as "leverage" was in changing medication times. Most clients expressed the desire to be medicated as early as possible. Many cited reasons related to working or other kinds of responsibilities that took up their daytime hours. If a client missed a counseling session or a group meeting, tested positive for drugs, or did not return a take-home bottle on time, they could face a medication time change as a punishment. Changing the client's medication time was a common sanction at Southside. The clients perceived this sanction as strictly punitive because they not only had to restructure their day to accommodate the change in medication time but it is likely that they also would suffer withdrawal symptoms, such as nausea, from not taking methadone at the usual time. Despite these physical repercussions, the staff saw the sanctions as "therapeutic," as promoting clients to take more responsibility in their treatment.

While this sanction was commonly used, Jerry, a therapist, expressed some reservations about the kind of message that it sent and what it said about the role of therapy in the program: "The medication is the whip that we crack. . . . It doesn't jive with my concept of therapy. I'd like to see the patient be in *therapy*. They have all sorts of paranoia about earning take-home bottles and medication times and all kinds of rules and regulations that they have to conform to. . . . I'd like to see therapy take the front seat." In the group sessions I observed, Jerry often treated the clients with a lot of respect and empathy. This might be due to his having worked previously at an outpatient treatment program for working professionals. That is, his perspective on addiction might be broader since he had seen its impact on both middle- and lower-class individuals. Some of the other therapists seemed to only be exposed to the clients at Southside, which in turn framed their whole understanding of opiate addiction.

The most threatening sanction was a forced detox from the program, where clients would receive dramatic reductions in their daily methadone dose over a few days until they were released from the program. This most often occurred for disciplinary reasons, such as fighting with another client, but also was a result of the client not following the clinic's rules around attendance and abstinence:

> SAM (Southside group, white male, probably mid-twenties): I don't know
> if I'm going to IOP, though, 'cause I might be getting detoxed.
> WENDY (therapist): Why?
> SAM: 'Cause I missed yesterday.
> CATHY (white female, probably mid-thirties): You missed an appoint-
> ment with your therapist?
> SAM: Yeah. So she said if I missed it, I'd be detoxed.
> WENDY [*looking a bit shocked, although not genuinely*]: So what are you
> going to do? Will you get sick?
> SAM: I don't know. I haven't stopped getting high, so . . . I'm going to pay
> what I owe and then get on another program.
> WENDY: What about going inpatient?
> SAM: Yeah, I'm gonna try to go away.
> [*Wendy tells Sam to go speak with his therapist, Linda, about getting
> another chance. He comes back to group a little while later and tells
> Wendy that he was going to be allowed to stay in the program.*]

In this case, Sam was threatened with detox as punishment for not attending a counseling session (and likely continued drug use, since he indicated that he was still getting high). However, after speaking again with his therapist, he was given another chance. While the medical director would likely have to approve such a measure, the client is led to believe that it is completely at the therapist's discretion whether or not he or she will continue on the program. This gives therapists an enormous amount of power over the clients.

In addition, forcing clients to feel withdrawal symptoms as a form of punishment could be detrimental to their own commitment to treatment. Most of the clients I encountered in the Southside program mentioned physical symptoms from opiate withdrawal as one of the indicators that made them recognize they had a drug problem in the first place. For instance, in an interview, Cathy, one of the Southside clients, discussed how she came to realize that she had a drug problem:

> CATHY: I can remember having hangovers and stuff like that, but not in the bathroom throwing my guts up like with [heroin].
> INTERVIEWER: So that was like a wake-up call?
> CATHY: Oh, yeah. . . . And there was times when I didn't want to do it, and I was so sick. I didn't want to do it, but what am I going to do not to be sick like this?

Nearly all of Southside's clients enrolled in the methadone program to avoid withdrawal symptoms. That the treatment staff then used physical discomfort in an effort to enforce responsibility was at odds with treating opiate addiction like a real medical problem.

While therapists suggested that a forced detox was a "last straw" due to continued problems with the client's behavior, there was some indication that it might be used as punishment even for one-time breaches of expected behavior. For instance, at one point while I was observing, several neighbors had complained to the clinic (and their state representative's legislative aide, who lived nearby) about clients from Southside standing on their sidewalks and being noisy in the morning. While this was a direct result of the clinic not having a waiting room where clients could go before receiving their medication, and also not permitting them to stand directly in front of the clinic before it opened, the clinic instead addressed the neighbors' concerns by creating a new rule that clients were not permitted to "loiter" anywhere in the vicinity of the facility. Jerry informed the pre-IOP group about that new rule: "So, this is serious. And something like this, they might try to get a sacrificial lamb, or maybe a couple of people. Throw them off the program to show they're serious. So don't be that sacrificial lamb." Jerry warned the group to take the new rule seriously, or face expulsion from the program. His statement also indicated that ordinarily such a violation would probably not entail being forcibly detoxed from Southside, but the clinic was taking this situation more seriously, likely because one of the neighbors had a relationship with a local political figure. That the program attached a criminal label, "loitering," to the clients waiting to be medicated in the morning also revealed the conflation of addiction with criminality. While loitering is a vague term, and sometimes difficult to assess criminally, it is generally defined as waiting somewhere for an extended period of time without any purpose. These clients obviously had a purpose: to pick up their daily dose of medication. The Westview program did not appear to have a similar issue with their clients waiting outside before group therapy, indicating that the structure of Southside (the lack of a waiting room) was actually the cause of the "criminal" behavior.

This rule of no loitering in front of the facility before it opened created additional problems for clients. Because many clients arrived before the clinic unlocked its doors, they created their own system of rules about who would be medicated first. This occasionally led to conflict between clients. Jerry spoke about a client who was recently kicked out of Southside's program:

> He was ecstatic because he and his girlfriend were going to move into their first apartment. They were going to look at it that morning, so he drove up at eight o'clock in the morning, got out of his car, stood by the door. Thought he was first in line. Guards got here and opened the door. Others got out of their cars [and started yelling at him]. "Number one? You're number twelve! You're supposed to check when you get here and see who's number one, two . . ." He reached in his back pocket and pulled out his knife. [The other client] told the guard about it when he got inside. And whether the knife was ever seen or not, I don't know. I asked the patient, and he said he just reached in his back pocket to make [the other client] think he had something.

While the clinic might argue that their not having a waiting room for clients receiving medication had to do with space restrictions, there was never any indication that they were trying to accommodate the clients to avoid potential conflict or issues with neighbors. It was this waiting outside the clinic that some clients also expressed as a further sign of the stigma associated with receiving methadone and how methadone programs were often dissociated from more "medical" treatment facilities. Once during group, clients discussed an incident where someone spray painted "methadone clinic" on the side of the plain gray building, and clients were still forced to stand in front of it waiting for their medication until the clinic removed the graffiti several days later.

The program used this system of incentives and sanctions because they viewed it as therapeutic for the client, in that it would ultimately encourage the client to become more responsible. Peter, a Westside therapist, discussed his perspective on how this method was often associated with methadone maintenance treatment in general:

> PETER: The whole methadone system is not where I would personally go. . . . It's a little bit more behaviorist than my orientation is. Not behaviorist, but more reward-punish oriented.
>
> INTERVIEWER: Do you think that about methadone maintenance treatment in general?
>
> PETER: Somewhat. Because it's like, OK. You're not doing this; we're going to withhold your medicine until a certain time. And that will change your behavior. So . . . It's more carrot-and-stick oriented. But that's what works, too [chuckles].

In this statement, Peter disagreed with the philosophy of therapeutic punishment, especially concerning how the methadone was dispensed, but at the same time mentioned that it was an effective tactic. There was some indication that this was the case from the groups I observed:

> JERRY: George, what did you learn from group today?
> GEORGE (Southside program, white male, mid-twenties): I guess I learned from the others' experiences. . . . I learned not to mess up because, like, his dose got cut.

George, a new client in the pre-IOP group, articulated that the possible punishments associated with the dispensing of methadone were a deterrent for him. He also framed it exactly the way the treatment staff did: if you follow the rules, you will get your medication as prescribed.

The use of a "carrot and stick" model for treatment is not restricted to just this methadone maintenance program. Other researchers, through interviews with methadone clients, have suggested that methadone treatment programs exert power and control over the individual by changing aspects of the medication (such as the dosage level) as punishment (for instance, Bourgois 2000). Such research suggests that therapeutic punishment exists in other methadone treatment programs across the United States, although Southside's regulations were particularly strict considering that federal regulations around methadone dispensing were less stringent.

Conclusion

The use of therapeutic punishment in both the drug court and the treatment programs was a logical conclusion to the labeling of drug addicts in our society as both diseased and immoral. Reinarman (2005) also argued that the disease concept gets used as a justification for punitive policies—that we must incarcerate some "for their own good" (317). On a broader level, therapeutic punishment reflects the simultaneous medicalization and criminalization of drugs that has occurred at the institutional level. If addiction is managed by both the treatment establishment and the criminal justice system, then staff in these settings will use both therapeutic and punitive means to achieve their goals.

Therapeutic punishment also was a result of, and at the same time perpetuated, the stigma associated with being a drug addict or a drug-using criminal. That is, clients were perceived as inherently irresponsible, even before staff in either the drug court or the treatment programs had evidence that this was the case. This was because the clients were labeled "addicts" when they first walked in the door of either the court or the treatment programs and the programs' conceptualization of "addict" related to the assumption that these clients were poorly socialized, lacked good values, and were not trustworthy. Clients, therefore, had to provide evidence through their behavior that they were not irresponsible and were deserving of the rewards built into the organization of the programs. At the same time, there was an interesting difference between the drug court and the treatment programs in how they used therapeutic punishment. In the drug court, clients were in a sense punished with *more* therapy (that is, having to attend twelve-step meetings or enter a recovery house), while punishment in the treatment programs was a *reduction* in therapy (that is, having to leave the Westview clinic if late or losing medication privileges). Despite this difference in structure, both used therapeutic punishment in an attempt to teach the client responsibility.

6

Conclusion

Reducing Stigma

Addiction is not a descriptive term, it is a stigmatizing term which is culturally conditioned. And it reflects not a property of the drug, but a property of the culture.

—Thomas Szasz, HBO studios, 1996

It is not that people who get high are pathological, but rather it is alleged that people who get high with a substance defined as criminal by the state are pathological. . . . The presumption of pathology is more a political claim than a scientific fact.

—Waldorf, Reinarman, and Murphy (1991: 281).

On Tuesday evening, November 4, 2008, while newly elected President Obama was in Chicago speaking victoriously about hope, change, and new leadership in America, the campaign named "People against the Proposition 5 Deception" also celebrated victory for defeating a California ballot proposition (the Nonviolent Offender Rehabilitation Act). This proposition would have required California to expand funding and drug treatment services for nonviolent drug offenders, while reducing the criminal consequences of some nonviolent drug offenses. Leading up to the election, Democratic senator Diane Feinstein appeared in television commercials calling Proposition 5 the "drug dealer's bill of rights." Similarly, actor Martin Sheen, who famously played the president of the United States on television's *The West Wing*, served as cochair of the anti-Proposition 5 campaign. He vociferously opposed the measure and wrote several op-ed pieces that asserted Proposition 5 would shift money from "quality" rehabilitative programs like drug courts to "harm reduction" techniques, which Sheen argued would only "make drug users better-informed consumers" (Sheen 2008). The campaign against Proposition 5 reveals another example of the conflict that Americans (even self-professed "liberals") have in determining what is the appropriate response to drug-related crime: should offenders be treated or punished? This book illustrates that most people prefer some combination of both. In both the court and treatment settings, therapy overlapped with punishment, a model that those working in both programs mostly embraced. This ambiguity of defining and managing addiction is directly related to the contradictions

inherent in our drug policy: offenders will be punished often, but only sometimes treated. This ambiguity is further enhanced by the criminal justice system's designation of which offenders "deserve" treatment. Today's criminal justice
system typically reserves treatment for "deserving offenders," or those who do not
have an extensive record of convictions. The "undeserving" addicts are those with
extensive criminal records or who have committed a violent offense. In a sense,
treatment is reserved for those whom the criminal justice system regards as
worthy of helping, or those they perceive as able to learn responsibility and eventually lead criminal-free lives. In this concluding chapter, I revisit the implications of the ambiguity in defining and managing addiction and offer several
policy implications that would help reduce the stigma associated with addiction.

The Institutionalization of Ambiguity

Substance abuse treatment is often proposed by liberal-minded individuals as
the answer to America's "drug problem." In addition, support for the expansion
of drug courts nationwide often crosses party lines because of the possible cost-
saving benefits. Many justify this position by saying that addiction is a disease
that needs to be treated just like any other. Recent polls also indicate that the
public believes we should place drug users in treatment rather than just in prison.
While it is likely that those in the treatment community would agree with that
response, based on the attitudes of those working at Southside and Westview
programs, this book reveals that drug treatment programs do not necessarily
exhibit the characteristics we would typically associate with "medical" treatment.
Instead, the stigma around drug use was often present within, and perpetuated
by, treatment programs. Interestingly, methadone maintenance, which is arguably the most medicalized way to deal with substance abuse, had additional
stigma from those within the treatment community. Before we advocate for more
funding for drug courts and treatment programs, we need to be confident that
the treatment programs themselves are not simply replacing the harsh punishment of prison life with judgmental policies thinly disguised as treatment.

Illness and Deviance also illustrates how the label of "addiction" was ambig-
uously defined in both drug treatment programs and a drug court; its application was not only to drug use but also to the so-called "drug lifestyle." This
ambiguity, which often centered on the role that individual responsibility played
in the development of addiction, led to the use of therapeutic punishment in
both settings. That is, punishment was packaged as therapy; the ultimate goal
was resocialization. This finding is perhaps not all that surprising given that the
history of drug policy in the United States shows an overlap of treatment and
punishment. Still, this combination of therapy and punishment, especially under
the guise of "treating" drug users, is problematic and deserves further evaluation.

The reconstruction of addiction to include other problems (what a sociologist would consider to be "social problems") also allowed the staff in both locations to view the drug court and treatment programs as helping an underserved

population access services that they needed to improve their lives. In interviews, the staff minimized a drug use problem that the client might have; they focused instead on drug "lifestyle" issues that if treated could turn the client into a productive, responsible citizen. Job-training programs, assistance with further education, parenting classes, and counseling are certainly much-needed services for those arrested (and for those in prison) if we want to reduce America's recidivism rate. However, it is problematic that these programs are only available to individuals who agree to go through a drug treatment program and be continually monitored by the criminal justice system. Such a program furthers the notion that the underlying problems that led to the initial arrest (such as lack of decent jobs, access to quality schools, family problems) are problems with individual, not structural, solutions. Furthermore, the criminal justice system's success in creating a program that incorporates the widely held view that drug addiction is a disease that needs treatment solidifies its position as the prime authority over those who use drugs and commit drug-related crime. They have convinced the public that we do not need to change our drug laws; instead, we can change how to deal with those who are arrested. The end result is that drug treatment courts and similar criminal justice initiatives become hegemonic means for dealing with drug users in the United States and effectively silence the debate around alternatives to dealing with drugs, such as harm reduction techniques or decreasing penalties for drug offenses. This position also is tied to the fact that the United States is the only nation at "war" with drugs, and as long as we consider any use of drugs to be "abuse" of some sort, our drug problem always will be significant.

Consequences of Ambiguity: Stigma and Therapeutic Punishment

The ambiguity surrounding the addiction label in both the drug court and the treatment programs led to the persistence of the stigma associated with drug addiction and the use of therapeutic punishment in both settings. The clients in the more medicalized treatment modality, methadone maintenance, were actually more stigmatized than those in other forms of treatment, a finding that challenges the notion that medicalization decreases stigma. The treatment program was somewhat responsible for the persistence of that stigma due to its structuring of how medication was dispensed and how clients earned take-home bottles. I first considered that such stigmatization was related to our American cultural ethic of hard work; that is, taking methadone allows one to not work very hard at getting better. However, since Americans have largely accepted pharmaceutical medication as the primary method of treating illnesses (and just about any other behavior that we consider to be deviant in some way), the way that methadone is stigmatized within the treatment community suggests a different phenomenon is at work. An alternative explanation could be that since those most resistant to such medications are often those in the twelve-step community (medications like methadone violate their notion of abstinence), the prevalence of twelve-step methods and philosophy within treatment programs means that resistance to medication has become institutionalized. Certainly, the treatment staff viewed those taking methadone as less trustworthy than the "drug-free" clients. In addition, combining the criminal justice system with treatment also leads to additional stigma since those referred to treatment from the criminal justice system are in effect stigmatized twice—first as a "criminal" and then as "sick."

Therapeutic punishment refers to the ways in which the addicts were sanctioned in both the treatment court and the treatment programs. While the programs viewed their responses as "helping" the clients become more responsible, the tactics were punitive in design. Often, they used therapy itself as a form of punishment. For instance, in the court, a recovery house was often used in response to severe violations like continued drug use or missed treatment sessions. While the court viewed it as an additional form of therapy that the client needed, the clients' outward resistance suggested that they instead viewed it as something not much different from prison itself (because of its strict structure). In the methadone maintenance program, the medication became a tool for leverage that the program staff used to maintain control over the clients' behavior. Violations of program rules resulted in changes in medication times or doses. Such methods led to clients often being distrustful of the staff in both programs, while the methods themselves seemed to be related to the staff members' initial distrust of the clients because of their "deviant" status as criminals, addicts, or both. This also was revealed in the images and language used to discuss clients by the court and the treatment programs (clients as dogs and childlike). Thus, just because something is labeled a "disease" and managed in a clinical setting does not mean that we do not continue to also incorporate punishment into its treatment.

The Continuing Expansion of Drug Courts: Is That All There Is?

The ever-growing number of drug courts in the United States, along with the expansion of the drug court model to other areas, is testament that the criminal justice system believes that drug courts are the best way to handle nonviolent drug offenders. However, this drug court explosion was driven by ideology, not by research. Figure 6.1 shows the evolution of drug courts along with the number of drug court evaluation studies completed (both are cumulative totals over time). The graph clearly shows that drug courts increased at a much greater rate than research could have guided.[1] Considering that drug courts can take years of planning before implementation makes the causal link between research and expansion even more tenuous. It is likely that there were more than four *dozen* drug courts either operating or in planning stages before the first four courts were fully evaluated. In addition, these earliest evaluation studies were

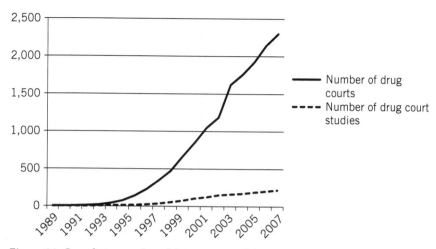

Figure 6.1 Cumulative number of drug courts and drug court evaluation studies, 1989–2008. *Sources*: National Association of Drug Court Professionals (2012), and National Criminal Justice Reference Service (2012).

flawed because of a lack of appropriate comparison groups and other methodological problems (Miethe, Lu, and Reese 2000). While recent research studies may support the expansion of drug courts, their explosion began long before the research caught up to them. Advocates can point to drug courts' success as evidence that stricter drug policies were not the problem; if anything, it was the lack of drug courts.

Drug offenders should have access to services like drug treatment, job training, and family counseling, but only as they are individually needed. At the same time, those who commit drug-related crimes should not have to be labeled "addicts" in order to access these services. An additional problem with this arrangement is that drug courts have tethered the economic survival of drug treatment programs to the criminal justice system. Currently, the criminal justice system is the largest referral source for those in treatment (SAMHSA 2010a). Many drug treatment programs have become dependent on those referrals, which further stigmatizes addiction by institutionalizing the link between the criminal justice system and drug treatment. As the executive director of the County Alcohol and Drug Program Administrators Association of California, Tom Renfree said in an interview, "Our system of care doesn't exist primarily to keep people out of prison. We would like to get to a place where treatment can be seen as more about public health, rather than tied to criminal justice" (*ADAW* 2009).

Drug courts are better than merely locking up offenders. But why are these our only two choices? By assuming that anybody who commits a drug offense has a deep-rooted pathology that needs treatment obscures the original intent of drug courts. It also results in a "one-size-fits-all" model for dealing with drug-related crime. This is unfortunate because many of these offenders do not need months of intensive (and expensive) drug treatment and counseling. However, the criminal justice system has effectively put all of its eggs into the drug court basket and actively opposes alternatives like expanding probation or decriminalization. While drug policy has expanded elsewhere beyond the two options of incarceration or drug courts, such as California's Proposition 36, these changes have been citizen driven and were often met with swift opposition from those within the criminal justice system, including drug court judges (Murphy 2012). Similarly, the National Association of Drug Court Professionals (NADCP) dismisses any critique of drug courts as either bad science or a veiled attempt to promote legalization (E. Sanders 2011). There are other approaches that also should be seriously considered and evaluated. In the face of no alternative except incarceration, of course "drug courts work."

Evaluating the Medicalization of Addiction

The overwhelming public support for viewing addiction as a disease, and the development of clinical and pharmaceutical methods to treat it, are evidence that drug addiction has been medicalized. Still, this book challenges some of the key notions that Conrad and Schneider ([1980] 1999) made about that medicalization process and its consequences. Specifically, my study challenges their notion that medicalization is a straightforward process (either forward or backward), that it results in less-punitive methods of handling the issue, and that an individual is not found to be responsible if he or she is suffering from a "disease." In the following, I address each of these issues separately and then consider what this means for the social construction of disease categories in general.

One of the problems with the medicalization thesis is that Conrad and Schneider ([1980] 1999) illustrate the process of medicalization or demedicalization, suggesting that if something were partially medicalized, it was moving in one direction or the other. My research instead reveals that this medical/legal/moral hybrid way of defining and managing drug addiction could be a rather stagnant designation and is not necessarily moving in either direction of becoming more or less medicalized. Having this hybrid definition does not produce much conflict at the institutional level, even though it produces a very ambiguous notion of what the causes of addiction are and who has the authority to manage it.

In addition, there are clear benefits to both institutions (the criminal justice system and the treatment establishment) of keeping this hybrid designation. Drug courts allow the criminal justice system to decrease its crowded caseload and prison population and at the same time successfully convince the public (and politicians of both political parties) that it is a beneficial program because it reduces recidivism and drug use of the arrestees and saves the taxpayer money. As a result, treatment programs have a steady influx of clients referred from the criminal justice system, ensuring that they have a steady stream of income.

While I do think that these benefits help prolong the relationship between the criminal justice system and treatment, I do not think that most individuals involved in these institutions are actively trying to protect this hybrid management of addiction. I believe that those working in both settings strongly believe that drug addiction requires treatment because it is a disease and that treatment is a more compassionate way to handle it. Still, it is quite remarkable how the criminal justice system has managed to retain its control over drug issues in the context of increasing medicalization.

The third criticism of the medicalization of addiction that this book offers involves the issue of responsibility someone has when labeled as "diseased." Conrad (1992) and Parsons (1951) contend that once a person is considered "ill," that person is not viewed as responsible for having the disease (or punished for it). In both the court and the treatment programs, however, I have illustrated the use of what I termed therapeutic punishment, which was very much tied to the idea of responsibility. Both the court and the treatment programs viewed individuals as responsible for being addicts: clients chose to consume a substance that they knew could have negative effects. This tied issues of self-control to responsibility and accountability for the drug problem. The client was instructed to simply stay away from "people, places, and things" (that is, triggers that could lead to relapse) as part of treatment. While a temporary relapse to using drugs was considered normal, prolonged use instead was characterized as a marker of irresponsibility and perhaps not trying hard enough. This criticism is illuminated by a 2006 USA Today/HBO poll of family members of drug/alcohol addicts. In this survey, 76 percent of respondents indicated that "addiction is a disease." Still, 82 percent of respondents indicated that "lacking willpower" was either a major or minor factor in their family member's addiction, which had far greater support than the 60 percent indicating that genetics was a major or minor factor (USA Today 2006). So even those who consider addiction to be a disease do not release the individual from being responsible for contracting the illness and for getting "better."

This notion of responsibility for acquiring a disease, in addition to being responsible for treating it, is surely not limited to drug or alcohol addiction. Those with diabetes, heart disease, lung cancer, and HIV/AIDS are all viewed as being somewhat responsible for their diseased state, except in rare instances (such as contracting HIV from a blood transfusion). Similarly, they are expected to follow a certain regimen of proper diet, exercise, and medication to keep the illness under control. Still, drug addiction often carries with it an additional stigma because drugs are illegal and viewed as immoral in our society. If one looks at the plethora of antidrug public service announcements from the past seventy years, you find similar themes throughout, such as people who use drugs are bad, those who use drugs fund our foreign enemies, and drugs make people do things that "normal" people would not do. Such themes surrounding drugs in American culture are ingrained in our news stories, our movies, our books, and our television programs. In the same way that the court and the treatment programs conflate any drug use with drug abuse, our cultural messages about drug use tell us that any drug use is bad or immoral. These designations have not changed over time, nor do I expect that they will change in the near future, even if more people accept the idea that addiction is a brain disease. That people have to choose to consume drugs in the first place will always make them have a level of responsibility for their "disease" that the medicalization of deviance thesis minimizes.

Study Limitations

The major limitations of this study are those that are common in other qualitative research. While the types of programs where I did research were the most common forms of treatment in the United States, and even though state licensing requirements standardize services to a large extent across states, I cannot generalize my findings to other outpatient treatment programs. The same is true for the drug court. While there are a number of characteristics that all drug courts have in common, it is likely that Capital City's drug court has some differences at the organizational level from other courts nationwide. Still, as a sociologist, I have to believe that human behavior is determined in large part by the social context under which we operate. For that reason, although my research methods do not permit me to generalize to larger populations, I would expect at least some of my analysis to apply to other treatment programs and drug courts (especially those in urban areas), and by extension, to deepen our understanding of how addiction is labeled and managed in similar institutions.

My observations also were limited to group sessions in the treatment programs and the public sessions of the court. I was never permitted to observe the "back stage" of the courtroom, where the court team discussed "problem" clients before court started. In addition, I did not observe individual sessions between counselors and clients in the treatment program or in case management sessions. I do not consider this a major limitation, however, since the focus of my analysis is on the negotiation of addiction issues at the institutional level. For that reason, what is communicated in public and in written records is more important.

One limitation to note is that I cannot be certain if I would have observed the same persistence of stigma and use of therapeutic punishment in treatment programs that cater to wealthier populations. There certainly seemed to be a mutual sense of distrust between the clients and the staff in both the court and the treatment programs because of obvious differences in race and class. The treatment staff also seemed to relate drug problems to characteristics of the surrounding neighborhood of the treatment facility, so I am not sure what would replace that conceptualization in a treatment facility located in a middle-class, white neighborhood (although treatment programs are far less prevalent in those locations).

While I should cite a similar limitation as far as the drug court I observed, I do believe that the criminal status of the individuals involved would largely dictate how the court staff treated them. In addition, arrest statistics show that those arrested (and imprisoned) for the types of drug-related offenses that drug courts target are disproportionately lower class and racial minorities. Therefore, while I recognize that I do not have data to support this, I think there would be more similarities than differences among courts, even considering different locations.

One of the benefits of qualitative research is that the researcher is able to investigate deeply into the meanings of concepts and how those meanings are negotiated and shared in certain settings. Because that sort of investigation is laborious and takes a long time, the researcher often does not have the time, money, or energy to include many sites in a research project. This study is also limited in scope because of the selection of only three sites for investigation. While the drug court is the criminal justice initiative that has the most direct overlap of criminal justice and treatment institutions, it would be presumptive to attempt to generalize my findings to the "criminal justice system" as a whole. Similarly, by only looking at outpatient drug treatment programs, even if they were similar to other programs in the city or the state, I cannot generalize to the "treatment establishment" overall. These were known limitations when I designed the research project. Since my focus was on understanding how addiction is defined and managed in specific settings, the method was the most appropriate for exploring the meanings of that concept.

Suggestions for Policy

I could make a list of policy recommendations that actually reflect the serious changes I think we need in our whole approach to dealing with drugs in American society, but those changes are too radical for our current social and political climate. Instead, I propose specific policy recommendations that could operate within our existing frameworks for dealing with drugs, while still pushing on those frameworks' boundaries to try to effect real change in our labeling and management of drug users. Just as the medicalization of drug addiction can only operate within the boundaries set by our drug laws and criminal justice approaches to drug issues, my own suggestions for change must operate within those same boundaries. I believe these changes, however, would have a positive impact on reducing the stigma of drug addiction and help individuals and communities affected by real drug problems.

1. *Invest more resources in quality, hospital-based drug treatment.* This policy recommendation has two parts: increasing access to treatment and increasing treatment quality. Data from the Substance Abuse and Mental Health Services Administration (SAMHSA) reveals that people living in poverty are not receiving the drug treatment they need compared to those who have more resources for treatment, like

health insurance coverage or the ability to pay out of pocket. The SAMHSA's data show that, in 2006 and 2008, only about 18 percent of those living in poverty who needed treatment actually received it (SAMHSA 2010b). Being arrested for a crime should not be the only way that these people can access drug treatment. The Web site of the NADCP reveals their perspective: "NADCP will not rest until there are Drug Courts within reach of every American in need." But the "need" should be about access to drug treatment *before* individuals become involved in the criminal justice system.

If those with true drug problems had access to quality treatment programs in medical centers and hospitals that already exist in their community, then they would be more likely to never enter the criminal justice system, saving taxpayers money, reducing incarceration rates, and improving people's lives. Drug treatment programs should not be ghettoized; they need to be integrated with other physical and mental health programs. This integration also means that physicians should have a more active role in screening and referring patients to treatment. President Obama's initial drug control strategy highlights the importance of better integrating treatment for drug abuse with existing medical treatment facilities. In addition to the health benefits of having a better coordinated system of care, this integration would help reduce the stigma of drug abuse. In order to accomplish this, however, primary-care and emergency physicians need to be better trained at assessing symptoms of drug abuse in a nonjudgmental way. They need to better communicate to their patients that they are a resource for drug and alcohol treatment issues. As my research showed, there was a lack of understanding about the research on drug addiction. Improving treatment quality also means integrating research into the structure of treatment (Miller and Carroll 2006).

The restrictions around methadone use also should be reevaluated to provide better access for those who could benefit from such treatment. Current regulations perpetuate the stigma of using pharmaceuticals to treat addiction and discourage many from seeking treatment. Research shows that the benefits from methadone treatment (reduced crime, disease, and so forth) far outweigh the risks (such as diversion) and policy should reflect that (Riley et al. 1999).

In addition, we need to invest in more resources for those in treatment to set them up for success, like job training, access to public education, and various skills training (that is, using the Internet effectively). These resources need to be better integrated into treatment. Just labeling drug abuse as a public health or "medical" problem is not enough; drug abuse is often tied to other mental health problems and a lack of opportunities for social advancement. One should not have to enter the criminal justice system to access these resources.

Drug treatment quality also would improve if those working in treatment programs were better paid and trained. While my research revealed that therapists themselves sometimes stigmatized clients, I believe that many of their attitudes could be changed with better training about research-based outcomes and the complex relationship between poverty, racism, drug policy, and addiction. The current system basically assigns drug treatment professionals an impossible task of curing a person's drug problem in twelve weeks. Considering the severe problems that may relate to the client's addiction, or be an underlying cause of it, it is no wonder that counselors ultimately feel defeated in their jobs. If drug treatment were not considered second-class medical care, perhaps the resources would meet the demands of such a difficult profession.

2. *Stop treating all drug use as drug abuse.* Experimental or infrequent drug use is not an addiction and our criminal justice system has to stop dealing with it like it is. Similarly, selling drugs is not the same as being addicted to drugs, but is the logical conclusion to the high demand for illegal drugs. Because of increasing arrest and incarceration rates, and the lengthening of prison sentences for drug-related crimes, our criminal justice system is overcrowded and overworked. In order to alleviate some of those consequences of our drug policy, we have created new initiatives to divert some of the "deserving" addicts into drug treatment. The fundamental flaw in this design is that just because somebody is arrested for drug possession does not mean that he or she requires drug treatment. Rather than send them to expensive (although cheaper than prison) drug treatment programs, they should just be fined for possessing small amounts of illicit drugs. In addition, police should not spend a great deal of time and resources targeting low-level drug users and sellers. This targeting has terrorized low-income neighborhoods and communities of color for too long and is one of the reasons for the disproportionate imprisonment rates of people of color.

The conflation of drug use and abuse is also a problem beyond the criminal justice system. There is not enough research being done that recognizes the nuances of drug use and abuse. One reason that drug use leads to further drug problems is that we do not discuss ways to control drug use or alternatives to either treatment or crime (Waldorf, Reinarman, and Murphy 1991). Many people experiment with legal and illegal drugs and develop norms for controlling use. Using drugs does not automatically turn a healthy person into a sick, demented monster who will stop at nothing for his or her next fix. Our discourse about drugs needs to reflect realities rather than fears.

3. *Use more diversion programs.* For those offenders who have genuine drug use problems, many should be diverted into programs that emphasize drug treatment rather than criminal sanctions. This means expanding supervised or unsupervised drug treatment (depending

on the individual and the offense) rather than filtering them into drug courts. California's Proposition 36, which gives low-level drug offenders multiple opportunities in treatment before becoming involved with the criminal justice system, is one such program. At the same time, these programs need to be fully funded or they will not be effective.

Because of their strict supervision and cost, drug courts should be reserved for more serious offenders who may require more frequent involvement with a judge and case manager. In many jurisdictions, this means widening the net of offenses that can be included into drug courts, including offenders with lengthy criminal records and those who have committed a violent offense. This also would help address the racial imbalance in drug courts. Because of the restrictions regarding who can enter a drug court program, people of color are more likely to be excluded from drug courts compared to their white counterparts. This is largely due to the requirement that many courts impose about excluding potential clients who have previous felony convictions. In addition, research suggests that black people do not do as well in drug court as whites, since they have lower graduation rates and are more likely to receive sanctions while in the program (Walsh 2011). Drug courts need to demonstrate effectiveness at reducing the recidivism of more serious offenders and address racial discrimination in their structure.

4. *Work toward eradicating the enduring stigma associated with drug abuse.* The federal government should not be spending tax money on public service announcements and "education" programs that merely attempt to scare American youths about drugs and drug users. Such attempts just paint those with drug problems as immoral and weak-willed and further stigmatize those who seek treatment. Our national conversations about drug use and addiction should be based on research and recognize complexity.

In addition to ending the perpetuation of a cultural stigma, we need to stop institutionalizing stigma. Those who are convicted for a drug offense should be able to fully rejoin society after their incarceration or graduation from drug court. We need to stop the "invisible punishments" (Cooper 2007; Travis 2002) applied to ex-cons for years after they serve their sentence, sometimes lasting an entire lifetime. This means that drug offenders should be able to access federal student loans for college or trade schools, be able to receive public assistance, and not be required to report a nonviolent drug conviction on job applications. These should be policy changes that the NADCP lobbies for; to date, the integration of drug court graduates back into society has not been a chief concern for the advocacy organization. These restrictions only perpetuate stigma and prevent the offender from fully reintegrating into society, a combination that ensures a large number of offenders will commit new crimes and return to prison. Whether the argument is fueled by a desire to save taxpayer money or for social justice, it is in everyone's best interest to reduce the stigma around drug abuse and addiction.

Appendix: Methods and Perspective

The purpose of this project was to investigate how competing medical and moral frameworks for labeling and managing addiction were used in a drug court and a drug treatment facility. Because the research focused on how these institutions communicated definitions of addiction to their clients, my research fit into the paradigm of "institutional ethnography" (Smith 2002, 2006a, 2006b). Institutional ethnography as a method focuses on how daily activities reflect larger social organization. Its purpose is not to generalize about people's experiences, but to try to find social processes that can be generalized (DeVault and McCoy 2006). While my research was conducted in only two settings, I argue that the processes I observed can be generalized to other similar settings. This is largely due to the discourses used in the settings and how they reflect our larger cultural discourse about addiction.

There is no single strategy for an institutional ethnography; I relied on traditional ethnographic methods for the research, including observations, interviews, and document analysis. The following explains in more detail how I conducted the research and reflects on the strengths and weaknesses of the methods I used.

CHOOSING THE SITES

Institutional ethnography aims to start with people's experiences rather than with theory (Smith 2002). The "grounded theory" method of conducting qualitative research also starts from a similar strategy (Glaser and Strauss 1967). I followed these approaches by choosing two research sites that labeled and managed addicts. In order to get a variety of experiences, I chose one site that was affiliated with the criminal justice system (a drug court) and one that was more "medicalized" (a drug treatment facility).

Capital City's adult drug court program began in 1997. During my observations, about four hundred individuals participated in the program at any given time. The court operated as a pre-plea program, meaning that participants entered a plea of guilty or nolo contendere as a condition of acceptance into the program. If clients were terminated from the program, the drug court judge determined their sentence and they were unable to appeal. The drug court program, like most programs across the country, was designed to take one year to complete and included monthly court supervision and drug treatment. Before beginning my observations, I contacted the court coordinator about my project. She enthusiastically invited me to observe court sessions.

While there was only one drug court program in Capital City, there were many drug treatment facilities to possibly include in this study. At the time I began this research, there were eighty-eight state-licensed drug treatment facilities in Capital City. Most (74 percent) housed outpatient programs, the most common type of formal drug treatment in the United States. From the list of programs, I contacted fifteen facilities that offered outpatient programs to the general population. I wanted programs that served as broad a population as possible, so I did not contact programs that worked exclusively with special populations, such as pregnant women. I phoned these facilities and asked them several questions about their programs and their clients to make sure that their programs also included clients referred from the criminal justice system. I also reviewed brochures from these facilities to better understand their treatment philosophy. From these conversations and brochures, it appeared that all of the programs were quite similar in their treatment philosophy and structure. All programs included individual counseling, group therapy sessions, and the use of twelve-step methods. Several programs also included methadone maintenance. I ultimately chose to study a treatment facility that housed two outpatient drug treatment programs, one focused exclusively on methadone maintenance and one that had intensive outpatient care. I chose these programs because they were under the same organizational management, a teaching hospital, and thought it would be useful for my research questions to analyze two different treatment modalities that operated within the same organization. In addition, the intensive outpatient program included clients referred from all of the various drug treatment–related criminal justice initiatives in Capital City. I had worked as a research assistant in this facility several years earlier, so I also had the benefit of having a positive relationship with a "gatekeeper" who was receptive to my studying the facility. Because the facility was affiliated with a hospital, I had to submit my proposal and questionnaires to their institutional review board (IRB) for approval. While this delayed my data collection at the facility, in the end, it proved to be beneficial. Those working in the programs seemed to view my project as more legitimate because I could show them the approval from their own IRB as well as the one from my university.

While it is not possible to generalize my findings from these two treatment programs to others in the city, the licensing requirements by the state, as well as the program-level components that must exist to be labeled a certain type of treatment program (that is, intensive outpatient), suggest it is likely that there are many similarities between these programs and others that offer the same treatment type. From my brief survey of other outpatient programs (through brochures and telephone conversations), it appeared that there was little variation in the general structure of the programs across the city. In addition, all of the programs were located in poorer residential neighborhoods in the city, many in predominantly African American neighborhoods.

OBSERVATIONS AND ROLES

Capital City's drug court operated on two days each week. On Tuesdays, court proceedings were mostly occupied with the public defender meeting eligible participants, explaining the program, and enrolling those who wanted to enter the program. Wednesday's sessions were typically filled with the monthly visits of program participants, as well as a graduation ceremony once each month. My role during these sessions was that of a complete observer; I sat in the back of the courtroom where the program participants awaited their hearing. As a result, I only observed the public interactions between the clients and court staff. The court coordinator was aware of my research, but almost all of the other participants were unaware that I was there observing. This covert role allowed me to "blend in" with the other observers (typically, family members of the clients in court that day) and have no impact on the court proceedings. For the purposes of my research, it was only necessary to observe these public interactions. Having an institutional ethnographic approach meant that I was concerned with how notions of addiction were organized within the setting. That is, I wanted to focus on the experiences of those going through the process of being labeled an addict. As a result, it was not necessary to observe the private meetings between the court staff because clients were never allowed to attend them. Institutional ethnography focuses on institutional discourse (Smith 2006b); in this study, the institutional discourse about addiction was mainly achieved through the public activities of the court.

During court proceedings, I took brief notes and wrote more detailed field notes afterward. I observed Capital City's drug court program initially for six months, from June 2005 through November 2005. After this intense period of observations, I spent about twelve months coding and analyzing field notes. In order to validate my initial conclusions about the drug court, I attended several more drug court proceedings between March and May 2007. I considered my data saturated at this point because I was not observing any different processes than what I had witnessed initially. Throughout my time observing drug court, I observed sessions that included approximately 150 different program participants and fourteen different court staff. This method of observing, analyzing, and observing again with the goal of data saturation is consistent with a grounded theory approach for qualitative research.

My role observing the Southside and Westview treatment programs was quite different. Institutional ethnography recognizes that there are no neutral spaces for the observer and that the researcher's standpoint is critical (Campbell 2010). In the treatment facility, I took on more of a combined participant-observer role. I attended group therapy sessions in both programs, sitting among the group members. I did not take any notes during these meetings because I thought doing so would be distracting to the group members. I also wanted group members to feel comfortable with my presence and not like they were being studied. I often arrived several minutes before the group meeting started and casually interacted with the group members. During this time, I also would introduce myself to new group members and ask them to sign a consent form for my research. I sought informed consent from every person in these group meetings, explaining the purposes of my research and my role as a researcher. Every person that I approached gave consent for me to observe with the exception of one person toward the end of my observations in the Southside program. This individual had just begun treatment and expressed verbal approval for me to observe the session, but refused to sign the consent form. I decided to discontinue observing the Southside program at that point. Fortunately, this incident occurred after I had observed the group sessions for three months and was preparing to stop observing at Southside so that I could instead begin observations in Westview's outpatient program.

I observed group therapy sessions at Southside for three months. At a given time, this group would usually have between eight and ten members. Two different counselors were in charge of the group, each running it on alternate days. Throughout the course of my observing, I encountered approximately thirty different people participating in the group. All of the people in this group session were new to the Southside program, with the exception of one member who had been a patient at the clinic for several years. Most were seeking treatment for heroin dependence, with several indicating that prescription opiates (that is, Oxycodone) was their drug of choice. Several cited polysubstance abuse problems (most often using benzodiazepines like Xanax or Valium and/or cocaine, along with heroin). Participants were expected to attend these group therapy sessions for two to four weeks and then enter the intensive outpatient program. All of the group members also were receiving daily doses of methadone.

The other program I observed was an intensive outpatient program to which I assigned the pseudonym "Westview." One of the defining features of intensive outpatient versus ordinary outpatient is the inclusion of multiple hours of group therapy each week. There were four different groups at Westview. I observed two of these groups; each group met three times a week. In total, I observed these groups for four months. Both groups were designed explicitly for individuals who were *not* receiving methadone as part of treatment. These groups included those who were self-referred to treatment and those referred from the criminal justice system (such as from drug court). According to the program coordinator, approximately half of the group members had been referred into treatment from the criminal justice system. A group session would typically have between seven and ten members and last two and a half hours. Throughout the course of my observations, I encountered about thirty different people participating in the groups at Westview.

While I had explained my role as a researcher to everyone at the treatment facility and all group members had signed consent forms, group members would occasionally confuse me for either another group member or as someone affiliated with the treatment facility. For example, before one group meeting started, a man sitting next to me turned in my direction and asked what drugs I was in treatment for. As I started to explain that I was not in treatment but instead an observer, another group member interjected that I was there doing research. The man who had initially confused me for someone in treatment then nodded that he remembered my role. This incident made me question whether or not I should reintroduce myself at every group meeting to remind those in treatment that I was only an observer. Ultimately, I decided against doing so because it felt like it would be too disruptive, and most of the group members never confused me for someone in treatment. On several other occasions, group members talked to me as if I worked at the facility. At these times, the group members recognized that I was there doing research, but they seemed to think that I was also affiliated with the program in some way, such as a counselor-in-training. These episodes usually involved the group member complaining to me about some aspect of the facility or relating information to me as if I were much more familiar with the facility (and the other counselors) than I was. Despite the occasional confusion about my exact role in the group meetings, I do not feel like my presence impacted these group sessions. The counselors who ran the groups commented to me that the clients acted similarly whether or not I was observing the group on a given day.

To maintain my rapport with the group members and to emphasize that I was not part of the institutional structure, I had to be particularly cautious about my interactions with those working in the programs. For instance, counselors often would try to casually speak to me while I was jotting down notes after a meeting. To avoid seeming like I was affiliated with the facility, I decided to enter and leave just as the clients did. That is, I walked in when other group members walked into the building and I left immediately after the group (even if that meant I had to wait several additional minutes before I could jot down any notes about what I had just observed). While the program coordinator told me I could park in the staff parking lot, I decided I would park on the street when I drove to the facility. Similarly, when I rode my bike, I locked it to one of the poles on the street, just as some of the other clients did. Staff members usually kept their bikes in their offices and

I likely could have parked mine inside the building, but I wanted to try to draw distinctions (however small they might be) between me and the staff members.

My being a young white woman could have contributed to the clients' association of me with the facility since all of the counselors in these programs were white and several also were in their mid- to late twenties. In addition, my social class certainly made me stand out in group meetings. In both the Southside and Westview programs, group members typically had not even completed high school, let alone held a postgraduate degree. Most were unemployed and on some form of public assistance. The neighborhood where the facility was located had one of the highest poverty rates in the city. While the Southside group was racially diverse, groups in Westview were disproportionately African American men and women. This was likely because Southside's methadone maintenance program attracted clients from a wider geographical area, whereas the Westview group members were more likely to come from the surrounding neighborhood. I do not believe that my race, class, gender, or age impacted what occurred at these group meetings, but it is likely that they impacted how the clients perceived me, especially when we interacted before or after group sessions.

INTERVIEWS

While the analyzed field notes from my observations were the bulk of the data I used for this book, I supplemented observations with key interviews in both the drug court and drug treatment programs. From the drug court, I interviewed the assistant public defender, the court evaluator (who assigned new clients to treatment), and Capital City's coordinator of drug treatment initiatives for criminal offenders. These interviews occurred at each person's office. I also interviewed five clients who were enrolled in the court program and one who had completed the program and returned to be a guest speaker at one of the graduations. The interviews with the clients took place at the Westview treatment program (I recruited them while observing group therapy sessions). I approached the drug court alum at the graduation where he spoke and we arranged an interview that took place in his home. These open-ended interviews typically lasted between one and two hours; I tape-recorded and transcribed the interviews verbatim. In addition, the case management supervisor responded in writing to a set of questions I e-mailed her. The judge and the assistant district attorney assigned to the drug court refused my requests for interviews. However, during the time I was observing the court, I came across an interview with the presiding judge of Capital City's drug court on a program of the local National Public Radio station. I transcribed verbatim this one-hour-long interview and included it in my analysis.

I also conducted face-to-face, open-ended interviews with group members and several people working in the Southside and Westview programs. I approached every counselor that I encountered in the group sessions for an interview; all four of them consented. I also interviewed the clinical supervisor of each program. I approached clients and asked to interview them after a group session. I would attempt to schedule the interview for that day or for the time immediately following the next group session, since clients were more likely to participate if they did not have to make a separate trip to the facility for the interview. My selection of group members to approach for an individual interview was rather unscientific. In general, I tried to include a broad range of client characteristics in order to get the most diverse group of interviewees. Therefore, if after one session I approached a male to interview, the next session I would approach a female. I also alternated my interview requests by race (when possible) and how long someone was in treatment. At the Southside clinic, I interviewed eight group members. At the Westview clinic, I also interviewed eight group participants. These interviews were tape-recorded and transcribed verbatim. Each interview lasted between one and two hours.

My role in each setting and my personal characteristics influenced the content and quality of these interviews. As a result, I rely on them differently in different contexts. For instance, while it was extremely helpful to talk with the court staff to learn more about the drug court practices and philosophy, most of them seemed suspicious about my intentions, as if I were evaluating their work or the program. One of those affiliated with the drug court even refused to tell me his educational background; he either interpreted my question as too personal or he did not want to waste time with a question he saw as irrelevant to how the court operated. Even those who were more forthcoming with personal opinions about the drug court program or general drug policy appeared reluctant to say anything negative about drug courts. For these reasons, when I present my analysis of the drug court, I use court observations as evidence more often than data from the interviews.

I had a very different experience conducting interviews with the treatment staff in the Southside and Westview programs. For the most part, these individuals were very open with me about the treatment programs and their impressions of the clients. Nobody seemed to hold back in these interviews and at times shared with me some very negative comments about clients. One therapist even told me that one of the group members was "a liar." These professionals tended to view me as "one of them," possibly because of my race and educational background. All of them also were white and most held advanced degrees in counseling or psychology. While I highlighted the "social distance" between them and the clients and how that led to a sense of mutual distrust (see Chapter 4), the social closeness between them and myself led to my accessing a great deal of private information about how this institution worked. Because of the insights that these interviews provided, I use them quite extensively as evidence when I discuss the treatment programs.

While those in treatment did not seem to alter their behavior when I observed group, I felt that some of them held back some of their true feelings during interviews. Ultimately, I do not believe I was able to shed the impression that I was somehow affiliated with the treatment facility despite my efforts to do so. While these interviews yielded some very useful data, I think that many of the interviewees were hesitant to reveal negative things to me about themselves and their impressions of the treatment programs. This was especially true for the clients participating in drug court. They tended to paint a very positive view of the drug court and drug treatment programs and seemed unwilling to admit to having attitudes or behaviors that could be seen as contradicting the drug court mission. It is not surprising that they would not want to reveal these things to me because of their fear of being sanctioned or possibly thrown out of the program. Because of these barriers, I do not rely very heavily on the client interviews when I present data and evidence for my thesis throughout the book.

DOCUMENT ANALYSIS

My third source of data (besides observations and interviews) comes from documents from Capital City's drug court and the National Association for Drug Court Professionals (NADCP), the main drug court advocacy organization. These texts included brochures, handbooks for new clients, published reports, and items found on their Web sites. In addition, I analyzed PowerPoint slides and handouts from sessions from two annual NADCP conferences that were posted on their Web site. These documents were important for understanding how drug courts conceptualize addiction and drug problems and their own perspective of their work. Capital City's drug court had the distinction of being designated a "model court" by the NADCP. This means that the NADCP encouraged those starting drug courts to look at Capital City's program as a good example. This institutional relationship suggests that the NADCP's very public perspective about addiction and drug courts is shared by those most central to the operations of Capital City's drug court.

DATA ANALYSIS AND PRESENTATION

My strategy for data analysis comes from the "grounded theory" method of collecting data and then examining them for emerging themes. Because I began the study with an exploratory research question, I did not have a theory in mind that I was trying to attach to the data. Similarly, I was open to unexpected findings. This method overlaps with my attempt to produce an institutional ethnography, where data collection and analysis are not completely planned out at the start of the project.

As for how I present the data from observations and interviews, the data from interviews are shown verbatim. Because I did not record the group meetings or drug court sessions, I relied on my own memory to reconstruct what I observed. I recognize that the words I attribute to various individuals may not be the exact ones used. The interviews, however, were tape-recorded and transcribed verbatim, so they represent the actual words that were spoken. I did occasionally omit words or phrases in the interview excerpts to shorten what could at times be very lengthy responses. I use ellipses to designate when I edited out parts of the transcript.

Institutional ethnography attempts to show how social processes reproduce inequality. Researchers who take this approach often are very critical of the institutions they study and see their research as one way to empower those who are oppressed. While my analysis is critical about how drug courts and treatment programs operate, I am not convinced that the participants in my research ultimately benefited more from this project than I did. I earned a doctoral degree because of their willingness to let me into their lives; they did not even get the recognition of their own name in this book. Still, I like to think that the research benefited them in small ways. Many expressed gratitude during our interviews that they had the chance to speak freely about issues that were bothering them. While it is not likely that this book will change large-scale social structures and how they operate, studies like this have the possibility of collectively challenging policy. As more critical analyses about our drug policy are published, those who are truly oppressed by these structures may get the social change they deserve.

Notes

CHAPTER 1

1. A recent commercial for a medication to treat fibromyalgia reminded me of this phenomenon. Marketing of the drug included persuading the viewer that fibromyalgia was a "real" condition that could be effectively treated. Barker (2002) studied how such individuals formed an illness identity in the context of the questionable legitimacy of the medical label for fibromyalgia syndrome.

2. I reluctantly use the term "abuse" throughout this book, recognizing that the word itself carries a moral condemnation. I refer to drug abuse that has been labeled as a clinical disorder as "addiction." I use both abuse and addiction in an effort to be consistent with the nomenclature used by various institutions (i.e., the criminal justice system and the *Diagnostic and Statistical Manual of Mental Disorders,* or *DSM*-IV). By "abuse," I am referring to alcohol and/or drug use that is considered excessive by the individual using the substance, by the larger society, or by some other institution (such as the criminal justice system).

3. Additional survey results support this contradictory view of addiction as both disease and deviance and the inconsistent ways that people define addiction (e.g., Furnham and Thomson 1996; Walters and Gilbert 2000).

4. One example of this would be the recent accounts of celebrities like David Duchovny and Tiger Woods, who reportedly entered residential rehabilitation programs for sex addiction.

5. Howard Becker (1974), largely considered the "father" of the labeling perspective of deviance, cautions that his early works were not to be considered a fully developed *theory* of deviance, but instead a shift in focus or a new perspective for studying deviance. For that reason, I resist the common use of the term "labeling theory" and instead refer to it as a perspective.

CHAPTER 2

1. From NIDA Director Reports, February 2008, available at http://www.drugabuse .gov/DirReports/DirRep208/DirectorReport14.html (accessed January 11, 2010).

2. Several years later there was an additional push to merge the National Institute on Drug Abuse (NIDA) with the National Institute on Alcohol Abuse and Alcoholism (NIAAA), renaming the new institution the "National Institute of Substance Use and Addiction Disorders" (Roan 2011). At the writing of this book, it appeared that the directors of NIDA and NIAAA had decided not to pursue such a merger.

3. For additional critiques of the disease model of addiction, see Davies (1998), Fingarette (1988), and Peele (1989).

4. He was essentially the first federal "drug czar," although that title would not be formally used until 1989.

5. The Obama administration downgraded the drug czar from a cabinet-level position in 2009.

6. According to the Uniform Crime Reports issued by the Federal Bureau of Investigation (FBI), drug abuse violations are defined as "state and/or local offenses relating to the unlawful possession, sale, use, growing, manufacturing, and making of narcotic drugs including opium or cocaine and their derivatives, marijuana, synthetic narcotics, and dangerous nonnarcotic drugs such as barbiturates" (Bureau of Justice Statistics 2006).

7. For a more thorough discussion of the moral panic around crack cocaine in the late 1980s, see Reinarman and Levine (1997).

8. A *Washington Post* columnist would publish a story two weeks later revealing that the "purchase" was actually a setup by drug enforcement officials, who took several weeks to orchestrate the event by luring a drug dealer to the area.

9. The coca plant is used to manufacture cocaine.

10. The budget reports also indicate that the total amount of funding for the treatment and prevention programs included funding for research, thus making the actual amount of money going toward these programs considerably less. There is no such inclusion of "research" funding associated with law enforcement and interdiction tactics.

11. Congress reinstated the ban on federal funding for needle exchange programs in 2011.

12. Several authors have presented convincing arguments that we are in the midst of a moral panic over methamphetamine use (for example, Linneman 2010; Shafer 2005; Weidner 2009). The characteristics of a moral panic are prevalent, with increased media reports about a supposed "epidemic" despite an extremely small number of users, and shocking images of the impact of the drug that include hypersexualized women and the supposed "meth mouth."

CHAPTER 3

Parts of this chapter originally appeared in "Drug Court as Both a Medical and Legal Authority," *Deviant Behavior* 32: 257–291. The journal granted permission to reprint those sections.

1. All names of persons, places, and institutions have been changed to protect their confidentiality.

2. "People, places, and things" are commonly cited as "triggers" for relapsing to alcohol and/or drug use, especially in twelve-step settings.

3. Others have discussed the implication of referring to drug court participants as "clients," rather than another term, like "offender" (Burns and Peyrot 2003; Steen 2002). It is clearly a conscious decision to differentiate the drug court from the traditional court setting and to promote a sense of "helping" within the court setting.

4. The presiding judge of the drug court refused my request to interview him, but I was able to locate and transcribe an hour-long interview from a local radio program that the judge participated in during my observations.

5. In this chapter, the word "drug" is defined as any substance (legal or illegal) that the court considered addictive and monitored its use. The most common drugs that clients used were marijuana, alcohol, opiates (heroin), and cocaine. Similarly, "drug treatment" refers to the formal or informal means that the court staff considered appropriate for handling the client's drug problem. Most often, this included participation in an out-patient drug/alcohol treatment program and attending twelve-step meetings (such as Alcoholics Anonymous or Narcotics Anonymous).

6. An evaluation of this drug court from 1998 to 2000 found that about 47 percent of clients reported marijuana as their primary drug of choice.

CHAPTER 4

1. Southside and Westview are pseudonyms for the actual treatment programs.

2. These figures were obtained from aggregating the 2000 census data in the three census tracts immediately surrounding the facility.

3. Those who indicated a level of drug use that required detoxification would be referred to another treatment facility.

4. A 2010 survey of substance abuse treatment programs nationwide found that 92 percent of outpatient programs used cognitive behavioral therapy (CBT) (SAMHSA 2010a).

5. The Westview Clinic ended its relationship with Capital City's drug court by the fall of 2007. Westview's program supervisor indicated that the number of people referred to Westview from the drug court had been declining over the previous two years, and that it got to the point where it was too much work on their end (such as going to court once a month) for the small number of clients that were being referred to them. When I asked him why he thought that the drug court was referring fewer people to Westview, knowing that in recent years the actual number of people in the court program had increased, he indicated that he thought some of the other treatment programs in the same area of the city were better connected politically to the drug court program, and were therefore receiving more referrals. Westview continued to accept clients from the other criminal justice initiatives that did not require as much additional work for the therapist.

6. "Maintenance" refers to the practice of prescribing methadone to a client for an extended period of time rather than just for detoxification purposes. Methadone suppresses withdrawal symptoms associated with discontinued opiate use and blocks the euphoric effects of opiates.

7. For descriptive purposes, I estimate the ages of the clients and the staff members. These are purely conjecture, however, and are not meant to be used in an analytical way.

8. Stanton Peele is a psychologist who has written at least six books on the topic of addiction. His books are critical of the treatment industry using biological models of addiction and twelve-step practices because they have little empirical evidence to prove their effectiveness. His use of the term "addiction" indicates that he does view it as something

that needs treatment, but insists that the most effective way is a "nondisease approach" (Peele 2008).

9. "Diversion" refers to the illegal selling of methadone by patients who obtained it through a prescription.

10. In the early years of drug courts, drug court judges actively resisted the use of methadone maintenance and in some courts would not permit clients to use it at all (Hora 2005).

11. Federal regulations mandate that those under the age of eighteen cannot be prescribed methadone.

12. Kevin, Westview's program coordinator, was substituting for Jerry and Wendy during this group meeting because both of them were out of the office.

13. While Wendy's analogy implied that addiction was a prize of some sort, I did not observe other therapists using such flip remarks.

14. The serenity prayer is attributed to theologian Reinhold Niebuhr. The first part, which is recited at most twelve-step meetings, reads: "God grant me the serenity to accept the things I cannot change, courage to change the things I can, and wisdom to know the difference."

15. Urging new members to attend ninety meetings in ninety days is standard advice for those new to twelve-step meetings.

16. I found it strange that the group was named "Methadone Anonymous" because the many twelve-step groups that exist (that is, Alcoholics Anonymous, Cocaine Anonymous, Gamblers Anonymous, Debtors Anonymous, and the like) tend to name the main "problem" or addiction that the group focuses on before the word "anonymous." I wonder how using that phrase might impact the stigma of methadone that the group seemingly was trying to combat within the addict community, since its name suggested that methadone is the problem. In addition, not permitting members to discuss medication issues ignored a likely reason why someone taking methadone might seek out such a group.

17. Wendy was referring to the practice where therapists could fill out a request form for an increase in methadone for a particular client. The doctor would review these request forms on a near-daily basis, often approving the request without examining the patient.

CHAPTER 5

1. I am not using the term to suggest that this form of punishment was in any way beneficial to the clients.

2. This was the only day when I observed court that Judge Gallo was not the presiding judge.

CHAPTER 6

Parts of this chapter originally appeared in "The Continuing Expansion of Drug Courts: Is That All There Is?" *Deviant Behavior* 33: 582–588. The journal granted permission to reprint those sections.

1. I calculated the number of research studies by searching for "drug court" or "drug treatment court" in the title of reports housed in the National Criminal Justice Reference Service. The numbers reported in Figure 6.1 likely overestimate the actual number of evaluation studies during that time period because multiple reports could have been produced from the single evaluation of one court. In addition, some of the studies included in the count were not actual evaluation studies, but summarized other research on drug courts.

References

Abide, Marcia, Herbert Richards, and Shula Ramsay. 2001. "Moral Reasoning and Consistency of Belief and Behavior: Decisions about Substance Abuse." *Journal of Drug Education* 31(4): 367–384.

Abt, Vicki, and Martin McGurrin. 1990. "Toward a Social Science of Addiction: A Critical Analysis of the Disease Model of Addictive Gambling." *Sociological Viewpoints* 5: 75–86.

Acharyya, Suddhasatta, and Heping Zhang. 2003. "Assessing Sex Differences on Treatment Effectiveness from the Drug Abuse Treatment Outcome Study (DATOS)." *American Journal of Drug and Alcohol Abuse* 29: 415–444.

Acker, Caroline Jean. 2002. *Creating the American Junkie: Addiction Research in the Classic Era of Narcotic Control.* Baltimore, MD: Johns Hopkins University Press.

Aharon, Itzhak, Nancy Etcoff, Dan Ariely, Christopher Chabris, Ethan O'Connor, and Hans C. Breiter. 2001. "Beautiful Faces Have Variable Reward Value: fMRI and Behavioral Evidence." *Neuron* 32(3): 537–551.

Akers, Ronald. 1992. *Drugs, Alcohol, and Society: Social Structure, Process, and Policy.* Belmont, CA: Wadsworth.

Alcoholism and Drug Abuse Weekly (ADAW). 2001. "CSAT Issues Landmark Methadone Regulations." January 22.

———. 2009. "Criminal Justice and Treatment: An Uneasy Alliance in California." August 24. Available at http://onlinelibrary.wiley.com/doi/10.1002/adaw.v21:33/issuetoc. Accessed February 21, 2012.

Anderson, Tammy, Holly Swan, and David Lane. 2010. "Institutional Fads and the Medicalization of Drug Addiction." *Sociology Compass* 4(7): 476–494.

Anglin, M. Douglas, Barry Brown, Richard Dembo, and Carl Leukefeld. 2009. "Criminality and Addiction: Selected Issues for Future Policies, Practice, and Research." *Journal of Drug Issues* 39(1): 89–99.

Anspach, Donald, and Andrew Ferguson. 2003. *Assessing the Efficacy of Treatment Modalities in the Context of Adult Drug Courts: Final Report.* Portland: University of Southern Maine.

Appleton, Lynn. 1995. "Rethinking Medicalization: Alcoholism and Anomalies." In *Images of Issues: Typifying Contemporary Social Problems*, 2nd ed., edited by Joel Best, 59–80. Hawthorne, NY: Aldine de Gruyter.

Armstrong, David. 1987. "Theoretical Tensions in Biopsychosocial Medicine." *Social Science and Medicine* 25: 1213–1218.

Armstrong, Edward. 2007. "Moral Panic over Meth." *Contemporary Justice Review* 10(4): 427–442.

Aronowitz, Robert A. 1991. "Lyme Disease: The Social Construction of a New Disease and Its Social Consequences." *Milbank Quarterly* 69(1): 79–112.

———. 1992. "From Myalgic Encephalitis to Yuppie Flu: A History of Chronic Fatigue Syndromes." In *Framing Disease: Studies in Cultural History*, edited by Charles Rosenberg and Janet Golden. New Brunswick, NJ: Rutgers University Press.

Ballard, Karen, and Mary Ann Elston. 2005. "Medicalisation: A Multi-Dimensional Concept." *Social Theory and Health* 3: 228–241.

Barker, Kristin. 2002. "Self-Help Literature and the Making of an Illness Identity: The Case of Fibromyalgia Syndrome (FMS)." *Social Problems* 49(3): 279–300.

Bayer, Ronald. 1992. "Introduction: The Great Drug Policy Debate—What Means This Thing Called Decriminalization?" *Milbank Quarterly* 69(3): 341–363.

Becker, Howard. 1963. *Outsiders: Studies in the Sociology of Deviance*. New York: Free Press.

———. 1974. "Labeling Theory Reconsidered." *Deviance and Social Control* 3: 41–76.

Beckerman, Adela, and Leonard Fontana. 2001. "Issues of Race and Gender in Court-Ordered Substance Abuse Treatment." In *Drug Courts in Operation: Current Research*, edited by James J. Hennessy and Nathaniel J. Pallone, 45–62. Binghamton, NY: Haworth Press.

Beckett, Katherine, Kris Nyrop, and Lori Pfingst. 2006. "Race, Drugs, and Policing: Understanding Disparities in Drug Delivery Arrests." *Criminology* 44(1): 105–137.

Beckett, Katherine, Kris Nyrop, Lori Pfingst, and Melissa Bowen. 2005. "Drug Use, Drug Possession Arrests, and the Question of Race: Lessons from Seattle." *Social Problems* 52(3): 419–441.

Begley, Sharon. 2004. "Scans of Monks' Brains Show Meditation Alters Structure, Functioning." *Wall Street Journal*, November 5. Available at http://psyphz.psych.wisc.edu /web/News/Meditation_Alters_Brain_WSJ_11-04.htm. Accessed October 3, 2012.

Belenko, Steven. 1998. "Research on Drug Courts: A Critical Review." *National Drug Court Institute Review* 1(1): 1–42.

———. 2002. "The Challenges of Conducting Research in Drug Treatment Court Settings." *Substance Use and Misuse* 37(12–13): 1635–1664.

Ben-Yehuda, Nachman. 2009. "Moral Panics—36 Years On." *British Journal of Criminology* 49: 1–3.

Berger, Peter, and Thomas Luckmann. 1966. *The Social Construction of Reality: A Treatise in the Sociology of Knowledge*. New York: Anchor Books.

Best, Joel. 2004. *Deviance: Career of a Concept*. Belmont, CA: Thomson Wadsworth.

BJA Drug Court Clearinghouse Project. 2006. "Summary of Drug Court Activity by State and County." Washington, DC: Justice Programs Office, School of Public Affairs, American University. Available at http://spa.american.edu/justice/map.php.

Blackwell, Judith Stephenson. 1983. "Drifting, Controlling and Overcoming: Opiate Users Who Avoid Becoming Chronically Dependent." *Journal of Drug Issues* 13: 219–235.

Blakeslee, Sandra. 2002. "Hijacking the Brain Circuits with a Nickel Slot Machine." *New York Times*, February 19.

Bobo, Lawrence D., and Victor Thompson. 2006. "Unfair by Design: The War on Drugs, Race, and the Legitimacy of the Criminal Justice System." *Social Research* 73(2): 445–472.

Boldt, Richard C. 2002. "The Adversary System and Attorney Role in the Drug Treatment Court Movement." In *Drug Courts in Theory and in Practice*, edited by James L. Nolan Jr., 115–144. New York: Aldine de Gruyter.

Bourgois, Philippe. 1997. "In Search of Horatio Alger: Culture and Ideology in the Crack Economy." In *Crack in America: Demon Drugs and Social Justice*, edited by Craig Reinarman and Harry G. Levine, 57–76. Berkeley: University of California Press.

———. 2000. "Disciplining Addictions: The Bio-Politics of Methadone and Heroin in the United States." *Culture, Medicine and Psychiatry* 24: 165–195.

Bowers, Josh. 2008. "Contraindicated Drug Courts." *UCLA Law Review* 55: 783–835.

Boyd, Susan C. 2004. *From Witches to Crack Moms: Women, Drug Law, and Policy.* Durham, NC: Carolina Academic Press.

Boyum, David, and Peter Reuter. 2001. "Reflections on Drug Policy and Social Policy." In *Drug Addiction and Drug Policy*, edited by Philip Heymann and William Brownsberger, 239–264. Cambridge, MA: Harvard University Press.

Braithwaite, John. 1989. *Crime, Shame, and Reintegration.* New York: Cambridge University Press.

———. 2000. "Shame and Criminal Justice." *Canadian Journal of Criminology* 42: 281–298.

Brecher, Edward M. 1972. *Licit and Illicit Drugs.* Boston: Little, Brown.

Brecht, Mary-Lynn, M. Douglas Anglin, and Michelle Dylan. 2005. "Coerced Treatment for Methamphetamine Abuse: Differential Patient Characteristics and Outcomes." *American Journal of Drug and Alcohol Abuse* 31: 337–356.

Brecht, Mary-Lynn, M. Douglas Anglin, and Jung-Chi Wang. 1993. "Treatment Effectiveness for Legally Coerced vs. Voluntary Methadone Maintenance Clients." *American Journal of Drug and Alcohol Abuse* 19(1): 89–106.

Broadus, Angela, Joyce Hartje, Nancy Roget, Kristy Cahoon, and Samantha Clinkinbeard. 2010. "Attitudes about Addiction: A National Study of Addiction Educators." *Journal of Drug Education* 40(3): 281–298.

Brownsberger, William. 1997. "Prevalence of Frequent Cocaine Use in Urban Poverty Areas." *Contemporary Drug Problems* 24: 349–371.

Buchanan, David, Susan Shaw, Amy Ford, and Merrill Singer. 2003. "Empirical Science Meets Moral Panic: An Analysis of the Politics of Needle Exchange." *Journal of Public Health Policy* 24: 427–444.

Bufe, Charles. 1998. *Alcoholics Anonymous: Cult or Cure?* Tucson, AZ: See Sharp Press.

Bureau of Justice Statistics. 2006. "Drugs and Crime." Available at http://ojp.usdoj.gov/bjs/. Accessed September 20, 2007.

Burke, Anna Celeste. 1992. "Between Entitlement and Control: Dimensions of U.S. Drug Policy." *Social Service Review* 66(4): 571–581.

Burke, Anna, and Thomas Gregoire. 2007. "Substance Abuse Treatment Outcomes for Coerced and Noncoerced Clients." *Health and Social Work* 32(1): 7–15.

Burns, Stacy Lee, and Mark Peyrot. 2003. "Tough Love: Nurturing and Coercing Responsibility and Recovery in California Drug Courts." *Social Problems* 50(3): 416–438.

Burrows, Cassandra. 2010. "C.R.A.C.K. Program—Personal Empowerment or Control of Certain Populations?" National Advocates for Pregnant Women, May 3. Available at http://advocatesforpregnantwomen.org/blog/2010/05/crack_program_personal _empower.php. Accessed December 1, 2012.

Bushway, Shawn, and Peter Reuter. 2011. "Deterrence, Economics, and the Context of Drug Markets." *Criminology and Public Policy* 10(1): 183–194.

Campbell, Marie L. 2010. "Institutional Ethnography." In *Qualitative Methods in Health Research*, edited by Ivy Bourgeault, Robert Dingwall, and Raymond DeVries, 497–512. Los Angeles: Sage.

Campbell, Nancy D. 2006. "A New Deal for the Drug Addict: The Addiction Research Center, Lexington, Kentucky." *Journal of the History of the Behavioral Sciences* 42: 135–157.

———. 2007. *Discovering Addiction: The Science and Politics of Substance Abuse Research.* Ann Arbor: University of Michigan Press.

Campbell, Nancy D., J. P. Olsen, and Luke Walden. 2008. *The Narcotic Farm: The Rise and Fall of America's First Prison for Drug Addicts.* New York: Abrams.

Carey, Shannon, Michael Finigan, Dave Crumpton, and Mark Wailer. 2006. "California Drug Courts: Outcomes, Costs and Promising Practices: An Overview of Phase II in a Statewide Study." *Journal of Psychoactive Drugs* 38: 345–356.

Caulkins, Jonathan, and Philip Heymann. 2001. "How Should Low-Level Drug Dealers Be Punished?" In *Drug Addiction and Drug Policy*, edited by Philip Heymann and William Brownsberger, 206–238. Cambridge, MA: Harvard University Press.

Caulkins, Jonathan, and Peter Reuter. 2006. "Reorienting U.S. Drug Policy." *Issues in Science and Technology* 23(1): 79–85.

Center for Health and Justice at TASC. 2007. "Brief Overview." Available at http://www.centerforhealthandjustice.org/BOPublicSupportforTreatment_October07.pdf. Accessed January 15, 2008.

Chambliss, William J. 1973. "The Saints and the Roughnecks." *Society* 11(1): 23–31.

Chavigny, Katherine. 2004. "Reforming Drunkards in Nineteenth-Century America." In *Altering American Consciousness: The History of Alcohol and Drug Use in the United States, 1800–2000,* edited by Sarah Tracy and Joan Acker. Boston: University of Massachusetts Press.

Cheung, Yuet W., Patricia G. Erickson, and Tammy C. Landau. 1991. "Experience of Crack Use: Findings from a Community-Based Sample in Toronto." *Journal of Drug Issues* 21: 121–140.

Chriss, James J. 2002. "The Drug Court Movement: An Analysis of Tacit Assumptions." In *Drug Courts in Theory and in Practice*, edited by James L. Nolan Jr., 189–214. New York: Aldine de Gruyter.

Cohen, Eric, and Gerald Stahler. 1998. "Life Histories of Crack-Using African-American Homeless Men: Salient Themes." *Contemporary Drug Problems* 25: 373–397.

Cohen, Mark, Roland Rust, and Sarah Steen. 2006. "Prevention, Crime Control or Cash? Public Preferences towards Criminal Justice Spending Priorities." *Justice Quarterly* 23(3): 317–334.

Cohen, Stanley. 1972. *Folk Devils and Moral Panics: The Creation of the Mods and Rockers.* London: McGibbon and Kee.

Conner, Kyaien O., and Daniel Rosen. 2008. "'You're Nothing but a Junkie': Multiple Experiences of Stigma in an Aging Methadone Maintenance Population." *Journal of Social Work Practice in the Addictions* 8(2): 244–264.

Conner, Kyaien O., Daniel Rosen, Sandra Wexle, and Charlotte Brown. 2010. "'It's Like Night and Day. He's White, I'm Black': Shared Stigmas between Counselors and Older Adult Methadone Clients." *Best Practice in Mental Health* 6(1): 17–30.

Conrad, Peter. 1975. "The Discovery of Hyperkinesis: Notes on the Medicalization of Deviant Behavior." *Social Problems* 23: 12–21.

———. 1992. "Medicalization and Social Control." *Annual Review of Sociology* 18: 209–232.

———. 2000. "Medicalization, Genetics, and Human Problems." In *Handbook of Medical Sociology*, 5th ed., edited by Chloe Bird, Peter Conrad, and Allen Fremont, 322–333. Upper Saddle River, NJ: Prentice Hall.

———. 2007. *The Medicalization of Society: On the Transformation of Human Conditions into Treatable Disorders*. Baltimore, MD: Johns Hopkins University Press.

Conrad, Peter, and Joseph Schneider. (1980) 1999. *Deviance and Medicalization: From Badness to Sickness*. Philadelphia, PA: Temple University Press.

Cooper, Caroline. 2007. "Drug Courts—Just the Beginning: Getting Other Areas of Public Policy in Sync." *Substance Use and Misuse* 42: 243–256.

Coordinating Office of Drug Abuse and Alcohol Programs (CODAAP). 2007. Available at http://www.phila.gov/health/units/codaap/.

Corrigan, Patrick W., Sachiko Kuwabara, and John O'Shaughnessy. 2009. "The Public Stigma of Mental Illness and Drug Addiction." *Journal of Social Work* 9(2): 139–147.

Courtwright, David. 2001. *Dark Paradise: A History of Opiate Addiction in America*. Cambridge, MA: Harvard University Press.

———. 2010. "The NIDA Brain Disease Paradigm: History, Resistance and Spinoffs." *BioSocieties* 5(1): 137–147.

Cullen, Francis T., Bonnie S. Fisher, and Brandon K. Applegate. 2000. "Public Opinion about Punishment and Corrections." *Crime and Justice* 27: 1–79.

Cummings, Nicholas. 1991. "Inpatient versus Outpatient Treatment of Substance Abuse: Recent Developments in the Controversy." *Contemporary Family Therapy* 13(5): 507–520.

Daniels, Tatiana Starr. 2012. "What Influences Some Black Males to Sell Drugs during Their Adolescence?" *McNair Scholar Journal* 19: 21–39.

Davenport-Hines, Richard. 2002. *The Pursuit of Oblivion: A Global History of Narcotics*. New York: W. W. Norton.

Davies, John Booth. 1998. *The Myth of Addiction: An Application of the Psychological Theory of Attribution to Illicit Drug Use*. 2nd ed. New York: Routledge.

DeLeon, George. 2000. *The Therapeutic Community: Theory, Model and Method*. New York: Springer.

Demuth, Stephen, and Darrell Steffensmeier. 2004. "Ethnicity Effects on Sentence Outcomes in Large Urban Courts: Comparisons among White, Black and Hispanic Defendants." *Social Science Quarterly* 85(4): 994–1011.

DeVault, Marjorie. 2006. "Introduction: What Is Institutional Ethnography?" *Social Problems* 53(3): 294–298.

DeVault, Marjorie, and Liza McCoy. 2006. "Institutional Ethnography: Using Interviews to Investigate Ruling Relations." In *Institutional Ethnography as Practice*, edited by Dorothy Smith, 15–44. New York: Rowman and Littlefield.

Dohan, Daniel. 2003. *The Price of Poverty*. Berkeley and Los Angeles: University of California Press.

Drug Policy Alliance. 2011. *Drug Courts Are Not the Answer: Toward a Health-Centered Approach to Drug Use*. New York: Drug Policy Alliance Headquarters.

Duckworth, Kenneth, John Halpern, Russell Schutt, and Christopher Gillespie. 2003. "Use of Schizophrenia as a Metaphor in U.S. Newspapers." *Psychiatric Services* 54(10): 1402–1404.

DuPont, Robert L. 2009. "Reflections on the Early History of National Institute on Drug Abuse (NIDA): Implications for Today." *Journal of Drug Issues* 39(1): 5–14.

Duster, Troy. 1970. *The Legislation of Morality: Law, Drugs and Moral Judgment*. New York: Free Press.

Epstein, Steven. 1996. *Impure Science: AIDS, Activism, and the Politics of Knowledge.* Berkeley: University of California Press.

Farabee, David, Michael Prendergast, and M. Douglas Anglin. 1998. "The Effectiveness of Coerced Treatment for Drug-Abusing Offenders." *Federal Probation* 62(1): 3–21.

Faupel, Charles, Alan Horowitz, and Greg Weaver. 2004. *The Sociology of American Drug Use.* Boston: McGraw Hill.

Fielding, Jonathan, Grace Tye, Patrick Ogawa, Iraj Imam, and Anna Long. 2002. "Los Angeles County Drug Court Programs: Initial Results." *Journal of Substance Abuse Treatment* 23(3): 217–224.

Fingarette, Henry. 1988. *Heavy Drinking: The Myth of Alcoholism as a Disease.* Berkeley: University of California Press.

Finigan, Michael, and Shannon Carey. 2001. *Analysis of 26 Drug Courts: Lessons Learned.* Portland, OR: NPC Research.

Fiorentine, Robert, and Maureen P. Hillhouse. 1999. "Drug Treatment Effectiveness and Client-Counselor Empathy: Exploring the Effects of Gender and Ethnic Congruency." *Journal of Drug Issues* 29(1): 59–74.

Fischer, Benedikt. 2003. "Doing Good with a Vengeance: A Critical Assessment of the Practices, Effects and Implications of Drug Treatment Courts in North America." *Criminal Justice* 3(3): 227–248.

Fletcher, Bennett W., and Redonna Chandler. 2006. *Principles of Drug Abuse Treatment for Criminal Justice Populations.* Washington, DC: National Institute on Drug Abuse, National Institutes of Health, U.S. Department of Health and Human Services.

Fox, Renee. 1977. "The Medicalization and Demedicalization of American Society." *Daedalus* 106: 9–22.

———. 1989. *The Sociology of Medicine: A Participant Observer's View.* Englewood Cliffs, NJ: Prentice Hall.

Frank, David. 2011. "The Trouble with Morality: The Effects of 12-Step Discourse on Addicts' Decision-Making." *Journal of Psychoactive Drugs* 43(3): 245–256.

Freed, Christopher. 2010. "Addiction Medicine and Addiction Psychiatry in America: Commonalities in the Medical Treatment of Addiction." *Contemporary Drug Problems* 37: 139–163.

Freidson, Eliot. 1970. *Profession of Medicine: A Study of the Sociology of Applied Knowledge.* New York: Dodd, Mead.

———. 1989. *Medical Work in America: Essays on Health Care.* New Haven, CT: Yale University Press.

Fulkerson, Andrew. 2009. "The Drug Treatment Court as a Form of Restorative Justice." *Contemporary Justice Review* 12(3): 253–267.

Furnham, Adrian, and Louise Thomson. 1996. "Lay Theories of Heroin Addiction." *Social Science and Medicine* 43(1): 29–40.

Furst, R. Terry, Bruce Johnson, Eloise Dunlap, and Richard Curtis. 1999. "The Stigmatized Image of the 'Crack Head': A Sociocultural Exploration of a Barrier to Cocaine Smoking among a Cohort of Youth in New York City." *Deviant Behavior* 20(2): 153–181.

Garland, David. 2001. *The Culture of Control: Crime and Social Order in Contemporary Society.* New York: Oxford University Press.

Gassman, Ruth A and Constance Weisner. 2005. "Community Providers' Views of Alcohol Problems and Drug Problems." *Journal of Social Work Practice in the Addictions* 5(4): 101–115.

Gerstein, Dean R., and Lawrence S. Lewin. 1990. "Treating Drug Problems." *New England Journal of Medicine* 323(12): 844–848.

Gfroerer, Joseph, and Marc Brodsky. 1992. "The Incidence of Illicit Drug Use in the United States, 1962–1989." *British Journal of Addiction* 87: 1345–1351.

Glaser, Barney, and Anselm Strauss. 1967. *The Discovery of Grounded Theory: Strategies for Qualitative Research.* Hawthorne, NY: Aldine de Gruyter.

Goerdt, John, and John Martin. 1989. "The Impact of Drug Cases on Case Processing in Urban Trial Courts." *State Court Journal* 13(4): 4–12.

Goffman, Erving. 1959. *The Presentation of Self in Everyday Life.* New York: Anchor Books.

———. 1963. *Stigma: Notes on the Management of Spoiled Identity.* New York: Simon and Schuster.

Goldberg, Peter. 1980. *The Federal Government's Response to Illicit Drugs, 1969–1978.* Drug Abuse Council. Available at www.druglibrary.org/schaffer/library/studies/fada/fada1.htm. Accessed January 23, 2008.

Goldkamp, John S. 1999. "Challenges for Research and Innovation: When Is a Drug Court Not a Drug Court?" In *The Early Drug Courts: Case Studies in Judicial Innovation,* edited by W. Clinton Terry III, 166–177. Thousand Oaks, CA: Sage.

Goldkamp, John S., Michael D. White, and Jennifer B. Robinson. 2001. "Do Drug Courts Work? Getting Inside the Drug Court Black Box." *Journal of Drug Issues* 31(1): 27–72.

Golub, Andrew, and Bruce D. Johnson. 2001. "Substance Use Progression and Hard Drug Abuse in Inner-City New York." In *Stages and Pathways of Involvement in Drug Use: Examining the Gateway Hypothesis,* edited by Denise Kandel, 90–112. New York: Cambridge University Press.

———. 2002. "The Misuse of the 'Gateway Theory' in U.S. Policy on Drug Abuse Control: A Secondary Analysis of the Muddled Deduction." *International Journal of Drug Policy* 13: 5–19.

Goode, Erich. 2008. *Drugs in American Society.* 7th ed. New York: McGraw-Hill.

Goode, Erich, and Nachman Ben-Yehuda. 1994. "Moral Panics: Culture, Politics and Social Construction." *Annual Review of Sociology* 20: 149–171.

Gossop, Michael. 2003. *Drug Addiction and Its Treatment.* New York: Oxford University Press.

Gottfredson, Denise, and M. Lyn Exum. 2000. *The Baltimore City Drug Treatment Court: First Evaluation Report.* College Park: University of Maryland, Department of Criminology and Criminal Justice.

Gourlay, Jane, Lina Ricciardelli, and Damien Ridge. 2005. "Users' Experiences of Heroin and Methadone Treatment." *Substance Use and Misuse* 40: 1875–1882.

Gove, Walter R. 1982. "The Current Status of the Labeling Theory of Mental Illness." In *Deviance and Mental Illness,* edited by Walter R. Gove, 273–300. Beverly Hills, CA: Sage.

Government Accountability Office (GAO). 2005. *Adult Drug Courts: Evidence Indicates Recidivism Reductions and Mixed Results for Other Outcomes.* Washington, DC: U.S. Government Accountability Office.

Grattet, Ryken. 2011. "Societal Reactions to Deviance." *Annual Review of Sociology* 37: 185–204.

Gross. 2010. "Effects of Net-Widening on Minority and Indigent Drug Offenders: A Critique of Drug Courts." The *University of Maryland Legal Journal Race, Religion, Gender and Class* 10: 161–178.

Haney, Lynne. 2010. *Offending Women: Power, Punishment, and the Regulation of Desire.* Berkeley: University of California Press.

Harrison, Lana. 1995. "The Validity of Self-Reported Data on Drug Use." *Journal of Drug Issues* 25: 91–111.

Hartley, Roger, and Randy Phillips. 2001. "Who Graduates from Drug Courts? Correlates of Client Success." *American Journal of Criminal Justice* 26(1): 107–119.

Hawdon, James. 2001. "The Role of Presidential Rhetoric in the Creation of a Moral Panic: Reagan, Bush, and the War on Drugs." *Deviant Behavior* 22: 419–445.

HBO Studios. 1996. "Do Drugs Cause Addiction?" Debatesdebates episode 113, August 26.

Hennessy, James J. 2001. "Introduction: Drug Courts in Operation." In *Drug Courts in Operation: Current Research,* edited by James J. Hennessy and Nathaniel J. Pallone, 1–10. Binghamton, NY: Haworth Press.

Herbert, Keith, and Julie Shaw. "Drug Courts Are Battling Addictions behind Crime." *Philadelphia Inquirer,* January 2, 2007, A1.

Heyman, Gene. 2001. "Is Addiction a Chronic, Relapsing Disease?" In *Drug Addiction and Drug Policy,* edited by Philip Heymann and William Brownsberger, 81–117. Cambridge, MA: Harvard University Press.

Hickman, Timothy. 2000. "Drugs and Race in American Culture: Orientalism in the Turn-of-the-Century Discourse of Narcotic Addiction." *American Studies* 41(1): 71–91.

Hiller, Matthew, Kevin Knight, Kirk Broome, and D. Dwayne Stimpson. 1998. "Legal Pressure and Treatment Retention: A National Sample of Long-Term Residential Programs." *Criminal Justice and Behavior* 25(4): 463–481.

Hoffman, Lisa, and Brian Coffey. 2008. "Dignity and Indignation: How People Experiencing Homelessness View Services and Providers." *Social Science Journal* 45: 207–222.

Hoffman, Morris B. 2000. "The Drug Court Scandal." *North Carolina Law Review* 78: 1437–1534.

———. 2002. "The Denver Drug Court and Its Unintended Consequences." In *Drug Courts in Theory and in Practice,* edited by James L. Nolan Jr., 67–88. New York: Aldine de Gruyter.

Holliday, Adrian. 2002. *Doing and Writing Qualitative Research.* Thousand Oaks, CA: Sage.

Holt, Martin. 2007. "Agency and Dependency within Treatment: Drug Treatment Clients Negotiating Methadone and Antidepressants." *Social Science and Medicine* 64: 1937–1947.

Hora, Peggy. 2002. "A Dozen Years of Drug Treatment Courts: Uncovering Our Theoretical Foundation and the Construction of a Mainstream Paradigm." *Substance Use and Misuse* 37: 1469–1488.

———. 2005. "Trading One Drug for Another? What Drug Treatment Court Professionals Need to Learn about Opioid Replacement Therapy." *Journal of Maintenance in the Addictions* 2(4): 71–76.

Horwitz, Allan. 1982. *The Social Control of Mental Illness.* New York: Academic Press.

Howard, Daniel, and William McCaughrin. 1996. "The Treatment Effectiveness of Outpatient Substance Misuse Organizations between Court-Mandated and Voluntary Clients." *Substance Use and Misuse* 31(7): 895–926.

Howard, Jenna. 2006. "Expecting and Accepting: The Temporal Ambiguity of Recovery Identities." *Social Psychology Quarterly* 69(4): 307–323.

Hser, Yih-Ing, M. Douglas Anglin, Christine Grella, Douglas Longshore, and Michael Prendergast. 1997. "Drug Treatment Careers: A Conceptual Framework and Existing Research Findings." *Journal of Substance Abuse Treatment* 14(6): 543–558.

Hubbard, R., S. Craddock, and J. Anderson. 2003. "Overview of Five-Year Follow-Up Outcomes in the Drug Abuse Treatment Outcome Studies (DATOS)." *Journal of Substance Abuse Treatment* 25(3): 125–134.

Humphries, Drew. 1999. *Crack Mothers: Pregnancy, Drugs, and the Media*. Columbus: Ohio State University Press.

Hunt, Dana E., Douglas S. Lipton, Douglas S. Goldsmith, David L. Strug, and Barry Spunt. 1986. "'It Takes Your Heart': The Image of Methadone Maintenance in the Addict World and Its Effect on Recruitment into Treatment." *International Journal of the Addictions* 20(11–12): 1751–1771.

Inciardi, James, and Steven Martin. 1993. "Drug Abuse Treatment in Criminal Justice Settings." *Journal of Drug Issues* 23: 1–6.

Inciardi, James, and Duane McBride. 1991. *Treatment Alternatives to Street Crime: History, Experiences, and Issues*. Washington, DC: National Institute on Drug Abuse, U.S. Department of Health and Human Services.

Jabr, Ferris. 2011. "Cache Cab: Taxi Drivers' Brains Grow to Navigate London's Streets." *Scientific American*, December 8. Available at http://www.scientificamerican.com /article.cfm?id=london-taxi-memory. Accessed October 3, 2012.

Jellinek, Elvin Morton. 1960. *The Disease Concept of Alcoholism*. New Brunswick, NJ: Hillhouse.

Jernigan, David, and Lori Dorfman. 1996. "Visualizing America's Drug Problems: An Ethnographic Content Analysis of Illegal Drug Stories on the Nightly News." *Contemporary Drug Problems* 23: 169–196.

Johnson, John, and Linda Waletzko. 1992. "Drugs and Crime: A Study in the Medicalization of Crime Control." In *Perspectives on Social Problems*, vol. 3, edited by James Holstein and Gale Miller, 197–219. Greenwich, CT: JAI.

Johnson, Kevin. 2012. "Prisoners Face Long Wait for Drug-Rehab Services." *USA Today*, December 4.

Jones, Rachel, and Ye Luo. 1999. "The Culture of Poverty and African-American Culture: An Empirical Assessment." *Sociological Perspectives* 42(3): 439–458.

Kakade, Meghana, Cristiane Duarte, Xinhua Liu, Cordelia Fuller, Ernest Drucker, Christina Hoven, Bin Fan, and Ping Wu. 2012. "Adolescent Substance Use and Other Illegal Behaviors and Racial Disparities in Criminal Justice System Involvement: Findings from a U.S. National Survey." *American Journal of Public Health* 102(7): 1307–1310.

Kalkhoff, Will, Kristina Djurich, and Jessica Burke. 2007. "Relational Distance and the Acceptance of Mental Health Evaluations: A Social Influence Approach to Deviant Labeling." *Sociological Perspectives* 50(4): 493–516.

Katz, Michael B. 1989. *The Undeserving Poor: From the War on Poverty to the War on Welfare*. New York: Pantheon.

Kelly, John, Sarah Dow, and Cara Westerhoff. 2010. "Does Our Choice of Substance-Related Terms Influence Perceptions of Treatment Need? An Empirical Investigation with Two Commonly Used Terms." *Journal of Drug Issues* 40(4): 805–818.

Kennedy, Bernice, Christopher Mathis, and Angela Woods. 2007. "African Americans and Their Distrust of the Health Care System: Healthcare for Diverse Populations." *Journal of Cultural Diversity* 14: 56–60.

Kennedy, Joseph. 2003. "Drug Wars in Black and White." *Law and Contemporary Problems* 66(3): 153–181.

King, Ryan S. 2008. *Disparity by Geography: The War on Drugs in America's Cities*. Sentencing Project, Washington DC. Available at http://www.sentencingproject.org /Admin/Documents/publications/dp_drugarrestreport.pdf. Accessed May 29, 2008.

King, Ryan, and Jill Pasquarella. 2009. *Drug Courts: A Review of the Evidence*. Sentencing Project, Washington, DC. Available at http://www.sentencingproject.org/doc/dp _drugcourts.pdf. Accessed February 6, 2012.

Kleiman, Mark A. R. 2001. "Controlling Drug Use and Crime with Testing, Sanctions, and Treatment." In *Drug Addiction and Drug Policy*, edited by Philip Heymann and William Brownsberger, 168–192. Cambridge, MA: Harvard University Press.

Klein, Barry. 1989. "Treatment Is Often the Sentence in Dade's Drug Court." *St. Petersburg Times*, August 6, A1.

Klypchak, Brad. 2012. "How You Gonna See Me Now: Recontextualizing Metal Artists and Moral Panics." *Popular Music History* 6: 38–51.

Knudsen, Hannah, Lori Ducharme, and Paul Roman. 2006. "Counselor Emotional Exhaustion and Turnover Intention in Therapeutic Communities." *Journal of Substance Abuse Treatment* 31: 173–180.

Knudsen, Hannah, Lori Ducharme, Paul M. Roman, and Tanja Link. 2005. "Buprenorphine Diffusion: The Attitudes of Substance Abuse Treatment Counselors." *Journal of Substance Abuse Treatment* 29: 95–106.

Kobak, Marianne. 2007. "Judge Leads Local War on Meth." Elko Daily Free Press, February 27. Available at http://elkodaily.com/news/local/judge-leads-local-war-on-meth/article_c91ead8d-ddaf-5ae6-8bba-e7b96d26cd3d.html. Accessed January 20, 2013.

Kohler-Hausmann, Julilly. 2010. "'The Attila the Hun Law': New York's Rockefeller Drug Laws and the Making of a Punitive State." *Journal of Social History* 44(1): 71–95.

Kramer, Ronald. 2010. "Moral Panics and Urban Growth Machines: Official Reactions to Graffiti in New York City, 1990–2005." *Qualitative Sociology* 33(3): 297–311.

Krinsky, Charles. 2008. *Moral Panics over Contemporary Children and Childhood*. London: Ashgate.

Lawson, Kenneth A., Richard E. Wilcox, John H. Littlefield, Keenan A. Pituch, and Carlton K. Erickson. 2004. "Educating Treatment Professionals about Addiction Science Research: Demographics of Knowledge and Belief Changes." *Substance Use and Misuse* 39(8): 1235–1258.

Leacock, Eleanor Burke. 1971. *The Culture of Poverty: A Critique*. New York: Simon and Schuster.

Lee, Shirley, and Avis Mysyk. 2004. "The Medicalization of Compulsive Buying." *Social Science and Medicine* 58(9): 1709–1718.

Leifer, Ronald. 1990. "Introduction: The Medical Model as the Ideology of the Therapeutic State." *Journal of Mind and Behavior* 11(3–4): 247–258.

Lemanski, Michael. 2001. *A History of Addiction and Recovery in the United States*. Tucson, AZ: Sharp.

Lender, Mark Edward, and James Kirby Martin. 1987. *Drinking in America: A History*. New York: Free Press.

Lewis, David C. 1992. "Medical and Health Perspectives on a Failing U.S. Drug Policy." *Daedalus* 121(3): 165–194.

Lewis, Marc. 2012. "Why Addiction Is NOT A Brain Disease." PLOS Blog, November 12, 2012. Available at http://blogs.plos.org/mindthebrain/2012/11/12/why-addiction-is-not-a-brain-disease/. Accessed November 27, 2012.

Li, Li, and Dennis Moore. 2001. "Disability and Illicit Drug Use: An Application of Labeling Theory." *Deviant Behavior* 22(1): 1–21.

Lindesmith, Alfred. 1965. *The Addict and the Law*. Bloomington: Indiana University Press.

Lindquist, Christine H., Christopher P. Krebs, and Pamela K. Lattimore. 2006. "Sanctions and Rewards in Drug Court Programs: Implementation, Perceived Efficacy, and Decision Making." *Journal of Drug Issues* 36(1): 119–146.

Link, Bruce. 1987. "Understanding Labeling Effects in the Area of Mental Disorders: An Assessment of the Effects of Expectations of Rejection." *American Sociological Review* 52: 96–112.

Link, Bruce, Francis Cullen, Elmer Struening, Patrick Shrout, and Bruce Dohrenwend. 1989. "A Modified Labeling Theory Approach to Mental Disorders: An Empirical Assessment." *American Sociological Review* 54: 400–423.

Link, Bruce, and Jo Phelan. 2001. "Conceptualizing Stigma." *Annual Review of Sociology* 27: 363–385.

Linneman, Travis. 2010. "Mad Men, Meth Moms, Moral Panic: Gendering Meth Crimes in the Midwest." *Critical Criminology* 18(2): 95–110.

Lock, Eric, Jeffrey Timberlake, and Kenneth Rasinski. 2002. "Battle Fatigue: Is Public Support Waning for 'War'-Centered Drug Control Strategies?" *Crime and Delinquency* 48: 380–398.

Loring, Marti, and Brian Powell. 1988. "Gender, Race, and *DSM*-III: A Study of the Objectivity of Psychiatric Diagnostic Behavior." *Journal of Health and Social Behavior* 29: 1–22.

Lowenkamp, Christopher, Alexander Holsinger, and Edward Latessa. 2005. "Are Drug Courts Effective? A Meta-Analytic Review." *Journal of Community Corrections* Fall: 5–10, 28.

Mack, Avram H., and Richard J. Frances. 2003. "Substance-Related Disorders." *Focus* 1(2): 125–127.

Mackinem, Mitchell, and Paul Higgins. 2008. *Drug Court: Constructing the Moral Identity of Drug Offenders*. Springfield, IL: Charles C. Thomas.

"Managed Care Not Stepping Up to Cover Methadone Treatment." 2000. *Alcoholism and Drug Abuse Weekly* 12 (April 24): 17.

Manning, Peter K. 1970. "Talking and Becoming: A View of Organizational Socialization." In *Understanding Everyday Life: Toward the Reconstruction of Sociological Knowledge*, edited by Jack Douglas, 239–256. Chicago: Aldine.

Marijuana Anonymous. 2001. "Life with Hope: A Return to Living through the Twelve Steps and Twelve Traditions of Marijuana Anonymous." Available at http://www .marijuana-anonymous.org/excerpts.shtml. Accessed August 30, 2009.

Markens, Susan. 1996. "The Problematic of 'Experience': A Political and Cultural Critique of PMS." *Gender and Society* 10(1): 42–58.

Markowitz, Fred E. 1998. "The Effects of Stigma on the Psychological Well-Being and Life Satisfaction of Persons with Mental Illness." *Journal of Health and Social Behavior* 39: 335–348.

Markowitz, Fred, Beth Angell, and Jan Greenberg. 2011. "Stigma, Reflected Appraisals, and Recovery Outcomes in Mental Illness." *Social Psychology Quarterly* 74(2): 144–165.

Marlowe, Douglas. 2010. *Research Update on Adult Drug Courts*. Washington, DC: National Association of Drug Court Professionals. Available at http://www.nadcp.org /sites/default/files/nadcp/Research%20Update%20on%20Adult%20Drug%20 Courts%20-%20NADCP_1.pdf. Accessed February 21, 2012.

Marlowe, Douglas, David Festinger, Karen Dugosh, Patricia Lee, and Kathleen Benasutti. 2007. "Adapting Judicial Supervision to the Risk Level of Drug Offenders: Discharge and Six-Month Outcomes from a Prospective Matching Study." *Drug and Alcohol Dependence* 88: S4–S13.

Marlowe, Douglas, David Festinger, and Patricia Lee. 2004. "The Judge Is a Key Component of Drug Court." *Drug Court Review* 4(2): 1–34.

Marschall, Melissa, and Paru Shah. 2007. "The Attitudinal Effects of Minority Incorporation." *Urban Affairs Review* 42: 629–658.

Martin, Emily. 1999. "Medical Metaphors of Women's Bodies: Menstruation and Menopause." In *Health, Illness and Healing: Society, Social Context, and Self*, edited by Kathy Charmaz and Diane Paternitti, 291–301. Los Angeles: Roxbury.

Massing, Michael. 1998. *The Fix*. New York: Simon and Schuster.

Mauer, Marc. 2004. "Race, Class and the Development of Criminal Justice Policy." *Review of Policy Research* 21(1): 79–92.

May, Carl. 2001. "Pathology, Identity and the Social Construction of Alcohol Dependence." *Sociology* 35: 385–401.

McBride, Duane, Yvonne Terry-McElrath, Henrick Harwood, James A. Inciardi, and Carl Leukefeld. 2009. "Reflections on Drug Policy." *Journal of Drug Issues* 39(1): 71–88.

McColl, William D. 2002. "Theory and Practice in the Baltimore City Drug Court." In *Drug Courts in Theory and in Practice*, edited by James L. Nolan Jr., 3–26. New York: Aldine de Gruyter.

McLellan, A. Thomas, Deni Carise, and Herbert Kleber. 2003. "Can the National Addiction Treatment Infrastructure Support the Public's Demand for Quality Care?" *Journal of Substance Abuse Treatment* 25: 117–121.

McLellan, A. Thomas, David Lewis, Charles O'Brien, and Herbert Kleber. 2000. "Drug Dependence: A Chronic Medical Illness." *Journal of the American Medical Association* 284: 1689–1695.

McNulty, Thomas, Carrie Oser, J. Aaron Johnson, Hannah Knudsen, and Paul Roman. 2007. "Counselor Turnover in Substance Abuse Treatment Centers: An Organizational-Level Analysis." *Sociological Inquiry* 77: 166–193.

McSweeney, Tim, Alex Stevens, Neil Hunt, and Paul Turnbull. 2007. "Twisting Arms or a Helping Hand? Assessing the Impact of 'Coerced' and Comparable 'Voluntary' Drug Treatment Options." *British Journal of Criminology* 47: 470–490.

Mechanic, David. 1995. "Sociological Dimensions of Illness Behavior." *Social Science and Medicine* 41: 1207–1216.

Merrall, Elizabeth, and Sheila Bird. 2009. "A Statistical Perspective on the Design of Drug-Court Studies." *Evaluation Review* 33(3): 257–280.

Merton, Robert. 1938. "Social Structure and Anomie." *American Sociological Review* 3: 672–682.

Miethe, Terance, Hong Lu, and Erin Reese. 2000. "Reintegrative Shaming and Recidivism Risks in Drug Court: Explanations for Some Unexpected Findings." *Crime and Delinquency* 46(4): 522–541.

Miller, Eric. 2004. "Embracing Addiction: Drug Courts and the False Promise of Judicial Interventionism." *Ohio State Law Journal* 65: 1479–1576.

Miller, William, and Kathleen Carroll, eds. 2006. *Rethinking Substance Abuse*. New York: Guilford.

Miller, William, and Reid Hester. 1986. "Inpatient Alcoholism Treatment: Who Benefits?" *American Psychologist* 41 (7): 794–805.

Mojtabai, R., and J. Zevin. 2003. "Effectiveness and Cost-effectiveness of Four Treatment Modalities for Substance Disorders: A Propensity Score Analysis." *Health Services Research* 38: 233–259.

Murphy, Jennifer. 2011. "Drug Court as Both a Legal and Medical Authority." *Deviant Behavior* 32: 257–291.

———. 2012. "Changing Attitudes toward Drug Policy: A Tale of Two Propositions." Paper presented at the annual meeting of the Pacific Sociological Association, San Diego, CA, March.

Musto, David. 1999. *The American Disease: Origins of Narcotics Control*, 3rd ed. New York: Oxford University Press.

———. 2002. *Drugs in America: A Documentary History*. New York: New York University Press.

National Association of Criminal Defense Lawyers. 2009. *America's Problem-Solving Courts: The Criminal Costs of Treatment and the Case for Reform*. Available at http://www.nacdl .org/WorkArea/DownloadAsset.aspx?id=20217. Accessed January 15, 2011.

National Association of Drug Court Professionals (NADCP). 1997. *Defining Drug Courts: The Key Components*. Washington, DC: Office of Justice Programs.

———. 2007. "13th Annual Training Conference." Available at http://www.nadcp.org /annual.html. Accessed October 9, 2007.

———. 2013. Association Web site, available at http://www.nadcp.org. Accessed February 29, 2013.

National Council on Alcoholism and Drug Dependence (NCADD). 2008. Council Web site, available at http://www.ncadd.org/index.html. Accessed January 15, 2008.

National Criminal Justice Reference Service. 2012. "NCJRS Abstracts Database." Available at https://www.ncjrs.gov/.

National Institute of Justice (NIJ). 2006. *Drug Courts: The Second Decade*. Washington, DC: Office of Justice Programs.

National Institute on Drug Abuse (NIDA). 1999. "Principles of Drug Addiction Treatment: A Research-Based Guide." Available at http://www.drugabuse.gov/publications /principles-drug-addiction-treatment-research-based-guide-third-edition/principles -effective-treatment. Accessed January 10, 2007.

———. 2006. *Principles of Drug Abuse Treatment for Criminal Justice Populations: A Research-Based Guide*. Available at https://www.drugabuse.gov/sites/default/files /podat_cj_2012.pdf. Accessed February 21, 2012.

———. 2008. Institute Web site, available at http://www.drugabuse.gov. Accessed March 31, 2008.

Neale, Joanne. 1998. "Drug Users' Views of Prescribed Methadone." *Drugs: Education, Prevention and Policy* 5(1): 33–45.

Neighbors, Harold, Steven Trierweiler, Briggett Ford, and Jordana Muroff. 2003. "Racial Differences in DSM Diagnosis Using a Semi-Structured Instrument: The Importance of Clinical Judgment in the Diagnosis of African Americans." *Journal of Health and Social Behavior* 43: 236–256.

Newman, Robert G. 1987. "Frustrations among Professionals Working in Drug Treatment Programs." *British Journal of Addiction* 82(2): 115–117.

Nolan, James. 2001. *Reinventing Justice: The American Drug Court Movement*. Princeton, NJ: Princeton University Press.

Norland, Stephen, Robin Sowell, and Albert DiChiara. 2003. "Assumptions of Coercive Treatment: A Critical Review." *Criminal Justice Policy Review* 14(4): 505–521.

NY Courts. 2010. Website. Available at http://www.courts.state.ny.us/. Accessed on January 20, 2013.

Office of National Drug Control Policy (ONDCP). 2002. *The President's National Drug Control Strategy*. Available at http://www.whitehousedrugpolicy.gov/publications /policy/03ndcs/pdf.html. Accessed December 15, 2007.

———. 2006. *The President's National Drug Control Strategy.* Available at http://www .whitehousedrugpolicy.gov/publications/policy/03ndcs/pdf.html. Accessed December 15, 2007.

———. 2007. "National Criminal Justice Reference Service." Available at http://www.ncjrs .gov/spotlight/drug_courts/summary.html.

———. 2009. *National Drug Control Strategy: FY 2010 Budget Summary.* Available at http://www.whitehouse.gov/ondcp/2010-national-drug-control-strategy. Accessed November 15, 2011.

O'Halloran, Sean. 2008. *Talking Oneself Sober: The Discourse of Alcoholics Anonymous.* Amherst, NY: Cambria.

O'Hear, Michael. 2009. "Rethinking Drug Courts: Restorative Justice as a Response to Racial Injustice." *Stanford Law and Policy Review* 20: 463–499.

"Ohio Survey: Many People Don't Think Addiction Is a Disease." 2010. *Alcoholism and Drug Abuse Weekly* 22(6): 7–8. Accessed via Academic Search Premier, March 2, 2011.

Oliver, Phillip, Robert Forrest, and Jenny Kean. 2007. "Does the Combined Use of Heroin or Methadone and Other Substances Increase the Risk of Overdose?" United Kingdom: National Treatment Agency for Substance Misuse. Available at http://www.nta .nhs.uk/uploads/nta_rb27_combined_opiate_overdose.pdf. Accessed November 20, 2012.

Olson, David E., Arthur J. Lurigo, and Stephanie Albertson. 2001. "Implementing the Key Components of Specialized *Drug* Treatment *Courts*: Practice and Policy Considerations." *Law and Policy* 23(2): 171–196.

Orcutt, James, and J. Blake Turner. 1993. "Shocking Numbers and Graphic Accounts: Quantified Images of Drug Problems in the Print Media." *Social Problems* 40(2): 190–206.

Padamsee, Tasleem Juana. 2011. "The Pharmaceutical Corporation and the 'Good Work' of Managing Women's Bodies." *Social Science and Medicine* 72(8): 1342–1350.

Pager, Devah. 2003. "The Mark of a Criminal Record." *American Journal of Sociology* 108(5): 937–975.

Paik, Leslie. 2006a. "Are You Truly a Recovering Dope Fiend? Local Interpretive Practices at a Therapeutic Community Drug Treatment Program." *Symbolic Interaction* 29(2): 213–234.

———. 2006b. "Organizational Interpretations of Drug Test Results." *Law and Society Review* 40(4): 931–960.

———. 2011. *Discretionary Justice: Looking Inside a Juvenile Drug Court.* New Brunswick, NJ: Rutgers University Press.

Parsons, Talcott. 1951. *The Social System.* New York: Free Press.

———. 1975. "The Sick Role and the Role of the Physician Reconsidered." *Milbank Memorial Fund Quarterly* 53: 257–278.

Paternoster, Raymond, and Leeann Iovanni. 1989. "The Labeling Perspective and Delinquency: An Elaboration of the Theory and an Assessment of the Evidence." *Justice Quarterly* 6(3): 359–394.

Payer, Lynn. 1996. *Medicine and Culture: Varieties in the United States, England, West Germany and France.* New York: Henry Holt.

Peele, Stanton. 1989. *The Diseasing of America: Addiction Treatment Out of Control.* Boston: Houghton Mifflin.

Peele, Stanton. 2008. The Stanton Peele Addiction Website. Available at www.peele.net. Accessed on March 31, 2008.

Peele, Stanton, and R. J. Degrandpre. 1998. "Cocaine and the Concept of Addiction: Environmental Factors in Drug Compulsions." *Addiction Research* 6(3): 235–263.

Pelissier, Bernadette, and Nicole Jones. 2005. "A Review of Gender Differences among Substance Abusers." *Crime and Delinquency* 51: 343–372.

Perron, Brian. 2007. "The Relationship between Legal Coercion and Dropout from Substance Abuse Treatment." *BMC Psychiatry* 7: 14.

Peters, Roger H., Amie Haas, and W. Michael Hunt. 2001. "Treatment 'Dosage' Effects in Drug Court Programs." In *Drug Courts in Operation: Current Research*, edited by James J. Hennessy and Nathaniel J. Pallone, 63–72. Binghamton, NY: Haworth Press.

Peyrot, Mark. 1984. "Cycles of Social Problem Development: The Case of Drug Abuse." *Sociological Quarterly* 25: 83–96.

Polcin, Douglas L. 2001. "Drug and Alcohol Offenders Coerced into Treatment: A Review of Modalities and Suggestions for Research on Social Model Programs." *Substance Use and Misuse* 36(5): 589–608.

Powell, Charlotte, Marilyn Christie, John Bankart, Deboarh Bamber, and Ira Unell. 2011. "Drug Treatment Outcomes in the Criminal Justice System: What Non-Self-Report Measures of Outcome Can Tell Us." *Addiction Research and Theory* 19(2): 148–160.

Prendergast, Michael, and Harry Wexler. 2004. "Correctional Substance Abuse Treatment Programs in California: A Historical Perspective." *Prison Journal* 84(1): 8–35.

Quinn, Mae C. 2000. "Whose Team Am I on Anyway? Musings of a Public Defender about Drug Treatment Court Practice." *New York University Review of Law and Social Change* 26: 37–75.

Radcliffe, Polly, and Alex Stevens. 2008. "Are Drug Treatment Services Only for 'Thieving Junkie Scumbags'? Drug Users and the Management of Stigmatised Identities." *Social Science and Medicine* 67: 1065–1073.

Ragoné, Heléna, and Sharla Willis. 2000. "Reproduction and Assisted Reproductive Technologies." In *Handbook of Social Studies in Health and Medicine*, edited by Gary Albrecht, Ray Fitzpatrick, and Susan Scrimshaw. London: Sage.

Rains, Prudence Mors. 2007. *Becoming an Unwed Mother: A Sociological Account*. Chicago: Aldine.

Reinarman, Craig. 2005. "Addiction as Accomplishment: The Discursive Construction of Disease." *Addiction Research and Theory* 13(4): 307–320.

Reinarman, Craig, and Harry Levine, eds. 1997. *Crack in America: Demon Drugs and Social Justice*. Berkeley: University of California Press.

———. 2004. "Crack in the Rearview Mirror: Deconstructing Drug War Mythology." *Social Justice* 31(1–2): 182–199.

Rempel, Michael, and Christine Depies Destefano. 2001. "Predictors of Engagement in Court-Mandated Treatment: Findings at the Brooklyn Treatment Court, 1996–2000." In *Drug Courts in Operation: Current Research*, edited by James J. Hennessy and Nathaniel J. Pallone, 87–124. Binghamton, NY: Haworth Press.

Rettig, Richard, and Adam Yarmolinsky, eds. 1995. *Federal Regulation of Methadone Treatment*. Washington, DC: National Academy Press.

Reuter, Peter. 1992. "Hawks Ascendant: The Punitive Trend of American Drug Policy." *Daedalus* 121(3): 15–52.

Reuter, Peter, and Harold Pollack. 2006. "How Much Can Treatment Reduce National Drug Problems?" *Addiction* 101: 341–347.

Riessman, Catherine Kohler. 1983. "Women and Medicalization: A New Perspective." *Social Policy* 14: 3–18.

Riley, Diane, Ed Sawka, Peter Conley, David Hewitt, Wayne Mitic, Christiane Poulin, Robin Room, Eric Single, and John Topp. 1999. "Harm Reduction: Concepts and Practice. A Policy Discussion Paper." *Substance Use and Misuse* 34(1): 9–24.

Rippere, Vicky. 1978. "Drug Addiction and Drug Dependence: A Note on Word Meanings." *British Journal of Addiction* 73: 353–358.

Roan, Shari. 2011. "Federal Substance-Abuse Agencies Lumber toward a Merger." *Los Angeles Times* Blog, June 19. Available at http://articles.latimes.com/2011/ jun/19/news/ la-heb-agency-merger-06192011. Accessed August 3, 2012.

Robins, Lee, John Helzer, Michie Hesslebrock, and Eric Wish. 2010. "Vietnam Veterans Three Years after Vietnam: How Our Study Changed Our View of Heroin." *American Journal on Addictions* 19: 203–211.

Rolider, Ahmos, Anne Cummings, and Ron Van Houten. 1991. "Side Effects of Therapeutic Punishment on Academic Performance and Eye Contact." *Journal of Applied Behavior Analysis* 24: 763–773.

Roman, Paul M., and J. A. Johnson. 2004. *National Treatment Center Study Summary Report: Public Treatment Centers.* Athens: University of Georgia, Institute for Behavioral Research.

Rooks, Judith Pence. 1997. *Midwifery and Childbirth in America.* Philadelphia, PA: Temple University Press.

Room, Robin. 2005. "Stigma, Social Inequality and Alcohol and Drug Use." Drug and Alcohol Review 24: 143–155.

Rosenberg, Charles. 1962. *The Cholera Years.* Chicago: University of Chicago Press.

———. 1986. "Disease and Social Order in America: Perceptions and Expectations." *Milbank Quarterly* 64(1): 34–55.

———. 2006. "Contested Boundaries: Psychiatry, Disease, and Diagnosis." *Perspectives in Biology and Medicine* 49(3): 407–424.

Rosenfield, Sarah. 1997. "Labeling Mental Illness: The Effects of Received Services and Perceived Stigma on Life Satisfaction." *American Sociological Review* 62: 660–672.

Rossol, Josh. 2001. "The Medicalization of Deviance as an Interactive Achievement: The Construction of Compulsive Gambling." *Symbolic Interaction* 24: 315–341.

Rothman, David. 1971. *The Discovery of the Asylum: Social Order and Disorder in the New Republic.* New York: Aldine de Gruyter.

———. 1980. *Conscience and Convenience: The Asylum and Its Alternative in Progressive America.* New York: Aldine de Gruyter.

Rush, Benjamin. 1785. "An Inquiry into the Effects of Ardent Spirits upon the Human Body and Mind." In *Drugs in America: A Documentary History,* edited by David Musto. New York: New York University Press.

Rychtarik, Robert, Gerald Connors, Kurt Dermen, and Paul Stasiewicz. 2000. "Alcoholics Anonymous and the Use of Medications to Prevent Relapse: An Anonymous Survey of Member Attitudes." *Journal of Studies on Alcohol* 61: 134–138.

Salmon, Ruth, and Raphael Salmon. 1983. "The Role of Coercion in Rehabilitation of Drug Abusers." *International Journal of the Addictions* 18(1): 9–21.

Sanders, Eli. 2011. "The War on Drug Courts." *All Rise: The Magazine of the National Association of Drug Court Professionals,* Fall. Available at http://www.ndci.org/all _rise_magazine/index.html. Accessed February 21, 2012.

Sanders, Jolene M. 2011. "Feminist Perspectives on Twelve-Step Recovery: A Comparative Descriptive Analysis of Women in Alcoholics Anonymous and Narcotics Anonymous." *Alcoholism Treatment Quarterly* 29: 357–378.

Sanford, J. Scott, and Bruce Arrigo. 2005. "Lifting the Cover on Drug Courts: Evaluation Findings and Policy Concerns." *International Journal of Offender Therapy and Comparative Criminology* 49(3): 239–259.

Satel, Sally. 2001. "Is Drug Addiction a Brain Disease?" In *Drug Addiction and Drug Policy*, edited by Philip Heymann and William Brownsberger, 118–143. Cambridge, MA: Harvard University Press.

Scheff, Thomas. 1966. *Being Mentally Ill: A Sociological Theory*. Chicago: Aldine.

———. 1999. *Being Mentally Ill: A Sociological Theory*. 3rd ed. New York: Aldine De Gruyter.

Schiff, Mara, and W. Clinton Terry III. 1997. "Predicting Graduation from Broward County's Dedicated Drug Treatment Court." *Justice System Journal* 19(3): 291–310.

Schneider, Joseph. 1978. "Deviant Drinking as a Disease: Deviant Drinking as a Social Accomplishment." *Social Problems* 25: 361–372.

Schur, Edwin. 1965. *Crimes without Victims: Deviant Behavior and Public Policy*. Englewood Cliffs, NJ: Prentice Hall.

Scott, Wilbur. 1990. "PTSD in *DSM*-III: A Case in the Politics of Diagnosis and Disease." *Social Problems* 37: 294–310.

Sechrest, Dale, and David Shicor. 2001. "Determinants of Graduation from a Day Treatment Drug Court in California." *Journal of Drug Issues* 31: 129–148.

Seddon, Toby. 2007. "Coerced Drug Treatment in the Criminal Justice System: Conceptual, Ethical, and Criminological Issues." *Criminology and Criminal Justice* 7(3): 269–286.

Semple, Shirley, Igor Grant, and Thomas Patterson. 2005. "Utilization of Drug Treatment Programs by Methamphetamine Users: The Role of Social Stigma." *American Journal on Addictions* 14: 367–380.

Sered, Susan, and Maureen Norton-Hawk. 2011. "Whose Higher Power? Criminalized Women Confront the Twelve Steps." *Feminist Criminology* 6(4): 308–332.

Shafer, Jack. 2005. "The Meth-Mouth Myth: Our Latest Moral Panic." Slate Web site, August 9. Available at www.slate.com/toolbar.aspx?action=print&id=2124160. Accessed January 15, 2008.

Sharp, Elaine. 1994. *The Dilemma of Drug Policy in the United States*. New York: Harper Collins.

Shavelson, Lonny. 2001. *Hooked: Five Addicts Challenge Our Misguided Drug Rehab System*. New York: New Press.

Sheen, Martin. 2008. "A Costly, Dangerous Drug Treatment Initiative." *Sacramento Bee*, September 5. Available at http://www.sacbee.com. Accessed April 1, 2011.

Simmons, James, and Barbara Reed. 1969. "Therapeutic Punishment in Severely Disturbed Children." *Current Psychiatric Therapies* 9: 11–18.

Slate, Steven. 2012. "Addiction is NOT a Brain Disease: It Is a Choice." Clean Slate Addiction Site. Available at http://www.thecleanslate.org/about-2/. Accessed October 3, 2012.

Smith, David, Dorothy Lee, and Leigh Dickerson Davidson. 2010. "Health Care Equality and Parity for Treatment of Addictive Disease." *Journal of Psychoactive Drugs* 42(2): 121–126.

Smith, Dorothy. 2002. "Institutional Ethnography." In *Qualitative Research in Action*, edited by Tim May, 17–52. Thousand Oaks, CA: Sage.

———, ed. 2006a. *Institutional Ethnography as Practice*. New York: Rowman and Littlefield.

———. 2006b. "Introduction." In *Institutional Ethnography as Practice*, edited by Dorothy Smith, 1–11. New York: Rowman and Littlefield.

Somers, Margaret. 1994. "The Narrative Constitution of Identity: A Relational and Network Approach." *Theory and Society* 23: 605–649.

Spillane, Joseph. 2000. *Cocaine: From Medical Marvel to Modern Menace in the United States, 1884–1920.* Baltimore, MD: Johns Hopkins University Press.

Spillane, Joseph, and William McAllister. 2003. "Keeping the Lid On: A Century of Drug Regulation and Control." *Drug and Alcohol Dependence* 70: S5–S12.

Spinak, Jane M. 2003. "Why Defenders Feel Defensive: The Defender's Role in Problem-Solving Courts." *American Criminal Law Review* 40(4): 1617–1623.

Stahler, Gerald, Eric Cohen, Mitchell Greene, Thomas Shipley, and David Bartelt. 1995. "A Qualitative Study of Treatment Success among Homeless Crack-Addicted Men: Definitions and Attributions." *Contemporary Drug Problems* 22: 237–264.

Stahler, Gerald, Eric Cohen, Thomas Shipley, and David Bartelt. 1993. "Why Clients Drop Out of Treatment: Ethnographic Perspectives on Treatment Attrition among Homeless Male 'Crack' Cocaine Users." *Contemporary Drug Problems* 20: 651–680.

Stahler, Gerald, Thomas Shipley, David Bartelt, Danielle Westcott, Ellen Griffith, and Irving Shandler. 1993. "Retention Issues in Treating Homeless Polydrug Users: Philadelphia." *Alcoholism Treatment Quarterly* 10(3–4): 201–215.

Stancliff, Sharon, Julie Elana Myers, Stuart Steiner, and Ernest Drucker. 2002. "Beliefs about Methadone in an Inner-City Methadone Clinic." *Journal of Urban Health: Bulletin of the New York Academy of Medicine* 79(4): 571–578.

Starr, Paul. 1982. *The Social Transformation of American Medicine.* New York: Basic.

Staton, Michele, Allison Mateyoke, Carl Leukefeld, Jennifer Cole, Holly Hopper, T. K. Logan, and Lisa Minton. 2001. "Employment Issues among Court Participants." In *Drug Courts in Operation: Current Research*, edited by James J. Hennessy and Nathaniel J. Pallone, 73–86. Binghamton, NY: Haworth Press.

Steen, Sara. 2002. "West Coast Drug Courts: Getting Offenders Morally Involved in the Criminal Justice Process." In *Drug Courts in Theory and in Practice*, edited by James L. Nolan Jr., 51–66. New York: Aldine de Gruyter.

Steen, Sara, Rodney Engen, and Randy Gainey. 2005. "Images of Danger and Culpability: Racial Stereotyping, Case Processing, and Criminal Sentencing." *Criminology* 43(2): 435–468.

Sterk, Claire, Kirk Elifson, and Katherine Theall. 2000. "Women and Drug Treatment Experiences: A Generational Comparison of Mothers and Daughters." *Journal of Drug Issues* 30(4): 839–862.

Substance Abuse and Mental Health Services Administration (SAMHSA). 2000. *Substance Abuse Treatment in Adult and Juvenile Correctional Facilities.* Available at http://www.oas.samhsa.gov/UFDS/ CorrectionalFacilities97/index.htm. Accessed January 15, 2008.

———. 2004. *Substance Use Disorders: A Guide to the Use of Language.* Available at www.naabt.org/documents/ languageofaddictionmedicine.pdf. Accessed November 15, 2012.

———. 2007. Buprenorphine. Available at http://buprenorphine.samhsa.gov/.

———. 2010a. *National Survey of Substance Abuse Treatment Services (N-SSATS).* Available at http://www.oas.samhsa.gov/DASIS/2k5nssats.cfm.

———. 2010b. *The NSDUH Report: Substance Use Treatment Need and Receipt among People Living in Poverty.* Rockville, MD: Office of Applied Studies. Available at www.oas.samhsa.gov/2k10/173/173PovertyHTML.pdf. Accessed March 1, 2011.

———. 2013. *National Survey of Substance Abuse Treatment Services (N-SSATS): 2011.* Available at http://www.samhsa.gov/data/DASIS/2k11nssats/NSSATS2011TOC.htm. Accessed June 4, 2013.

Szalavitz, Maia. 2007. "So, What Made Me an Addict?" *Washington Post*, August 8, p. HE01. Available at http://www.washingtonpost.com/wpdyn/content/article/2007/08/24/AR2007082401699.html. Accessed May 1, 2008.

Szasz, Thomas. 1974. *The Myth of Mental Illness*. Rev. ed. New York: Harper and Row.

———. 1975. *Ceremonial Chemistry*. Garden City, NY: Anchor.

———. 1984. *The Therapeutic State*. Buffalo, NY: Prometheus.

———. 1991. "The Medicalization of Sex." *Journal of Humanistic Psychology* 31(3): 34–42.

———. 1992. *Our Right to Drugs: The Case for a Free Market*. New York: Praeger.

———. 1994. "Mental Illness Is Still a Myth." *Society* 31(4): 34–39.

———. 2001. *Pharmacracy: Medicine and Politics in America*. Westport, CT: Praeger.

Taxman, Faye S. and Jeffrey A. Bouffard. 2003. "Substance Abuse Counselors' Treatment Philosophy and the Content of Treatment Services Provided to Offenders in Drug Court Programs." *Journal of Substance Abuse Treatment* 25(2): 75–84.

Taxman, Faye, Matthew Perdoni, and Lana Harrison. 2006. "Drug Treatment Services for Adult Offenders: The State of the State." *Journal of Substance Abuse Treatment* 32: 239–254.

Terry, W. Clinton III. 1999. "Judicial Change and Dedicated Treatment Courts: Case Studies in Innovation." In *The Early Drug Courts: Case Studies in Judicial Innovation*, edited by W. Clinton Terry III, 1–18. Thousand Oaks, CA: Sage.

Thoits, Peggy. 2011. "Resisting the Stigma of Mental Illness." *Social Psychology Quarterly* 74(1): 6–28.

Tiet, Quyen, Mark Ilgen, Hilary Byrnes, Alex Harris, and John Finney. 2007. "Treatment Setting and Baseline Substance Use Severity Interact to Predict Patients' Outcomes." *Addiction* 102: 432–440.

Tiger, Rebecca. 2011. "Drug Courts and the Logic of Coerced Treatment." *Sociological Forum* 26(1): 169–182.

———. 2013. *Judging Addicts: Drug Courts and Coercion in the Justice System*. New York: New York University Press.

Tonry, Michael. 1994. "Racial Politics, Racial Disparities, and the War on Crime." *Crime and Delinquency* 40(4): 475–495.

———. 1996. *Malign Neglect: Race, Crime and Punishment in America*. New York: Oxford University Press.

———. 2011. *Punishing Race: A Continuing American Dilemma*. New York: Oxford University Press.

Tonry, Michael, and Matthew Melewski. 2008. "The Malign Effects of Drug and Crime Control Policies on Black Americans." *Crime and Justice* 37(1): 1–44.

Townsend, Elizabeth. 1998. *Good Intentions Overruled: A Critique of Empowerment in the Routine Organization of Mental Health Services*. Toronto: University of Toronto Press.

Tracy, Sarah. 2005. *Alcoholism in America: From Reconstruction to Prohibition*. Baltimore, MD: Johns Hopkins University Press.

Tracy, Sarah, and Caroline Jean Acker. 2004. "Introduction: Psychoactive Drugs—An American Way of Life." In *Altering American Consciousness: The History of Alcohol and Drug Use in the United States, 1800–2000*, edited by Sarah Tracy and Joan Acker, 1–32. Boston: University of Massachusetts Press.

Travis, Jeremy. 2002. "Invisible Punishment: An Instrument of Social Exclusion." In *Invisible Punishment: The Collateral Consequences of Mass Incarceration*, edited by Marc Mauer and Meda Chesney-Lind, 15–36. New York: New Press.

Treloar, Carla, Suzanne Fraser, and Kylie Valentine. 2007. "Valuing Methadone Takeaway Doses: The Contribution of Service-User Perspectives to Policy and Practice." *Drugs: Education, Prevention and Policy* 14(1): 61–74.

Turner, Ralph. 1972. "Deviance Avowal as Neutralization of Commitment." *Social Problems* 19(3): 308–321.

Turner, Susan, Douglas Longshore, Suzanne Wenzel, Elizabeth Deschenes, Peter Greenwood, Terry Fain, Adele Harrell, Andrew Morral, Faye Taxman, Martin Iguchi, Judith Greene, and Duane McBride. 2002. "A Decade of Drug Treatment Court Research." *Substance Use and Misuse* 37(12–13): 1489–1527.

United States Department of Health and Human Services. Substance Abuse and Mental Health Services Administration. Center for Behavioral Health Statistics and Quality. 2010a. *Treatment Episode Data Set-Discharges (TEDS-D)*. Ann Arbor, MI: Inter-university Consortium for Political and Social Research (distributor). Available at http://doi.org/10.3886/ICPSR34898.v1. Accessed November 21, 2013.

———. 2010b. *National Survey of Substance Abuse Treatment Services (N-SSATS)*. Ann Arbor, MI: Inter-university Consortium for Political and Social Research (distributor). Available at http://doi.org/10.3886/ICPSR32723.v3. Accessed April 25, 2014.

Unnever, James D., Francis T. Cullen, and James D. Jones. 2008. "Public Support for Attacking the 'Root Causes' of Crime: The Impact of Egalitarian and Racial Beliefs." *Sociological Focus* 41(1): 1–33.

USA Today. 2006. "*USA Today*/HBO Drug Addiction Poll." July 19. Available at http://www.usatoday.com/news/polls/2006-07-19-addiction-poll.htm. Accessed May 1, 2008.

Vaillant, George. 2001. "If Addiction Is Involuntary, How Can Punishment Help?" In *Drug Addiction and Drug Policy*, edited by Philip Heymann and William Brownsberger, 144–167. Cambridge, MA: Harvard University Press.

Valentine, Charles A. 1971. "The 'Culture of Poverty': Its Scientific Significance and Its Implications." In *The Culture of Poverty: A Critique*, edited by Eleanor Burke Leacock, 193–225. New York: Simon and Schuster.

Valverde, Mariana. 1998. *Diseases of the Will: Alcohol and the Dilemmas of Freedom*. Cambridge: Cambridge University Press.

Vastag, Brian. 2003. "Addiction Poorly Understood by Clinicians." *JAMA* 290(10): 1299–1303.

Venkatesh, Sudhir. 1997. "The Social Organization of Street Gang Activity in an Urban Ghetto." *American Journal of Sociology* 103(1): 82–111.

Volkow, Nora. 2007. "This Is Your Brain on Food (Interview by Kristen Leutwyler-Ozelli)." *Scientific American* 297: 84–85.

———. "Talk of the Nation." National Public Radio, February, 25, 2011.

Volkow, Nora, Joanna Fowler, and Gene-Jack Wang. 2003. "The Addicted Human Brain: Insights from Imaging Studies." *Journal of Clinical Investigation* 111(10): 1444–1451.

Volkow, Nora, and Ting-Kai Li. 2005. "Drugs and Alcohol: Treating and Preventing Abuse, Addiction, and Their Medical Consequences." *Pharmacology and Therapeutics* 108: 3–17.

Volpicelli, Joseph, and Maia Szalavitz. 2000. *Recovery Options: The Complete Guide*. New York: John Wiley.

Wacquant, Loic. 2001. "Deadly Symbiosis: When Ghetto and Prison Meet and Mesh." *Punishment and Society* 3(1): 95–133.

Waldorf, Dan, Craig Reinarman, and Sheigla Murphy. 1991. *Cocaine Changes: The Experience of Using and Quitting*. Philadelphia, PA: Temple University Press.

Walley, Alexander, Julie Alperen, Debbie Cheng, Michael Botticelli, Carolyn Castro-Donlan, Jeffrey Sarnet, and Daniel Alford. 2008. "Office-Based Management of Opioid Dependence with Buprenorphine: Clinical Practices and Barriers." *Journal of General Internal Medicine* 23(9): 1393–1398.

Walsh, Nastassia. 2011. "Addicted to Courts: How a Growing Dependence on Drug Courts Impacts People and Communities." Washington, DC: Justice Policy Institute.

Walters, Glenn. 1999. *The Addiction Concept: Working Hypothesis or Self-Fulfilling Prophecy?* Boston: Allyn and Bacon.

Walters, Glenn, and Alice Gilbert. 2000. "Defining Addiction: Contrasting Views of Clients and Experts." *Addiction Research* 8(3): 211–220.

Weidner, Robert. 2009. "Methamphetamine in Three Small Midwestern Cities: Evidence of a Moral Panic." *Journal of Psychoactive Drugs* 41(3): 227–239.

Weinberg, Darin. 2000. " 'Out There': The Ecology of Addiction in Drug Abuse Treatment Discourse." *Social Problems* 47(4): 606–621.

Weinman, Beth A., and Dorothy Lockwood. 1993. "Inmate Drug Treatment Programming in the Federal Bureau of Prisons." In *Drug Treatment and Criminal Justice*, edited by James A. Inciardi, 194–208. Newbury Park, CA: Sage.

Welsh, Wayne, and Gary Zajac. 2004. "A Census of Prison-Based Drug Treatment Programs: Implications for Programming, Policy, and Evaluation." *Crime and Delinquency* 50: 108–133.

Wertz, Richard W., and Dorothy C. Wertz. 1989. *Lying-In: A History of Childbirth in America*. New Haven, CT: Yale University Press.

West, Steven, Keri O'Neal, and Carolyn Graham. 2000. "A Meta-Analysis Comparing the Effectiveness of Buprenorphine and Methadone." *Journal of Substance Abuse* 12: 405–414.

Western, Bruce. 2006. *Punishment and Inequality in America*. New York: Russell Sage Foundation.

Wexler, David, and Bruce Winick. 1996. *Law in a Therapeutic Key: Developments in Therapeutic Jurisprudence*. Durham, NC: Carolina Academic Press.

Wexler, Harry. 1994. "Progress in Prison Substance Abuse Treatment: A Five-Year Report." *Journal of Drug Issues* 24: 349–360.

Wexler, Harry, and Bennett Fletcher. 2007. "National Criminal Justice Drug Abuse Treatment Studies (CJ-DATS) Overview." *Prison Journal* 87(1): 9–24.

White, William. 1998. *Slaying the Dragon: The History of Addiction Treatment and Recovery in America*. Bloomington, IL: Chestnut Health Systems.

———. 2004. "The Lessons of Language: Historical Perspectives on the Rhetoric of Addiction." In *Altering American Consciousness: The History of Alcohol and Drug Use in the United States, 1800–2000*, edited by Sarah Tracy and Joan Acker, 33–60. Boston: University of Massachusetts Press.

Whiteacre, Kevin. 2008. *Drug Court Justice: Experiences in a Juvenile Drug Court*. New York: Peter Lang.

Wilson, David B., Ojmarrh Mitchell, and Doris L. MacKenzie. 2006. "A Systematic Review of Drug Court Effects on Recidivism." *Journal of Experimental Criminology* 2(4): 459–487.

Wilson, William Julius. 1996. *When Work Disappears: The World of the New Urban Poor*. New York: Alfred A. Knopf.

Wisotsky, Steven. 1992. *A Society of Suspects: The War on Drugs and Civil Liberties*. Policy Analysis No. 180. Washington, DC: CATO Institute.

Wolfe, Ellen, Joseph Guydish, and Jenna Termondt. 2002. "A Drug Court Outcome Evaluation Comparing Arrests in a Two Year Follow-Up Period." *Journal of Drug Issues* 22: 1155–1172.

Wolfer, Loreen. 2006. "Graduates Speak: A Qualitative Exploration of Drug Court Graduates' Views of the Strengths and Weaknesses of the Program." *Contemporary Drug Problems* 33: 303–320.

Wolfer, Loreen, and James C. Roberts. 2008. "A Theoretical Exploration of a Drug Court Program Based on Client Experiences." *Contemporary Drug Problems* 35: 481–507.

Yamaguchi, K., and D. B. Kandel. 1984. "Patterns of Drug Use from Adolescence to Young Adulthood II: Sequences of Progression." *American Journal of Public Health* 74: 668–672.

Zarkin, Gary, Laura Dunlap, Steven Belenko, and Paul Dynia. 2005. "A Benefit-Cost Analysis of the Kings County District Attorney's Office Drug Treatment Alternative to Prison (DTAP) Program." Justice Research and Policy 7(1): 1–26.

Zhang, Zhiwei. 2003. "Drug and Alcohol Use and Related Matters among Arrestees." National Institute of Justice. Available at http://www.ncjrs.gov/nij/adam/ADAM2003.pdf.

Zinberg, Norman E. 1984. *Drug, Set and Setting: The Basis for Controlled Intoxicant Use.* New Haven, CT: Yale University Press.

Zlotnick, Caron, Jennifer Clarke, Peter Friedmann, Mary Roberts, Stanley Sacks, and Gerald Melnick. 2008. "Gender Differences in Comorbid Disorders among Offenders in Prison Substance Abuse Treatment Programs." *Behavioral Sciences and the Law* 26: 403–412.

Zola, Irving. 1972. "Medicine as an Institution of Social Control." *Sociological Review* 20: 487–504.

Index

Jennifer Murphy is Associate Professor of Sociology at California State University, Sacramento.